# Exam Ref MS-900
# Microsoft 365
# Fundamentals

Craig Zacker

# Exam Ref MS-900 Microsoft 365 Fundamentals

Published with the authorization of Microsoft Corporation by
Pearson Education, Inc.

ISBN-13: 978-0-13-648487-5
ISBN-10: 0-13-648487-5

Library of Congress Control Number: 2019956209

ScoutAutomatedPrintCode

## TRADEMARKS

## WARNING AND DISCLAIMER

## SPECIAL SALES

For information about buying this title in bulk quantities, or for special sales opportunities (which may include electronic versions; custom cover designs; and content particular to your business, training goals, marketing focus, or branding interests), please contact our corporate sales department at corpsales@pearsoned.com or (800) 382-3419.

For government sales inquiries, please contact governmentsales@pearsoned.com.

For questions about sales outside the U.S., please contact intlcs@pearson.com.

Printed and bound by CPI Group (UK) Ltd, Croydon CR0 4YY

## CREDITS

**EDITOR-IN-CHIEF**
Brett Bartow

**EXECUTIVE EDITOR**
Loretta Yates

**ASSISTANT SPONSORING EDITOR**
Charvi Arora

**DEVELOPMENT EDITOR**
Rick Kughen

**MANAGING EDITOR**
Sandra Schroeder

**SENIOR PROJECT EDITOR**
Tracey Croom

**COPY EDITOR**
Rick Kughen

**INDEXER**
Erika Millen

**PROOFREADER**
Charlotte Kughen

**TECHNICAL EDITOR**
J. Boyd Nolan

**EDITORIAL ASSISTANT**
Cindy Teeters

**COVER DESIGNER**
Twist Creative, Seattle

**COMPOSITION**
codeMantra

# Contents at a glance

# Contents

# Introduction

The Microsoft 365 Certified Fundamentals certification is the initial entry point into a hierarchy of Microsoft 365 certifications. The MS-900 Microsoft 365 Fundamentals exam tests the candidate's knowledge of the components and capabilities of the Microsoft 365 products without delving into specific administrative procedures. With the Fundamentals certification in place, IT pros can then move up to Associate level certifications that concentrate on specific areas of Microsoft 365 administration, such as messaging, security, desktop, and teamwork. The ultimate pinnacle in the hierarchy is the Enterprise Administrator Expert certification, achievable by passing the MS-100 and MS-101 exams.

This book covers all the skills measured by the MS-900 exam, with each of the four main areas covered in a separate chapter. Each chapter is broken down into individual skill sections, which cover all the suggested topics for each skill. It is recommended that you access a trial version of Microsoft 365 as you work your way through this book. Nothing can replace actual hands-on experience, and Microsoft provides a fully functional evaluation platform of Microsoft 365 Enterprise—all the components of which are accessible in the cloud and require no hardware other than a computer with Internet access. Microsoft also provides a wealth of documentation for all the Microsoft 365 components at *docs.microsoft.com*. With these tools, as well as some time and dedication, you can prepare yourself for the MS-900 exam and the first step toward your Microsoft 365 career.

## Organization of this book

This book is organized by the "Skills measured" list published for the exam. The "Skills measured" list is available for each exam on the Microsoft Learn website: *http://microsoft.com/learn*. Each chapter in this book corresponds to a major topic area in the list, and the technical tasks in each topic area determine a chapter's organization. If an exam covers four major topic areas, for example, the book will contain four chapters.

# Microsoft certifications

Microsoft certifications distinguish you by proving your command of a broad set of skills and experience with current Microsoft products and technologies. The exams and corresponding certifications are developed to validate your mastery of critical competencies as you design and develop, or implement and support, solutions with Microsoft products and technologies both on-premises and in the cloud. Certification brings a variety of benefits to the individual and to employers and organizations.

> **MORE INFO    ALL MICROSOFT CERTIFICATIONS**
>
> For information about Microsoft certifications, including a full list of available certifications, go to *http://www.microsoft.com/learn*.

# Errata, updates, & book support

We've made every effort to ensure the accuracy of this book and its companion content. You can access updates to this book—in the form of a list of submitted errata and their related corrections—at:

*MicrosoftPressStore.com/ExamRefMS900/errata*

If you discover an error that is not already listed, please submit it to us at the same page.

For additional book support and information, please visit *http://www.MicrosoftPressStore.com/Support*.

Please note that product support for Microsoft software and hardware is not offered through the previous addresses. For help with Microsoft software or hardware, go to *http://support.microsoft.com*.

# Stay in touch

Let's keep the conversation going! We're on Twitter: *http://twitter.com/MicrosoftPress*.

# Important: How to use this book to study for the exam

Certification exams validate your on-the-job experience and product knowledge. To gauge your readiness to take an exam, use this Exam Ref to help you check your understanding of the skills tested by the exam. Determine the topics you know well and the areas in which you need more experience. To help you refresh your skills in specific areas, we have also provided "Need more review?" pointers, which direct you to more in-depth information outside the book.

The Exam Ref is not a substitute for hands-on experience. This book is not designed to teach you new skills.

We recommend that you round out your exam preparation by using a combination of available study materials and courses. Learn more about available classroom training and find free online courses and live events at http://microsoft.com/learn. Microsoft Official Practice Tests are available for many exams at http://aka.mspracticetests.

This book is organized by the "Skills measured" list published for the exam. The "Skills measured" list for each exam is available on the Microsoft Learn website: http://aka.ms/examlist.

Note that this Exam Ref is based on this publicly available information and the author's experience. To safeguard the integrity of the exam, authors do not have access to the exam questions.

# About the Author

**Craig Zacker** is the author or coauthor of dozens of books, manuals, articles, and websites on computer and networking topics. He has also been an English professor, a technical and copy editor, a network administrator, a webmaster, a corporate trainer, a technical support engineer, a minicomputer operator, a literature and philosophy student, a library clerk, a photographic darkroom technician, a shipping clerk, and a newspaper boy. He lives in a little house with his beautiful wife and a neurotic cat.

# CHAPTER 1

# Understand cloud concepts

The cloud is one of the biggest buzzwords ever to emerge from the IT industry, but it is a term that is difficult to define in any but the most general terms. For a simple definition, you can say that the *cloud* is an Internet-based resource that provides subscribers with various types of IT services on demand. For users, the cloud enables them to run applications, stream video, download music, read email, and perform any number of other tasks, all without having to worry about where the servers are located, what resources they utilize, how much data is involved, and—in most cases—whether the service is operational. Like the electricity or the water in your house, you turn it on, and it is there—most of the time. For IT professionals, however, defining the cloud can be more difficult.

## Skills in this chapter:

- Detail and understand the benefits and considerations of using cloud services
- Understand the different types of cloud services available

## Skill 1.1: Detail and understand the benefits and considerations of using cloud services

System administrators, software developers, database administrators, and user-support personnel all see the cloud in a different light and use it for different purposes. Cloud providers, such as Microsoft, Google, and Amazon, typically offer a wide variety of resources and services. They can provide virtualized hardware, such as servers, storage, and networks; software in the form of back-end server and user applications; as well as tools for messaging, content management, collaboration, identity management, analytics, and others. Services are provided on an *à la carte* basis, with the subscribers only paying for what they use.

> **This section covers how to:**
> - Understand cloud services
> - Understand the advantages of cloud computing

# Understanding cloud services

Different types of IT professionals understand the cloud in different ways. For a system administrator, the cloud can provide virtual machines that function as servers, in place of or alongside physical servers in the organization's data center. For software developers, the cloud can provide a variety of preconfigured platforms and development environments for application deployment and testing. For a database administrator, the cloud can provide complex storage architectures and preconfigured database management solutions. Cloud services can then organize the data and use artificial intelligence to develop new uses for it. For user support technicians, the cloud can provide productivity applications and other software, such as Office 365, that are more easily deployed than standalone applications, automatically updated on a regular basis, and accessible on any device platform.

In each of these specializations, cloud services can eliminate the tedious set-up processes that administrators often have to perform before they can get down to work. For example, the process of adding a new physical server to a data center can require many separate tasks, including assessing the hardware needs, selecting a vendor, waiting for delivery, assembling the hardware, and installing and configuring the operating system and applications. These tasks can result in days or weeks wasted before the server is even ready for use. With a cloud provider, the process of adding a new virtual server takes only a matter of minutes. A remote management interface, such as the Windows Azure portal shown in Figure 1-1, enables the subscriber to select the desired virtual hardware resources for the server, and within a few minutes, the new server is running and ready for use.

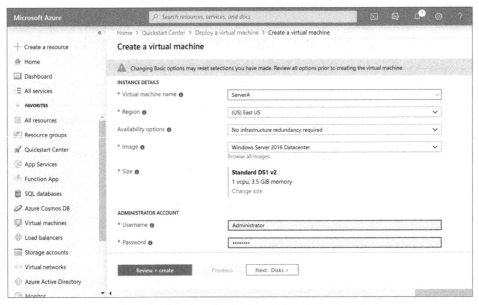

**FIGURE 1-1** The Create a Virtual Machine interface in the Windows Azure Portal

# Advantages of cloud computing

When an organization is building a new IT infrastructure or expanding an existing one, the question of whether to use on-premises resources or subscriber-based cloud services is a critical decision to make these days. Cloud-based services might not be preferable for every computing scenario, but they can provide many advantages over on-premises data centers. When designing an IT strategy, a business should consider both the practical needs of the organization, including data security and other business factors, as well as the relative costs of the required services.

Some of the advantages that cloud computing can provide are discussed in the following sections.

## Economy

Cloud services incur regular charges, but the charges are usually based solely on the subscribers' needs and what they use at a particular time. The monetary savings that result from using cloud services can be significant. Some of the expenses that can be reduced or eliminated by using cloud services include the following:

- **Hardware**   The high-end server hardware used by a large enterprise, aside from the standard computer components, can include elaborate storage arrays and other hardware that is an expensive initial outlay before any actual work starts. The fees for equivalent virtualized hardware in the cloud are amortized over the life of project for which it is used.

- **Upgrades**   In a large enterprise, servers and other hardware components have a documented life expectancy, after which they must be replaced. Cloud hardware is virtual, so the subscriber is isolated from the maintenance costs of the provider's physical hardware. Those costs are, of course, factored into the price of the service, but they eliminate another substantial hardware outlay for the subscriber.

- **Software**   Software licenses are a significant expense, especially for server-based products. In addition to operating systems and applications, utility software for firewalls, antivirus protection, and backups adds to the expenditure. As with hardware, software furnished on a subscription basis by a cloud provider requires little or no initial outlay. Typically, cloud-based software also includes updates applied by the provider on a regular basis.

- **Environment**   Outfitting a large data center often involves much more expenditure than the cost of the computer hardware alone. In addition to the cost of the square footage, a data center typically needs air conditioning and other environmental controls, electricity and power regulation equipment, racks and other mounting hardware, network connectivity equipment, and a physical security infrastructure. Depending on the needs of the organization, these costs can range from significant to astronomical. None of these expenses are required for cloud-based services, although their costs are certainly factored into the fees paid by the subscriber.

- **Network**   A data center requires an Internet connection and may also require cross-connections between locations within the data center. The size and functionality of the data center determine how much throughput is required and what technology can best supply it. More speed costs more money, of course. Cloud-based resources eliminate this expense because connectivity is part of the service. Internet access is still required to administer the cloud resources, but the amount of data transferred is relatively small.

- **Redundancy**  Depending on the needs of the organization, fault tolerance can take the form of backup power supplies, redundant servers, or even redundant data centers in different cities, which can cause the operational costs to grow exponentially. Typically, cloud providers can provide these various types of fault tolerance at a substantial savings. A contract with a cloud provider can include a service level agreement (SLA) with an uptime availability percentage that insulates the subscriber from the actual fault tolerance mechanisms employed and simply guarantees that the contracted services will suffer no more than a specified amount of downtime. For example, a contract specifying 99 percent uptime (colloquially called a *two nines contract*) allows for 3.65 days of downtime per year. A 99.9 percent (or *three nines*) contract allows for 8.76 hours of downtime per year. Contract stipulations go up from there, with the cost rising as the allowed downtime goes down. A 99.9999 percent (or *six nines*) contract allows only 31.5 seconds of downtime per year. Typically, if the provider fails to meet the uptime percentage specified in the SLA, the contract calls for a credit toward part of the monthly fee.

- **Personnel**  A data center requires trained people to install, configure, and maintain all the equipment. While cloud-based service equivalents do require configuration and maintenance performed through a remote interface, the elimination of the need for hardware maintenance greatly reduces the manpower requirements.

The costs of cloud-based services are not insignificant, but the nature of the financial investment is such that many organizations find them to be more practical than building and maintaining a physical data center. The initial outlay of cloud services is minimal, and the ongoing costs are easily predictable.

## Consolidation

Originally, IT departments provided services to users by building and maintaining data centers that contained servers and other equipment. One of the problems with this model was that the servers often were underutilized. To accommodate the increased workload of the "busy season," servers were often built with resources that far exceeded their everyday needs. Those expensive resources therefore remained idle most of the time. Virtual machines (VMs), such as those administrators can create using products like Microsoft Hyper-V and VMware ESX, are a solution to this problem. Virtual machines make it possible to consolidate multiple servers into one physical computer. Administrators can scale virtual machines by adding or subtracting virtualized resources, such as memory and storage, or they can move the virtual machines from one physical computer to another, as needed.

Cloud providers use this same consolidation technique to provide subscribers with virtual machines. For example, when a subscriber to Microsoft Azure creates a new server, what actually happens is that the Azure interface creates a new virtual machine on one of Microsoft's physical servers. The subscriber has no access to the underlying physical computer hosting the VM, nor does the subscriber even know where the computer is physically located. The virtual machines on the physical server are completely isolated from each other, so if even the fiercest competitors were to have VMs running on the same host computer, they would never know it. The provider can—and probably does—move VMs from one host computer to another when necessary, but this process is completely invisible to the subscribers.

The end result of this consolidation model is that each VM receives exactly the virtual hardware resources it needs at any particular time. Subscribers pay only for the virtualized resources they are using. Nothing goes to waste.

## Scalability

Business requirements change. They might increase or decrease over a course of years, and they might also experience regular cycles of activity that are seasonal, monthly, weekly, or even daily. A physical data center must be designed to support the peak activity level for the regular business cycles and also anticipate an expected degree of growth over several years. As mentioned earlier, this can mean purchasing more equipment than the business needs for most of its operational time, leaving that excess capacity often underused.

Cloud-based services avoid these periods of underutilization by being easily scalable. Because the hardware in a virtual machine is itself virtualized, an administrator can modify its resources through a simple configuration change. An on-premises (that is, noncloud) virtual machine is obviously limited by the physical hardware in the computer hosting it and the resources used by other VMs on the same host. In a cloud-based VM, however, these limitations do not apply. The physical hardware resources are invisible to the cloud subscriber, so if the resources the subscriber desires for a VM are not available on its current host computer, the provider can invisibly move the VM to another host that does have sufficient resources.

A cloud-based service is scalable in two ways:

- **Vertical scaling** Also known as *scaling up*, vertical scaling is the addition or subtraction of virtual hardware resources in a VM, such as memory, storage, or CPUs. The scaling process is a simple matter of adjusting the VM's parameters in a remote interface; it can even be automated to accommodate regular business cycles. Therefore, the subscriber pays only for the resources that the VMs are actually using at any given time.

- **Horizontal scaling** Also known as *scaling out*, horizontal scaling is the addition or subtraction of virtual machines to a cluster of servers running a particular application. For example, in the case of a cloud-based web server farm, incoming user requests can be shared among multiple VMs. If the web traffic should increase or decrease, the administrators can add or subtract VMs from the cluster, as needed.

## Reliability

In an on-premises data center, data backup, disaster recovery, and fault tolerance are all expensive services that require additional hardware, deployment time, and administration. A small business might require only a backup storage medium and software. However, for businesses with highly critical IT requirements, these services can call for anything up to duplicate data centers in different cities with high-speed data connections linking them.

In the case of a large-scale cloud provider, however, this is exactly what their infrastructure entails. Therefore, cloud providers are in an excellent position to provide these elaborate services without the need for infrastructure upgrades, and they often can do it for fees that are much less than would be required for businesses to provide them themselves.

For example, Microsoft Azure provides the following reliability mechanisms for its cloud-based services:

- Azure maintains three redundant copies of all data, with one of those copies located in a separate data center.
- Azure provides automatic failover to a backup server to minimize downtime in the event of an outage.
- Azure hosts all applications on two separate server instances to minimize downtime caused by hardware failure.

## Manageability

Because subscribers do not have physical access to the servers hosting their cloud services, they must access them remotely. This is common for organizations with on-premises servers as well, particularly those with large data centers. It is often far more convenient for administrators to access servers from their desks than travel to a data center that might be on another floor, in another building, or even in another city. Today's remote management typically provides comprehensive and reliable access to all server functions.

There are various remote management tools available for both cloud and on-premises resources, but the large third-party cloud providers typically provide a secured web-based portal that enables administrators to access all their subscription services using one interface, such as the one for Microsoft Azure shown in Figure 1-2.

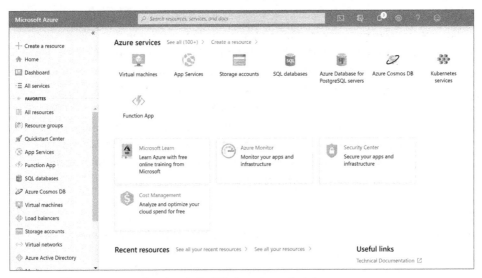

**FIGURE 1-2** The management interface in the Windows Azure Portal

A web-based portal enables administrators to access their services from any location, including from home or while traveling.

## Security

Security is a major issue for any data center, which administrators typically address by concerning themselves with issues such as data loss and unauthorized access. These are important concerns whether the data center is local or virtual. However, in the case of an on-premises data center, there is another potential attack vector: the physical. Servers and other equipment can be stolen outright, damaged by fire or other disasters or physically accessed by intruders. Therefore, there are additional security measures that might be required, such as door locks, surveillance equipment, access credentials, or even manned security checkpoints.

Cloud-based services eliminate the need for physical security, which is furnished by the provider. There is still the issue of software-based security, however, and cloud providers nearly always provide an array of controls and services that enable you to harden the security of your servers and applications to accommodate your business needs.

> **NOTE** **YOU ARE ALWAYS RESPONSIBLE FOR YOUR DATA**
>
> Organizations using cloud resources to implement their servers must be conscious of the fact that they are still responsible for the security and privacy of their data. For example, if an organization stores patient medical records on a cloud-based file server, the organization remains responsible for any data breaches that occur. Therefore, contracts with cloud providers should stipulate the security policies they must maintain.

## Infrastructure

In an on-premises data center, the administrators are responsible for all aspects of the servers and other equipment, including hardware installation and maintenance, operating system configuration and updates, and application deployment and management. Cloud-based services enable subscribers to specify which elements of the infrastructure they are responsible for maintaining.

For example, a subscriber can contract with a provider for a virtual machine running a server operating system, so that the subscriber is responsible for the entire operation and maintenance of the server. The subscriber does not have direct access to the physical hardware of the host system, of course, but he or she does have control over the virtual hardware on which the server runs, as well as all the software running on the server, including the operating system. In some situations, this is desirable, or even essential.

In other situations, cloud-based services can take the form of preinstalled server platforms or applications. In this case, the subscriber might have limited access to the server or no access at all. In the case of a subscriber contracting for Microsoft Exchange Online, the provider grants the subscriber with administrative access to the Exchange Server application, but it does not grant subscriber access to the underlying operating system on which the server application is running. For an Office 365 subscriber, the provider grants access only to the Office applications themselves. The subscriber knows nothing about the servers on which the applications are running or their operating systems.

These options enable cloud service subscribers to exercise administrative responsibility over specific components only in situations in which their business requirements demand it. For the elements administered by the service provider, contracts typically stipulate hardware maintenance requirements and software update policies. The end result can be substantial savings in time and training for the subscriber's in-house IT personnel.

### Alleged Disadvantages of Cloud Computing

There are some IT professionals who persist in stating that cloud-based services are inferior to on-premises services. They might say that an on-premises data center is more secure, more reliable, provides greater access to equipment, or suffers less downtime. While one cannot say that the cloud is always a preferable solution, these arguments mostly date from a time when the cloud was a new and immature technology. They have now largely been debunked by years of proven performance.

There are still reasons why businesses can and should maintain on-premises data centers. For example, they might have special security requirements, or they might have already made a large investment in facilities and equipment. However, each year sees a greater percentage of servers deployed in the cloud and clients accessing cloud-based services. Microsoft 365 is the next step in bringing the cloud to the desktop productivity environment.

## Skill 1.2: Understand the different types of cloud services available

Flexibility is an important aspect of cloud computing, and Microsoft 365 can accommodate a wide variety of IT environments. While some organizations might be building a Microsoft 365 deployment from scratch, others might have existing infrastructure that they want to incorporate into a Microsoft 365 solution. Before it is possible to explore how this can be done, it is important to understand the various types of cloud architectures and service models.

> **This section covers how to:**
> - Position Microsoft 365 in a SaaS, IaaS, PaaS, Public, Private, and Hybrid scenario

## Cloud architectures

Organizations today use cloud resources in different ways and for various reasons. A new business or division of a business might decide to build an entirely new IT infrastructure using only cloud-based resources. Meanwhile, a business that has already invested in a traditional IT infrastructure might use the cloud for expansions or for the addition of selected services. Organizations planning their infrastructures can use any of the three cloud architecture permutations described in the following sections.

## Public cloud

A *public cloud* is a network of servers owned by a third-party service provider at a remote location, which provides subscribers with access to virtual machines or services through the Internet, often for a fee. Prices are based on the resources or services you use. Microsoft Azure, Amazon Web Services, and Google Cloud are all examples of public cloud service providers that organizations use to host their virtual machines and access other services.

> **NOTE**   **PUBLIC DOES NOT MEAN UNPROTECTED**
>
> The term *public cloud* is something of a misnomer; it does not mean that the virtual machines an organization creates in a provider's cloud are public—that is, open to access by anyone. It means only that the provider furnishes services to the public by subscription, which are accessible from any location at any time via the Internet.

These major players in the public cloud industry maintain thousands of servers in data centers located around the world. They can accommodate large enterprise clients by providing services on a global scale. There are other, smaller cloud providers offering the same services, which might not be able to function on such a massive scale, but these can have their advantages as well. Because the cloud service providers are responsible for managing and maintaining the physical servers, the subscribers save a great deal of time, expense, and human resources.

There are two basic types of public cloud deployment that organizations can use, as follows:

- **Shared public cloud**   Subscribers access services that a third-party provider implements on hardware that might be used by other subscribers at the same time. For example, a physical host server at a provider site can run virtual machines belonging to different subscribers simultaneously, as shown in Figure 1-3. The VMs are secured individually and functionally isolated from each other. This is what is typically meant by a public cloud.

- **Dedicated public cloud**   Subscribers contract with a third-party provider for a hardware infrastructure that is dedicated to their exclusive use. (See Figure 1-4.) The services provided are the same as those in a shared public cloud; the only difference is the hardware the provider uses to furnish the services. Obviously, this arrangement is more expensive than a shared public cloud, but some organizations need the additional security and fault tolerance provided by having hardware dedicated to their own use.

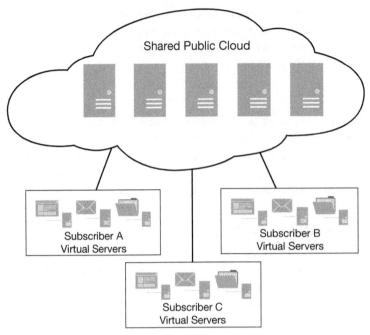

**FIGURE 1-3** Virtual servers running in a shared public cloud

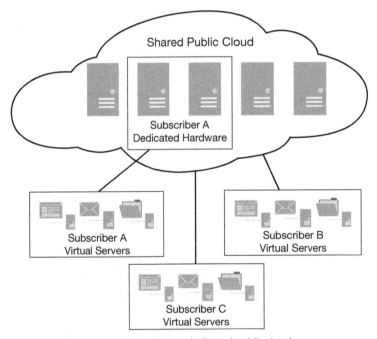

**FIGURE 1-4** Virtual servers running in a dedicated public cloud

Therefore, the term *public cloud* can refer to a provider that enables businesses to build their IT networks virtually instead of physically. Microsoft 365 subscribers can make use of these services to implement all or part of their productivity infrastructure. However, this is not the only function of the public cloud. When people stream movies to their televisions, use web-based banking services, access their email online, or use the Office 365 productivity applications, they are using public cloud providers. The difference in these cases is that the provider is furnishing specific services instead of an IT infrastructure.

## Private cloud

A *private cloud* is a network of servers owned and operated by a business solely for its own use. While the services can be the same and appear identical to their end users, the primary difference is that the organization has control over the physical hardware as well.

In a public cloud deployment of an IT infrastructure, either the subscriber creates virtual machines on the provider's servers and uses them to install and run specific applications or contracts with the provider for access to services running on the provider's own virtual machines. A private cloud deployment usually works in much the same way. The organization still creates and utilizes virtual machines to run its applications in most cases, but it creates those virtual machines on physical host servers that it owns.

Another variation on the private cloud is the *hosted private cloud*, in which hardware that is owned or leased by an organization is housed and managed by a third-party provider. The organization has exclusive use of the hardware and avoids the expenses of building and managing a data center. They do have to pay ongoing fees to the provider, and this arrangement might not satisfy all data storage stipulations, but the overall cost is likely to be less than an on-premises private cloud.

> **NOTE** **PRIVATE CLOUDS AND INTERNET TRAFFIC**
>
> The term *private cloud* can be something of an oxymoron. Typically, the definition of the cloud includes access to services over the Internet. In a public cloud, both administrative and user access to the cloud resources are through the Internet. While a private cloud can provide users and administrators with access to services via the Internet, it typically does not use the Internet when the administrators and users are located at the same site as the data center housing the cloud.
>
> When a large enterprise maintains facilities at multiple locations, users at all those facilities can access a private cloud using the Internet. However, a small- or medium-sized organization running Microsoft 365 Business at a single location can conceivably run what is technically called a private cloud without the need for user and administrator traffic to ever leave the facility.

The private cloud architecture can provide a level of security and privacy that a public cloud provider might not be able to meet. An organization might have government contract stipulations or legal requirements that compel them to maintain their own hardware and store sensitive data on site rather than use third-party hardware that is not subject to the same stipulations or requirements. For example, the Health Insurance Portability and Accountability Act (HIPAA) dictates how medical data must be secured and protected in the United States. Whether a third-party cloud provider is involved, a company is legally responsible for all the data stored on its servers. An organization might also need to run a legacy application that requires a specific hardware or software configuration that a third-party provider cannot supply.

A private cloud also provides a greater degree of customization than public cloud resources. Public cloud providers are successful because of the scale of their businesses; their services are configurable using the options that are most desired by most of their clients. They are not likely to provide access to obscure software options that only a few of their clients will need. In the case of a private cloud, an organization has access to any and all the customization options provided by the software they choose to install.

**EXAM TIP**

The difference between a private cloud and a dedicated public cloud is who owns and operates the hardware. Exam candidates should be aware that some documentation uses the term *private cloud*, instead of *dedicated public cloud*, to describe hardware owned and operated by a third-party provider for the exclusive use of one subscriber.

The advantages of a private cloud are its disadvantages as well. The owner of the hardware is responsible for purchasing, housing, deploying, and maintaining that hardware, which can add greatly to the overall expense, as described earlier in this chapter. There are no ongoing subscriber fees for a private cloud, as there are with a public cloud provider, but there are ongoing fees for operating a data center, including floor space, power, insurance, and personnel.

The organization is also responsible for purchasing and maintaining licenses for all the software products needed to provide the necessary services. This can include operating system licenses, application server licenses, and user licenses, as well as the cost of additional software utilities. Typically, the overall costs of a private cloud infrastructure are higher than that of a public cloud and can be enormously higher. It is up to the organization to determine whether the advantages of the private cloud are worth the additional expense.

## Hybrid cloud

A *hybrid cloud* combines the functionality of a public and a private cloud, enabling an organization to enjoy the best of both architectures. There are a variety of scenarios in which an organization might prefer to implement a hybrid cloud architecture.

If an organization has existing services implemented on its own physical hardware, it might want to maintain those services while adding others from a public cloud provider. For example, the organization might have reached the physical capacity of its own data center and does not want to invest in a major facility expansion.

An organization might also use public cloud resources to extend the capacity of its private cloud or its in-house network during temporary periods of greater need, such as seasonal business increases. This technique, called *cloudbursting*, eliminates the need for the organization to pay for hardware and other resources that are only required for brief periods of time. Because it is possible to connect the public and private services, the resources can interact in any way that is necessary. For example, a business with an e-commerce website implemented in a private cloud can add public cloud-based servers to its web server farm to accommodate the increase in traffic during its Christmas busy season.

Another possibility is that an organization might be subject to the type of data storage or other security requirements described in the previous section, but they do not want to build out their entire infrastructure in a private cloud. In this scenario, the organization could conceivably deploy a database containing the sensitive data in a private cloud and use a public cloud provider for a website implementation that is linked to the database. This way, the network can comply with the storage requirements without having to go to the expense of deploying web servers and other services in the private cloud. The same is true for a variety of other services; organizations can keep their sensitive data and services in the private cloud and use the public cloud for the nonsensitive services. Organizations can also use private cloud resources to run legacy equipment or applications, while all the other services run on a less expensive public cloud.

Some cloud providers supply tools that enable administrators to manage their public and private cloud resources through a single interface. Microsoft Azure provides Azure Active directory, for example, which enables a subscriber to use the same directory service for public and private cloud resources, so that administrators can access both with a single sign-on. Azure also provides management and security interfaces, both of which have built-in support for hybrid cloud architectures.

## Cloud service models

The offerings of cloud service providers are typically broken down into service models, which specify what elements of the cloud infrastructure are included with each product. There are three primary cloud service models, called Infrastructure as a Service (IaaS), Platform as a Service (PaaS), and Software as a Service (SaaS).

A cloud infrastructure can be broken down into layers forming a stack, as shown in Figure 1-5. The functions of the layers are as follows:

- **People**   The users working with the application
- **Data**   The information that the application creates or utilizes
- **Application**   The top-level software program running on virtual machine
- **Runtime**   An intermediate software layer, such as .NET or Java, that provides the environment in which applications run
- **Middleware**   A software component that provides intermediate services between an operating system and applications

- **Operating system**   The software that provides the basic functions of a virtual machine
- **Virtual network**   The logical connections between virtual machines running on servers
- **Hypervisor**   The software component on the physical servers that enables virtual machines to share the server's physical resources
- **Servers**   The physical computers that host the virtual machines that provide cloud services
- **Storage**   The hard drives and other physical components that make up the subsystem providing data storage for the physical servers
- **Physical network**   The cables, routers, and other equipment that physically connect the servers to each other and to the Internet

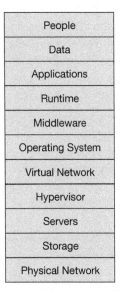

| People |
| Data |
| Applications |
| Runtime |
| Middleware |
| Operating System |
| Virtual Network |
| Hypervisor |
| Servers |
| Storage |
| Physical Network |

**FIGURE 1-5** The layers of the cloud infrastructure

In an organization that uses its own on-premises servers for everything, there is no cloud involved, and the organization is obviously responsible for managing all the layers of the stack. However, when an organization uses cloud-based services, the cloud service provider manages some layers of the stack, and the organization manages the rest. This is called a *shared responsibility model.* Which layers are managed by the organization and which are managed by the provider depends on the service model used to furnish the cloud product. The three basic cloud service models are described in the following sections.

## IaaS

*Infrastructure as a Service (IaaS)* is a cloud computing model in which a cloud service provider furnishes the client with the physical computing elements: the network, the storage subsystem, the physical servers, and the hypervisor running on the servers. This provides subscribers with everything they need to create their own virtual machines and manage them by themselves.

Therefore, all the cloud infrastructure layers above the hypervisor are the responsibility of the subscriber, as shown in Figure 1-6.

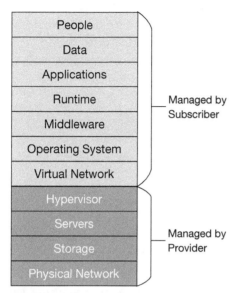

FIGURE 1-6 The shared responsibility model for IaaS

For example, when a subscriber uses Microsoft Azure to create a virtual machine, the provider is furnishing access to a physical server with hypervisor software—presumably Microsoft Hyper-V—running on it. The server has a physical storage subsystem and is connected to a physical network that provides it with access to the provider's other servers and to the Internet. Using the management tools that Azure provides, the subscriber can create a virtual machine containing a specific amount of memory and storage, and a number of CPUs, all of which are realized virtually.

> **NEED MORE REVIEW?** **CLOUD COMPUTING WITH MICROSOFT AZURE**
>
> For more information on cloud computing as realized in Microsoft Azure, see https://azure.microsoft.com/en-ca/overview/what-is-cloud-computing.

The end result is a virtual machine that the subscriber can install, configure, and use to run applications just like a VM running on an on-premises server. The difference is that the subscriber does not have to outfit a data center, build a network, procure a physical computer, and install the hypervisor. Instead, the subscriber pays a regular fee for the actual resources that the VM uses. The subscriber can add memory, storage, and CPUs to the VM or remove them, as needed, and the subscriber can configure many other settings through a remote management interface. Additional resources incur additional fees, but the process of building a new server takes a matter of minutes instead of days or weeks.

With the IaaS model, the provider is responsible for the physical servers and the physical network, but the subscriber is responsible for managing and maintaining its virtual machines and the virtual network on which they run, as shown earlier in Figure 1-6. Therefore, the provider installs operating system updates on the physical servers, but the subscriber must install any operating system and application updates needed on the virtual machines. Any other VM software, maintenance, and management issues that arise also are the subscriber's responsibility.

> **NOTE   VM UPDATE MANAGEMENT**
>
> For an additional fee, Microsoft Azure can provide an Update Management solution that automates the installation of updates and patches on a subscriber's virtual machines.

Of all the cloud service models, IaaS places the greatest amount of responsibility on the subscriber, and in many instances, this is how administrators want it. By creating and configuring their own virtual machines, administrators can duplicate the environment of their on-premises servers, creating a hybrid cloudbursting infrastructure that can handle overflow traffic during a busy season.

Organizations with high traffic websites often use a dedicated web hosting service provider to run their sites. However, building the site using virtual machines furnished by a cloud service provider using the IaaS model often can be a far less expensive proposition.

Subscribers can also use IaaS to create a testing and development environment for applications. Rapid deployment and modification of VMs makes it possible for administrators to create multiple temporary evaluation and testing platforms and take them down just as easily.

IaaS can also provide subscribers with VMs containing massive amounts of virtual hardware resources that would be impractical to implement in on-premises servers. Large data sets and high-performance computing can require huge amounts of memory and processing power to perform the tasks required for applications, such as weather patterning, data mining, and financial modeling. The resources of a high-end cloud service provider make it far less expensive to equip VMs with the necessary virtual hardware than to build equivalent physical servers.

## PaaS

In what is sometimes referred to as a *tiered cloud* service model infrastructure, *Platform as a Service (PaaS)* is the second tier, in that it builds on the provider's responsibilities from the first (IaaS) tier. PaaS is designed to provide subscribers with a ready-made developmental platform that enables them to avoid spending time repeatedly building out the hardware and software infrastructure for a test system before they can run a new application.

Because the platform is accessible through the Internet like all cloud services, an organization with multiple developers working on the same project can provide them all with access to the test environment, even if they are located at different sites.

The PaaS model expands the responsibility of the cloud service provider over the IaaS model by adding the virtual network, operating system, middleware, and runtime layers, as shown in Figure 1-7. The greater the responsibility of the provider, the less that of the subscriber.

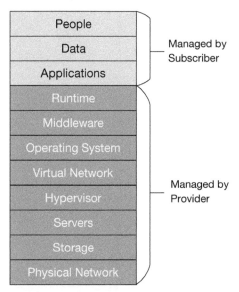

**FIGURE 1-7** The shared responsibility model for PaaS

Unlike virtual machines on the IaaS model, the cloud provider is entirely responsible for the VM operating system, applying updates and patches and performing maintenance as needed. The platform can also include (for an extra fee) additional components specified by the subscriber, such as development tools, middleware, and database management systems. The object of the PaaS model is to eliminate the need for software developers to do anything but actually develop, build, customize, test, and deploy their applications.

## Serverless

The fees for PaaS and IaaS virtual machines are typically based on the resources they are configured to use and the time they are running. However, there is another cloud service model for application development, related to PaaS, called *serverless computing*. In serverless computing (sometimes known as *Function as a Service*, or FaaS), the cloud provider takes on even more of the server management responsibility by dynamically allocating virtual machine resources in response to application requests or events.

Pricing is based on the VM resources as they are actually used. Therefore, this model can be less expensive than a PaaS VM that is incurring charges all the time it is running. The term *serverless*, in this instance, does not mean that there is no server involved; the name derives from the fact that the cloud subscriber does not have to provision a virtual machine on which the developer's code will run.

## SaaS

*Software as a Service (SaaS)* is the third tier of the cloud service model infrastructure, and in this model, the cloud provider is responsible for nearly all the layers. Only the people and data layers are left to the subscriber, as shown in Figure 1-8. This means that the provider is responsible for the applications, as well as all the layers beneath.

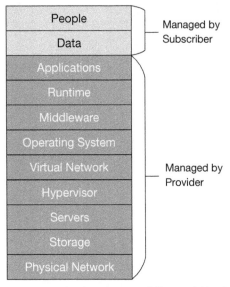

**FIGURE 1-8** The shared responsibility model for SaaS

The SaaS model enables endusers to access cloud-based applications using a web or other thin-client interface, without the need to install the applications first. Office 365 is an example of an SaaS product, as are Microsoft Teams and other Microsoft 365 components. While Office 365 makes it possible to install its productivity applications on a client computer, it is not necessary for the user to do so. The applications are accessible directly through a web browser, with everything but the user's own data files provided through the cloud.

**EXAM TIP**

The MS-900 exam requires you to understand the role of the public, private, and hybrid architectures, as well as the IaaS, PaaS, and SaaS service models, in cloud computing. However, be sure also to understand how these elements fit in with the Microsoft 365 product.

# Summary

- Cloud computing can provide organizations with many benefits, including economy scalability, reliability, manageability, and security.
- There are three basic cloud architectures:
    - **Public** Cloud resources are furnished by a third-party provider on the Internet.
    - **Private** An organization provides its own cloud resources.
    - **Hybrid** The public and private architectures are combined.
- There are three cloud service models—IaaS, PaaS, and SaaS, which specify how much of the resource management is the responsibility of the cloud provider and how much is the responsibility of the subscriber.

# Thought experiment

In this thought experiment, demonstrate your skills and knowledge of the topics covered in this chapter. You can find answer to this thought experiment in the next section.

Wingtip Toys has a website on which they sell their products to customers worldwide; it is the company's primary source of sales. The website is hosted on a server farm in the company's data center, which is a small room in the building's basement. The incoming traffic is distributed among the servers by a load-balancing switch. Richard, the administrator of the site, regularly monitors the website traffic and, as the holiday season approaches, he sees the traffic level rise almost to the point at which the servers are overwhelmed.

There is no budget for the purchase of additional web server computers, and there is also no room for more servers in the data center. Reading about cloud options, Richard thinks that there might be a solution there. How can Richard expand the web server farm to handle the increased traffic for the least expense by using the cloud?

# Thought experiment answer

For a minimal expenditure, Richard can create additional web servers using cloud-based virtual machines and add them to his web server farm, forming a hybrid cloud architecture. The cloud-based servers can help to handle the busy season web traffic, and when the traffic levels go down, Richard can remove the VMs from the server farm until they are needed again.

# CHAPTER 2

# Understand core Microsoft 365 services and concepts

At the most basic level, the Microsoft 365 product is documented as consisting of the following components:

- Office 365 Enterprise
- Windows 10 Enterprise
- Enterprise Mobility + Security

The object of the product is to provide users with a comprehensive workflow that combines cloud-based services, artificial intelligence, and machine learning capabilities. To do this, these three components actually consist of a variety of front-end and back-end applications and services, as described in the sections of this chapter.

## Skills in this chapter:

- Describe the core Microsoft 365 components
- Compare core services in Microsoft 365 with corresponding on-premises services
- Understand the concept of modern management
- Understand Office 365 ProPlus
- Understand collaboration and mobility with Microsoft 365
- Describe analytics capabilities in Microsoft 365

## Skill 2.1: Describe the core Microsoft 365 components

Microsoft 365 is not just a collection of workstation applications; it's designed more to be a comprehensive productivity solution for users, as well as a management solution for administrators. For users, the most visible element of Microsoft 365 is Office 365 Pro Plus, with the same familiar Outlook, Word, Excel, and PowerPoint applications they've probably been using for years. However, there are many Microsoft 365 components operating beneath the immediately visible applications, which help to protect the users and their data and provide them with intelligent communication and collaboration services.

# Windows 10 Enterprise

Windows 10 is the operating system that enables users to access both the Office 365 productivity applications and the services provided by the other Microsoft 365 components. The Microsoft 365 Enterprise product plans include the Enterprise edition of Windows 10. The Enterprise edition of Windows 10 includes security measures, deployment tools, and manageability functions that go beyond those of Windows 10 Pro, providing administrators of enterprise networks with centralized and automated protection of and control over fleets of workstations.

Some of the additional features included in Windows 10 Enterprise are described in the following sections.

## Security

All Windows 10 editions include Windows Defender, which protects the operating system from various types of malware attacks. However, compared to Windows 10 Pro, Windows 10 Enterprise includes several enhancements to the Windows Defender software, including the following functions:

- **Windows Defender Application Guard**   This enables enterprise administrators to create lists of trusted Internet sites, cloud resources, and intranet networks. When a user accesses an untrusted site using Microsoft Edge or Internet Explorer, Windows 10 automatically creates a Hyper-V container and opens the untrusted resource within the protected environment that the container provides. The result is that if the untrusted resource turns out to be malicious, the attacker is isolated within the container and the host computer remains protected.

- **Windows Defender Application Control (WDAC)**   This provides defense against malicious applications by reversing the standard trust model in which applications are assumed to be trustworthy until they are proven otherwise. WDAC prevents a system from running any applications, plug-ins, add-ins, and other software modules that have not been identified as trusted using a policy created with Microsoft Intune or Group Policy.

- **Microsoft Defender Advanced Threat Protection (ATP)**   Windows 10 includes the client-side components of ATP, a private cloud-based threat prevention, detection, and response engine. Windows 10 includes endpoint behavioral sensors, which collect behavioral information from the operating system and forward it to the ATP back-end servers in the enterprise's private cloud for analysis. ATP also protects the files in key system folders from unauthorized modification or encryption by ransomware and other attacks, applies exploit mitigation techniques to protect against known threats, enhances the network protection provided by Windows Defender SmartScreen, and performs automated real-time investigation and remediation of security breaches.

## Updates

Windows 10 performs system updates differently from previous Windows versions, replacing the major service packs released every few years with semi-annual feature updates.

The Windows Update process is automated by default for the typical Windows user, but network administrators can still intervene in the process for the purpose of testing update releases before they are generally deployed.

Microsoft provides the following tools for the administration of updates:

- **Windows Update for Business**   This is a free cloud-based service that enables administrators to defer, schedule, and pause update deployments to specific workstations. Administrators can use the service to allow the installation of updates on designated test systems only, and then deploy the updates later if no problems arise. If there are problems with particular updates, administrators can pause their deployments indefinitely.

- **Windows Server Update Service (WSUS)**   This is a free, downloadable service that enables administrators to manage system updates internally by downloading releases to a WSUS server as they become available, testing them as needed, and then deploying them to workstations on a specific schedule. WSUS not only enables administrators to exercise complete control over the update deployment process, it also reduces the Internet bandwidth used by the update process by downloading releases only once and then distributing them using the internal network. Administrators can install multiple WSUS servers and distribute update preferences and release schedules among them, making the system highly scalable.

While administrators can use these tools to manage updates on workstations running any version of Windows, there are additional enhancements for Windows 10 Enterprise workstations, including its manageability with the Desktop Analytics tool. *Desktop Analytics* is an enhanced service incorporating all of the upgrade compatibility and upgrade monitoring functionality of Windows Analytics, along with deeper integration into the Microsoft management tools, such as System Center Configuration Manager (SCCM), and a "single pane of glass" interface that provides administrators with a comprehensive view of Windows 10 and Office 365 update status.

Some of the update monitoring functions supported by Desktop Analytics are as follows:

- **Upgrade Readiness**   Desktop Analytics collects information about Windows, Office 365, and other applications and drivers and analyzes it to identify any compatibility issues that might interfere with an upgrade.

- **Update Compliance**   Desktop Analytics gathers Windows 10 information about the progress of operating system update deployments, as well as Windows Defender Antivirus signature and result data, Windows Update for Business configuration settings, and Delivery Optimization usage data. After analyzing the information, Desktop Analytics reports any update compliance issues that might need administrative attention.

- **Device Health**   A Desktop Analytics solution that uses the enhanced diagnostic data generated by Windows 10 to identify devices and drivers that are causing regular crashes. The tool also provides potential remediations, such as alternative driver versions or application replacements.

Windows 10 Enterprise also supports Windows 10 LTSC Access. The Long Term Servicing Channel (LTSC), formerly called the Long Term Servicing Branch (LTSB), is an update model that enterprise administrators can use for special purpose systems that perform a single task, such as kiosks. LTSC systems receive standard monthly quality updates, but they do not receive the semi-annual feature updates. There are LTSC feature updates made available every two to three years, but administrators can choose when or whether to install them. This enables the LTSC system to maintain a consistent feature set throughout its life cycle, so that it remains compliant with its designated function.

## Management

Microsoft 365 provides many enhancements to the enterprise management environment that enable administrators to simplify the process of deploying and configuring Windows 10 Enterprise workstations. One of the primary objectives of Microsoft 365 is to automate many of the routine tasks that occupy a great deal of an administrator's time.

- **Windows Autopilot**   This is a cloud-based feature that is designed to simplify and automate the process of deploying Windows 10 workstations on an enterprise network. Instead of having to create and maintain images and drivers for every computer model, Autopilot uses cloud-based settings and policies to reconfigure the OEM-installed operating system into a user-ready workstation, even installing applications and applying a new product key to transform Windows 10 Pro to the Windows 10 Enterprise edition.

- **Microsoft Application Virtualization (App-V)**   This enables Windows workstations to access Win32 applications that are actually running on servers instead of local disks. Administrators must install the App-V server components and publish the desired applications. A client component is necessary as well, and Windows 10 Enterprise (version 1607 or higher) includes the App-V client by default, so no additional installation is necessary. The client does have to be activated, however; administrators can activate clients using either Group Policy settings or the *Enable-App* cmdlet in Windows PowerShell.

- **Microsoft User Experience Virtualization (UE-V)**   This is the feature that enables Windows workstations to store user-customized operating system and application settings on a network share and sync them across multiple devices. Administrators still must install the UE-V server components, but as of version 1607, the UE-V client is included in Windows 10 Enterprise edition.

## Windows 10 Business

The Microsoft 365 Business plan does not include the full Windows 10 package because the assumption is that potential deployers already have or will be purchasing computers with a Windows OEM operating system installed. However, Windows 10 is required for the end-user workstations to function with the Microsoft 365 services, so the Microsoft 365 Business plan does include upgrade benefits to Windows 10 Pro for computers that are currently running Windows 7 or Windows 8.1 Pro.

Microsoft 365 Business also includes an enhancement called Windows 10 Business, which enables Windows 10 Pro to function with the cloud-based management and security controls in Microsoft 365, including Microsoft Autopilot.

> **NOTE  MICROSOFT 365 PLAN COMPONENTS**
>
> For more information about the components included in the various Microsoft 365 plans, see Chapter 4, "Understand Microsoft 365 pricing and support."

# Exchange Online

Exchange Online is a cloud-based implementation of Microsoft's flagship messaging and collaboration server product. All of the Microsoft 365 Enterprise and Microsoft 365 Business plans include access to Exchange Online for all of their users. This eliminates the need for organizations to install and maintain their own on-premises Exchange servers.

As with Microsoft Azure, Exchange Online uses shared servers in Microsoft data centers to host the mailboxes and other services for multiple subscribers. The Exchange Online services available include the following:

- **Mailboxes**   Each user is provided with mail storage, the amount of which is based on the Microsoft 365 plan. An In-Place Archive provides additional storage for mail. Exchange also supports shared mailboxes for groups of users that share responsibility for incoming mail.

- **Calendars**   Users can maintain events and appointments and share them with other users to create a unified scheduling and collaboration environment.

- **Shared calendars**   Users can share their calendars for scheduling, task management, and conference room booking. Exchange Online also provides a global address book, group management, and mailbox delegation.

- **Exchange Online Protection (EOP)**   EOP scans incoming email for spam and malicious code and forwards, deletes, or quarantines potentially dangerous messages based on rules established by administrators.

- **Unified Messaging (UM)**  UM enables administrators to combine email message with voice mail, so that both message types are stored in a single mailbox for each user. UM provides standard voice mail features, including call answering, and enables users to listen to their messages from the Outlook Inbox or by using Outlook Voice Access from any telephone.

- **Data Loss Prevention (DLP)**  DLP enables administrators to create DLP policies that protect sensitive company information by using deep content analysis to filter messaging traffic based on keywords, regular expressions, dictionary terms, and other criteria, and then take specific actions based on the type of information detected. For example, a DLP policy can identify email messages that contain credit card numbers and either notify the sender, encrypt the messages, or block them outright. More complex policies can identify specific types of company documents and use virtual fingerprinting to identify their source.

Microsoft maintains two Exchange Online subscription plans: Plan 1 that is included with Microsoft 365 Business, and Plan 2, which has additional features and is included with Microsoft 365 Enterprise. The features included in each plan are listed in Table 2-1.

**TABLE 2-1** Exchange Online plans for Microsoft 365

| EXCHANGE ONLINE PLAN 1 (MICROSOFT 365 BUSINESS) | EXCHANGE ONLINE PLAN 2 (MICROSOFT 365 ENTERPRISE) |
|---|---|
| 50 GB of mailbox storage per user | 100 GB of mailbox storage per user |
| In-Place Archive | Unlimited additional user storage in In-Place Archive |
| Access via desktop Outlook, Outlook on the web, and Outlook Mobile | Access via desktop Outlook, Outlook on the web, and Outlook Mobile |
| Individual user calendars | Individual user calendars |
| Shared calendars | Shared calendars |
| Exchange Online Protection | Exchange Online Protection |
| | Unified Messaging |
| | Data Loss Prevention |

Users can access Exchange Online services using the Microsoft Outlook application included with Office 365, the web-based Outlook client, or Outlook Mobile. This enables users to access their mail, calendars, and other services with virtually any device, including smartphones and tablets running iOS, Android, or Windows 10.

Microsoft 365 administrators do not have direct access to the Exchange Online servers, but they can access the Exchange Admin Center from a link in the Microsoft 365 Admin Center to manage Exchange-specific settings using a web-based interface, as shown in Figure 2-1.

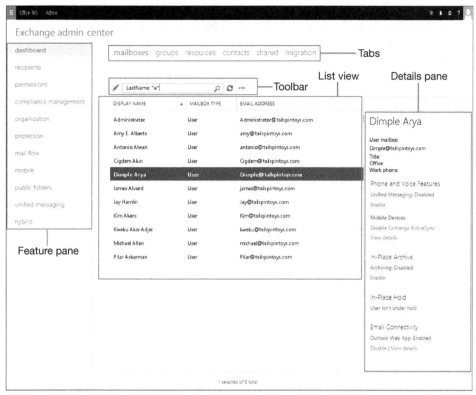

**FIGURE 2-1** The Exchange Admin Center interface

In this interface, administrators can perform tasks such as the following:

- Create and manage user accounts
- Grant management role permissions for administrators and users
- Configure mail flow options to integrate on-premises mail servers or third-party mail services into the message handling solution
- Enable calendar sharing with outside organizations or between users on-premises and in the cloud
- Manage hierarchical and offline address books, address lists, and address book policies
- Create and manage a public folder hierarchy for document sharing and collaboration
- Create and manage client access rules to restrict access to Exchange Online based on client platform, IP address, authentication type, location, and other criteria.

## SharePoint Online

Microsoft SharePoint is a web-based collaboration tool that was originally introduced in 2001 as an on-premises server product. SharePoint Online is the cloud-based equivalent that is included with all Microsoft 365 plans.

SharePoint Online is a service that administrators and workers can use to create websites for document management, distribution, and collaboration. At its simplest, SharePoint Online users can create a document library on the web and upload their files to it. The files are then accessible from any device that has access to the site. As SharePoint Online is part of Office 365, editing a library document opens it in the appropriate Office application, whether installed on a desktop or part of Office Online.

Users can share their library files with other users with varying degrees of access by assigning permissions to them. A scenario in which an organization or user wants to post documents to a library for many users to access is called a *communication site*. For example, a company could use SharePoint Online to create a library of human resources documents for all employees to access. SharePoint includes customization capabilities that enable administrators to design websites with modern graphical components, as shown in Figure 2-2.

**FIGURE 2-2** A sample SharePoint Online site

Even more useful, multiple people can edit a single SharePoint Online document at the same time, providing a collaborative environment that enables groups to work together. By creating a *team site*, a designated group of users can work simultaneously on documents that only they can access. SharePoint maintains multiple versions of the files in a library, so that users can review the iterations of a document throughout its history.

Communication sites and team sites are linked together in SharePoint Online by *hub sites*, which provide centralized navigation to the subordinate sites and downstream searching.

The SharePoint Online service included in Microsoft 365 can host multiple hub, collaboration, and team sites, as shown in Figure 2-3.

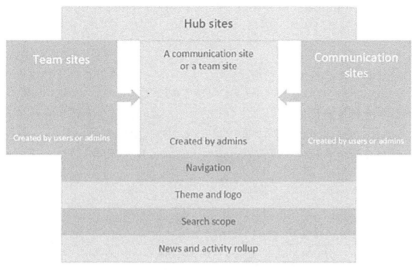

**FIGURE 2-3** SharePoint Online site types

Because SharePoint Online is integrated with the other Microsoft 365 components, users can take advantage of their security and manageability features. The documents uploaded to SharePoint Online sites are protected against malicious code by the same antimalware engine used by Exchange, as well as Data Loss Prevention. Outlook integration enables users to schedule team events and deliver them to members' calendars. SharePoint also can control group memberships and document permissions with user identities taken from Active Directory and Azure Active Directory.

The SharePoint Online plan included with Microsoft 365 Enterprise includes 1 TB of storage for the organization plus 10 GB for each license purchased. An organization can also purchase additional storage, up to a maximum of 25 TB per site collection. An organization can create up to one million site collections.

A SharePoint Online library can have up to 30 million files and folders, although there are limitations when the number goes beyond 100,000. Individual files can be up to 15 GB in size, and SharePoint can maintain up to 50,000 versions of each file. SharePoint groups can have up to 5,000 users, and a user can be a member of up to 5,000 groups. Therefore, SharePoint Online can support enormous installations that service as many as 500,000 users.

## Microsoft Teams

Microsoft Teams is another multiplatform collaboration tool included with Microsoft 365 that enables users to communicate and work together in real time, using document libraries, group and private chat, scheduled and unscheduled meetings, and audio/video calls. Teams is a client interface that works together with the other Microsoft 365 services to create a unified collaboration environment, as shown in Figure 2-4.

**FIGURE 2-4** The Microsoft Teams desktop interface

The Teams client provides real-time chat and the ability to make and receive calls, but the other tools incorporated into the client are provided by other Microsoft 365 services, as shown in Figure 2-5.

| Identity | Storage | Mail/Scheduling | Web Site | Chat | Calls | Video |
|----------|---------|-----------------|----------|------|-------|-------|
| Office 365 Groups | OneDrive for Business | Exchange Online/Outlook | SharePoint Online | Teams | Teams | Streams |

**FIGURE 2-5** Microsoft 365 services used by Microsoft Teams

The messaging functionality that Teams provides enables users to create *channels*, which are individual chat sessions shared by a team's members. A channel enables its members to post text and images, as well as information from outside social media services. Teams messaging is an independent service that does not rely on email or SMS messaging for communication. Teams also supports the transmission of private one-to-one messages between users.

The calling capability in Teams can use Voice over IP (VoIP) or standard Public Switched Telephone Network (PSTN) connections. Video conferencing is also possible within the Teams client software. Office 365 provides Teams with access to features such as Phone System, Direct Routing, and Calling Plan, which can perform functions typically left to standard telephony hardware, such as a private branch exchange (PBX).

Membership and authentication in Microsoft Teams is provided by Office 365 groups, which store their identity information in Azure Active Directory. Teams can store their documents and other files in the cloud using OneDrive for Business. Team websites, implemented using SharePoint Online, are also accessible through the Teams client. Group mailboxes and event and meeting scheduling are provided by Exchange Online and accessed via Outlook. To host and preserve meetings on video, Teams can use the Microsoft Stream service.

Teams is highly scalable and can support collaborative environments ranging from small workgroups to large departments to gigantic presentations, webinars, and conferences. Teams is also customizable, enabling administrators to incorporate third-party applications and services into a team's collaborative environment. For example, multiple vendors are working on H.323 video conferencing solutions that will enable teams to collaborate with outside partners.

> **NOTE** **MICROSOFT TEAMS IS REPLACING SKYPE FOR BUSINESS ONLINE**
>
> The instant messaging, meeting, and peer-to-peer voice and video functions formerly provided by the Skype for Business Online service are now being incorporated into Microsoft Teams. Skype for Business Online is being deprecated. Current users must switch to Microsoft Teams when their current Skype for Business Online terms expires.

# Enterprise Mobility + Security

Microsoft 365 is a suite of applications that is designed to provide users with advanced, cross-platform collaboration capabilities. In achieving this end, the product incorporates two current technologies that introduce new security and access control issues: the cloud and portable computing devices. For the features highlighted in Microsoft 365 to function as intended, users must be able to access their colleagues and their data from any location, using any device. For the administrators of Microsoft 365, the users must be able to do their work securely and reliably, even when they are using devices not supplied by the company.

Because Microsoft 365 takes the enterprise beyond the organization's physical perimeter and into the cloud, as well as into users' pockets and bags, a new security paradigm is needed, which is provided by *Enterprise Mobility + Security (EMS)*. EMS is a cloud-based management and security suite that consists of several components that were at one time separate products. Together, these components supply services to Microsoft 365 in the following primary areas:

- Identity and access management
- Mobile device and application management
- Information management and protection
- Cybersecurity and risk management

The components that make up EMS are described in the following sections.

## Azure Active Directory Premium

Active Directory (AD) is a directory service that has been a part of the Windows Server product since the Windows 2000 Server release. A directory service is a database of objects, including users and computers, that provides authentication and authorization services for network resources. *Azure Active Directory (Azure AD or AAD)* is a cloud-based equivalent that can provide Microsoft 365 users with single-sign on capability that enables them to access all of their SaaS applications and services, including Office 365 and any third-party products that administrators have integrated into their Microsoft 365 environment, from any device, at any location.

Azure AD provides a Microsoft 365 deployment with identity and access management services that extend beyond the on-premises network into the cloud. Azure AD enhances the security of the Microsoft 365 environment by supporting multifactor authentication, which requires users to verify their identities in two or more ways, such as with a password and a biometric factor, such as a fingerprint.

Azure AD can also provide authentication and authorization services for internal resources, such as on-premises applications and services. For organizations with an existing Windows Server–based AD infrastructure, Azure AD can connect to internal domain controllers, to create a hybrid directory service solution that shares the advantages of both implementations.

> **NEED MORE REVIEW?**
>
> For more information on how Azure Active Directory provides security services to a Microsoft 365 environment, see Chapter 3, "Understand security, compliance, privacy, and trust in Microsoft 365."

## Microsoft Intune

*Microsoft Intune* is a cloud-based device and application management tool that is integrated with the authentication and authorization functions provided by Azure Active Directory. While administrators can use Intune to manage their in-house computers and applications, the primary innovation of the product is its ability to manage BYOD, or user-owned, devices, such as smartphones, tablets, and laptops, and enable them to access the organization's protected services, applications, and data securely.

Intune can manage devices running any of the major mobile operating systems, including Android, iOS, MacOS, and of course Windows. Using Intune, even operating systems that are not able to join an Active Directory domain can access protected resources. Intune uses the mobile operating system's protocols and APIs to communicate, building an inventory of devices that can access company applications and data.

Administrators can use Intune to create standards for the configuration of security settings that a device must meet before it can access protected resources. For example, an administrator can require that a device uses a particular type of authentication or specify that only certain applications can access company data. Intune can even ensure that sensitive data is removed from a device when an app shuts down. This type of control enables Microsoft 365 to maintain the security of its resources without the need for administrators to take complete control over user-owned devices.

## Azure Information Protection

*Azure Information Protection (AIP)* is a system that enables users and administrators to apply labels to documents and emails that classify the information they contain. The labels can be configured to specify how applications treat the information and, optionally, take steps to protect it.

AIP can apply labels to specific documents, or it can follow rules created by administrators to identify sensitive data in any document. For example, an administrator can create a rule that identifies data patterns associated with credit card or social security numbers in a Word document as a user is creating it. When the user attempts to save the document, AIP warns the user to apply the label, as shown in Figure 2-6.

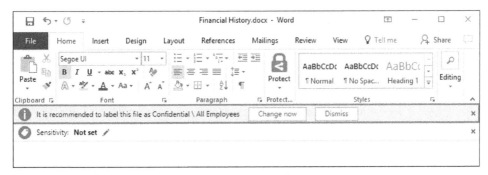

**FIGURE 2-6** An AIP labeling recommendation in a Word document

Administrators can also configure AIP labels to be visible in the documents to which they are applied. When a user agrees to classify a document as sensitive, the application can apply a watermark or other visual indicator, which will persist in the document wherever it is stored.

AIP can also use *Azure Rights Management (Azure RMS)* to protects documents or emails that have been labeled as sensitive. Based on the rules created by administrators, documents labeled by AIP can be protected using encryption, identity restrictions, authorization policies, and other methods. For example, when an email message contains sensitive data, AIP can exercise control over the email client application, preventing users from clicking the **Reply All** or **Forward** button. In the same way, AIP can restrict Office 365 documents to nonprinting or read-only status.

## Microsoft Advanced Threat Analytics

Advanced Threat Analytics (ATA) is an on-premises solution that uses information gathered from a wide variety of enterprise sources and uses it to anticipate, detect, and react to security threats and attacks. ATA receives log and event information from Windows systems, and also captures network traffic generated by security-related protocols, such as Kerberos and NTLM. This traffic provides ATA with information about user authentication and authorization patterns.

Using this gathered information, ATA builds up profiles of applications, services, and users. By examining the normal behavior of these entities, ATA can detect anomalous behavior when it occurs and ascertain whether that behavior is suspicious, based on known attack patterns. When it suspects or detects a security breach, ATA displays an alert in the ATA dashboard, such as the one shown in Figure 2-7.

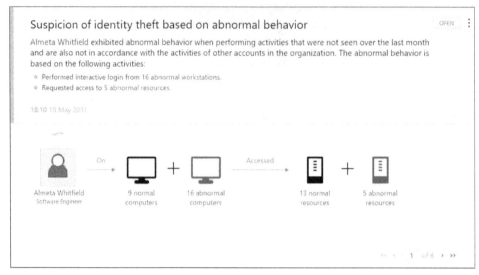

**FIGURE 2-7** A Microsoft Advanced Threat Analytics alert to abnormal behavior

ATA is one of several Microsoft 365 technologies that uses advanced intelligence to anticipate user needs before they occur. In this case, the need is for intervention, whether automated or human, in a potentially dangerous security situation.

## Cloud App Security

Microsoft's research has determined that, of the hundreds of cloud applications that large enterprises use today, a large percentage of them are unknown to the IT department and therefore are unmanaged by them. Microsoft has started calling these clandestine cloud apps Shadow IT, and they obviously present a security hazard.

Cloud App Security is a cloud access security broker (CASB) product that enables Microsoft 365 administrators to scan their networks for the cloud apps that users are accessing, assess their security vulnerability, and manage them on an ongoing basis.

Cloud App Security examines traffic logs and firewall and proxy information to discover the cloud apps in use. After determining whether the apps present a danger to data, identities, or other resources, administrators can then sanction or unsanction specific apps to allow or prevent user access to them. For apps that administrators have sanctioned, Cloud App Security uses the apps' own APIs to connect to them and monitor user activity.

### Azure Advanced Threat Protection

As with the Microsoft Defender Advanced Threat Protection feature included in Windows 10, Microsoft Azure has its own ATP, as do Office 365, Exchange Online, SharePoint Online, Teams, and OneDrive. Each ATP engine is designed to use machine intelligence to prevent, detect, and respond to the security threats unique to its environment. In Azure, the primary vulnerability is the identities stored in Azure Active Directory, so the Azure ATP engine looks for anomalous user behavior and compares it to standardized patterns used by attackers.

# Skill 2.2: Compare core services in Microsoft 365 with corresponding on-premises services

Microsoft 365 is based primarily on cloud services, but some of the services are also available as on-premises products. For example, an organization can use Exchange Online for email and scheduling or install its own servers and run an on-premises version of Exchange. The same is true for SharePoint Online, Azure Active Directory, and Office 365. As with any trade-off situation, there are advantages and disadvantages to both sides.

## Deployment

A cloud-based service is always simpler to deploy than an on-premises server-based product because the service is provided to the subscriber in an installed and operational state. There is no need to design an infrastructure, obtain hardware, or install server software. An administrator can begin to work with the service immediately after subscribing to it, creating user objects, Exchange mailboxes, or SharePoint sites that are up and running in minutes, instead of days or weeks.

## Updates

One significant advantage to using the cloud-based version of any of these applications or services is that they are regularly and automatically updated with the latest version of the software. Administrators are relieved of the need to download, evaluate, and deploy updates as they are released. With a cloud-based solution, an organization is subscribing to a service, not to a software product, so the provider is responsible for maintaining and updating the service's functionality. In many cases, the cloud-based version of a service receives new features sooner, and on-premises software products might not receive certain features at all.

For an on-premises service installation, a responsible update strategy requires testing and evaluation of new software releases and might require service downtime for the actual update deployments.

## Cost

Cost is another decisive factor in the deployment of any of these services. Cloud-based services require the payment of a regular subscription fee, and sometimes there are additional fees for add-on features. This enables an organization to implement a service with a minimal initial outlay, as there are no hardware costs or server licenses required.

Fees for cloud-based services are predictable and simplify the process of budgeting. Installing the equivalent on-premises service is a more complicated affair. An organization obviously first must purchase the server software license and the computers on which the software will run, as well as an operating system license and client access licenses for all the users. This can be a significant initial outlay.

Depending on the requirements of the organization, there might be additional costs as well. A large enterprise might require multiple servers to support different physical sites, which multiplies the initial outlay cost. Backing up data and storing it also adds to the cost.

There are also the issues of fault tolerance and disaster recovery to consider. Most cloud-based services from Microsoft are supplied with a 99.9% service level agreement (SLA) by default. This means that the service will experience no more than 0.1% of downtime in a given period. What infrastructure Microsoft uses to maintain that consistent performance is of no concern to the subscriber. To duplicate that performance level with on-premises servers will require redundant hardware and possibly even redundant data centers. Not every organization requires this same level of consistent performance, but even a more modest uptime guarantee will increase the expenditure for an on-premises solution.

Finally, there is the issue of the people needed to design, install, and maintain on-premises services. For example, deploying Exchange servers is not a simple matter of just installing the software and creating user accounts. Depending on the size of the organization, multiple servers might be needed at each location, and the design and configuration process can require advanced skills. These people will be an ongoing expense throughout the life of the service.

While cloud-based services can provide a great deal of performance for the price, this is not to say that they are always cheaper than on-premises servers. In the long term, cloud-based services can reach a point where they are more expensive. Cloud service fees are ongoing and perpetual, and while expenditures for on-premises servers might begin with a large initial outlay, they can come down to a much lower level once the servers and the software have been purchased and deployed.

A comparison of the relative costs also depends on the requirements of the organization and their existing infrastructure. For a large enterprise that already maintains data centers in multiple locations with experienced personnel, deploying a new service in-house might be relatively affordable. For a newly formed company with no existing IT infrastructure, the initial outlay for an on-premises service might be unfeasible.

## Administration

Compared to on-premises server administrators, who can work with server software controls directly, Microsoft 365 administrators work with cloud services using web-based remote interfaces. Microsoft 365 Admin Center provides access to the various tools for all the services included in the product, such as Exchange Online Admin Center and SharePoint Online Admin Center, as shown in Figure 2-8. These tools make it possible to manage configuration settings and create virtual resources, such as mailboxes and directory service objects.

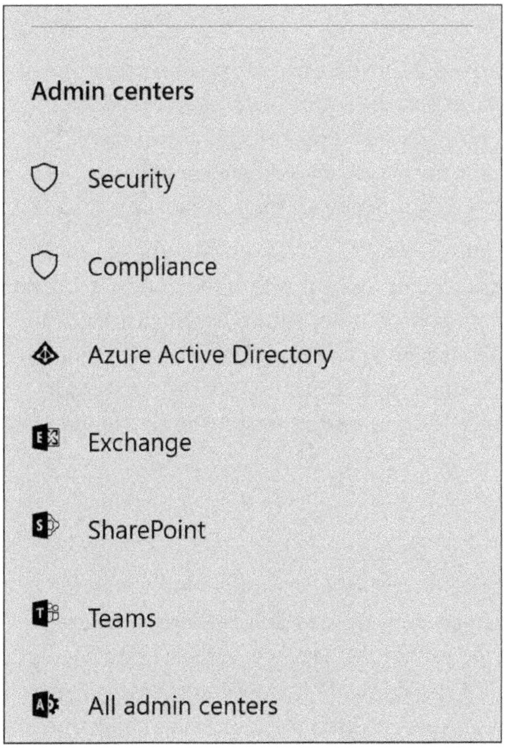

**FIGURE 2-8** Admin center access through Microsoft 365

However, administrators of cloud services do not have access to the underlying resources on which the services run. They cannot access the operating system of the computers on which their services are running, nor do they have direct access to the files and databases that form their service environments. For example, while administrators can create mailboxes for users in Exchange Online Admin Center, they do not have access to the mailbox databases that contain the users' messages. The experience can be similar to that of a pilot accustomed to feeling the tactile feedback of a plane's mechanical controls who suddenly has to transition to the indirect controls of a "fly-by-wire" system.

The web-based interfaces are not necessarily a drawback for all administrators. It is entirely possible to manage a cloud-based service without ever requiring access to the service's underlying data structures. In addition, Microsoft maintains responsibility for those data structures, ensuring their availability and security. In an on-premises service deployment, it is up to the local administrators to replicate the data structures for availability and implement a load balancing solution to maintain a similar level of performance.

Here again, the differences between the two service environments depend on the experience and preferences of the people responsible for them. Experienced Exchange Server administrators, for example, might be wary of using a cloud-based Exchange implementation that would isolate them from the servers, the operating system, and the traditional Exchange controls. An administrator relatively new to Exchange, however, might welcome the simplified access that the Exchange Online Admin Center provides.

# Security

One of the most critical factors in the decision to use cloud-based or on-premises services is the location of sensitive data. For many organizations, the security of their data is not just a matter of their own benefit. In some cases, contractual and legal constraints can make cloud-based data storage an impossibility. A company with a government contract, for example, might be required to maintain personal responsibility for their stored data; they cannot pass that responsibility on to a third-party cloud provider.

However, in cases where there are no legal constraints, storing data in the cloud can provide protection that is the equivalent of several different on-premises security products. Antivirus protection, message encryption, Information Rights Management, and Data Loss Prevention are just some of the security mechanisms that the Microsoft 365 cloud services can provide, all of which would require additional maintenance and expense to implement for on-premises servers.

# Service comparisons

Not all the cloud services included in Microsoft 365 are available in on-premises versions. Microsoft Teams and Microsoft Streams, for example, only exist as cloud services. However, some the core Microsoft 365 services have existed as standalone server software products for years, and organizations planning a Microsoft 365 deployment might want to compare the cloud services to their corresponding on-premises versions, as in the following sections, before committing to one or the other.

## Office 365

The Microsoft Office suite is a collection of productivity applications that has been available as a standalone product for many years. Office 365 was then introduced as a subscription-based product that enables users to access the same applications in several different ways. In most of the Office 365 plans, it is still possible to install the applications on a computer for online or offline use, but they are also available in the cloud for use on any device, using a web browser. In addition, there are also non-Windows versions of the applications available for use on Android and iOS devices.

With the standalone Office product, currently called Office 2019, you pay only once and receive the productivity applications, such as Word, Excel, PowerPoint, and Outlook, but that's all. The Office 2019 license is limited to a single device installation, while Office 365 enables you to install the applications on up to five devices.

Free security updates to the current versions of the applications are released on a regular basis, but not as frequently as the updates for Office 365, which can also include new features. In the event of a major upgrade release, such as from Office 2016 to Office 2019, there is an additional charge for the standalone product. An Office 365 subscription ensures that you always have the latest version of the software.

Office 2019 is available in several versions targeted at different audiences, with differing price points. Basic versions, such as Office Home & Student 2019, include some of the applications, while Office Professional 2019 includes the entire suite. At this point in the life of the Office product, Microsoft is targeting Office 2019 at enterprises that "are not ready for the cloud" and that purchase volume licenses for the entire organization. Because Office 2019 is feature-locked, the applications do not change, which is something that corporate licensees might prefer, to avoid interrupting their users' productivity with new feature releases.

Office 365 is available in several different plans that provide other services in addition to the applications, such as Exchange-based online email and extra OneDrive storage. The version included in Microsoft 365, called Office 365 ProPlus, is integrated with all the cloud services described earlier in this chapter, including Exchange Online, SharePoint Online, OneDrive for business, and Teams. The integration of the Office applications with these services provides users with advanced intelligence and collaboration features that are not available with Office 2019.

## Exchange

All the issues described earlier in this section apply to a comparison of Exchange Online with the on-premises version of Exchange. An Exchange Server deployment can be an elaborate and expensive affair requiring multiple servers and extensive configuration, while administrators can have Exchange Online up and running in less than a day.

Exchange Online provides each user with 50 or 100 GB of storage. In an on-premises exchange installation, the size of users' mailboxes is regulated by the administrators, who often do not want to expend that much storage space, which many users might never need.

Also, unlike Exchange Server, Exchange Online can create Office 365 groups, which enable users to work together with shared resources. This can be a valuable resource for administrators. For example, a technical support team can have its members added to an Office 365 group. Administrators then grant the group the permissions necessary to access a shared Exchange mailbox, a SharePoint team site, and other resources. When members enter or leave the group, the permissions to access those resources are automatically granted or revoked.

On Exchange Server, by default, user mailboxes exist on one server and are therefore vulnerable to hardware failures, system faults, and other disasters that can render them temporarily unavailable or even lead to data loss. For this reason, an enterprise exchange deployment often requires additional servers to maintain duplicate mailboxes, a reliable backup strategy, and in some cases duplicate data centers, all of which add to the cost of the installation. Exchange Online, by default, replicates mailbox databases across servers and data centers, ensuring the continuous availability of the service. This, too, is an issue that some Exchange administrators would prefer to address themselves, rather than leave it to a service provider, but the market for organizations that like the idea of a turnkey solution and are willing to trust cloud services is growing constantly.

## SharePoint

As with Exchange, SharePoint is available both as an on-premises server product and as the cloud-based SharePoint Online service. The main advantages of the cloud version are the same as those of the other services: simplified deployment, automatic updating, data redundancy, web-based administration, and so forth.

Microsoft is presenting its cloud-based products as the next wave in business computing, and SharePoint Online is now the flagship of the venerable SharePoint product. New features, such as the Modern experience in site design, appear in SharePoint Online first. However, in the case of SharePoint, this does not mean that SharePoint Server is being left behind.

SharePoint Server 2019 includes features that enable it to work together with Microsoft 365 cloud services. For example, administrators can redirect the MySites link in SharePoint Server to OneDrive for Business, so that users will be directed to cloud storage, rather than to the on-premises server. There is also a hybrid cloud search capability that causes an Office 365 search to incorporate the index from an on-premises server into the standard cloud search.

## Active Directory

Beginning with the Windows 2000 Server release, Active Directory Domain Services (AD DS) functioned as an identity management solution for enterprise resources. After creating an AD DS domain controller out of a Windows server, administrators create a hierarchy of forests and domains and populate them with logical objects representing users, computers, applications, and other resources. With those objects, AD DS functions as an intermediary between users and network resources, providing authentication and authorization services when users attempt to access them. Azure Active Directory (Azure AD or AAD) is an Identity as a Service (IDaaS) mechanism that performs the same basic authentication and authorization functions for the Microsoft 365 cloud services, but it does so in a different way.

There are no forests or domains in Azure AD. After an organization subscribes to Microsoft 365 (or any of the individual Microsoft cloud services), an administrator creates a tenant, using the Create Directory page, as shown in Figure 2-9. In Azure AD, a *tenant* is a logical construct that represents the entire organization. Administrators of the tenant can then use the Azure portal to create user accounts and manage their properties, such as permissions and passwords. The accounts provide users with single-sign on capability for all the Microsoft services.

**FIGURE 2-9** Creating a tenant

AD DS uses protocols such as Kerberos and NT LAN Manager (NTLM) for communication between domain controllers and the other computers involved in an authentication or authorization. This is appropriate for its functions because AD DS functions only within the organization's premises; it is not designed to work with users outside of the enterprise or manage cloud-based services like those in Microsoft 365.

Azure AD, obviously, is designed to manage cloud services and can work with users located anywhere, employing different security protocols, such as Security Assertion Markup Language (SAML) and Open Authorization (OAuth). Because they are so different, Azure AD and AD DS are not functionally interchangeable, as are the cloud-based and on-premises versions of services such as Exchange and SharePoint.

Thus, for any organization that has an existing on-premises AD DS deployment and is considering implementing Microsoft 365, the administrators will have to work with both AD DS and Azure AD. Fortunately, this does not mean that it will be necessary to create duplicate user accounts in each of the directory services. Microsoft provides a tool called *Azure AD Connect* that creates a link between the two and provides each user with a single *hybrid identity* that spans both on-premises and cloud-based services. This provides the user with single sign-on capability for all applications and services.

# Skill 2.3: Understand the concept of modern management

*Modern management* is a term that was coined by Microsoft, but which is rapidly being accepted throughout the IT industry. Described by Microsoft using the motto "mobile first; cloud first," it is intended to be a replacement for—or at least an evolution of—the traditional management practices that enterprise IT administrators have been using for years.

The traditional approach to IT device management consists of a paradigm in which all devices are owned, deployed, and managed by the enterprise IT department. This management typically includes the following elements:

- **Deployment**   IT administrators create and maintain system image files and deploy them on new computers using a management tool, such as System Center Configuration Manager (SCCM). Administrators must create and store separate images and drivers for each model of computer purchased and update them whenever the software configuration changes.

- **Updates**   Administrators manage operating system and application updates, typically using an elaborate download, evaluation, and deployment process, using a tool such as Windows Server Update Services (WSUS).

- **Identity**   Active Directory is a database of identities and other network resources that provide authentication and authorization services for internal users, services, and applications.

- **Configuration**   Administrators use Group Policy to deploy configuration settings as they connect and log on to the internal network.

This traditional management paradigm has worked for a long time, and many IT professionals are extremely reluctant to abandon it, particularly when adopting a new modern management concept requires them to learn to use new tools and technologies.

The problem, however, is that modern management is not just a fix for something that isn't broken. The idea of users all working on enterprise-owned and managed devices located in a company site is rapidly becoming a relic of the past. Vast numbers of users are working outside the office using their own devices, such as laptops, tablets, and smartphones, which cannot be readily deployed, updated, and configured to the specifications of an IT department using traditional tools.

The other motivation for modernizing IT management is the increased ubiquity of cloud-based applications in the enterprise. As software manufacturers shift their marketing emphasis to the cloud, it is becoming increasingly difficult for IT administrators to provide the services their users need with traditional, on-premises applications and services.

Modern management is designed to replace the traditional tools with new ones that can work with cloud-based resources, managing users' own devices, and simplifying the deployment, update, and management processes. The object is to replace the traditional reactive management processes with modern proactive processes. Microsoft 365 includes tools that do all these things, such as the following:

- **Deployment**  Windows AutoPilot is a cloud-based service that eliminates the need for separate system images and SCCM and simplifies the process of deploying new computers by automating the process of installing, activating, and configuring Windows 10.

- **Updates**  The Windows as a Service update program provides Windows 10 workstations with regularly scheduled feature and quality updates that are automatically applied. Microsoft has also implemented technologies to reduce the size of the update downloads, mitigating the burden on networks and Internet connections.

- **Identity**  Azure Active Directory moves user identities from the local network to cloud, enabling administrators to manage them from anywhere and providing users with single-sign on capability to all cloud-based services and applications.

- **Configuration**  Microsoft Intune expands an enterprise's management perimeter to include non-Windows devices and devices that are accessible through the cloud. However, Intune can also replace Group Policy for configuring Windows 10 computers because it has also been enhanced with hundreds of mobile device management (MDM) APIs that enable Intune and similar tools to control them through the cloud.

## Transitioning to modern management

New organizations or divisions that choose Microsoft 365 as their initial IT solution can, obviously, adopt Microsoft's modern management tools and techniques from scratch. Microsoft calls this the "cloud first" option. Administrators, even if they have a previous history with traditional management tools, can adapt to the new ones without any conflict between the two models. However, when an organization has an existing infrastructure based on the traditional model, they must decide whether to change to modern management and how they should do it.

A transition to the modern management model requires new tools and also new skills for administrators. Microsoft has designed three approaches to a transition from traditional to modern management, as follows:

- **Big switch**  In the big switch transition, an organization abandons all the traditional management tools and modalities and begins using modern management tools exclusively. While this might be a feasible option for a relatively small organization, large enterprises will likely find a sudden transition impractical.

- **Group-by-group**  In a group-by-group transition, an organization classifies its users by department, location, or workload and converts one group of users at a time to the modern management environment. In many cases, the transition process will be determined by the applications users require and whether they can readily be managed from the cloud.

- **Co-management**  The co-management model calls for administrators to maintain both the traditional and modern management paradigms for an extended period. This makes it possible for the organization to transition gradually from traditional applications and procedures to those that support modern management.

Co-management has become a widely accepted solution for enterprises that are reluctant to give up their traditional management model or that have applications and services that are not manageable using the modern tools. From Microsoft's standpoint, the objective of co-management is to form a bridge from the traditional to the modern management model. Administrators can continue to use elements of their traditional, on-premises infrastructure, such as Active Directory Domain Services and System Center Configuration Manager, and gradually migrate to modern tools, such as Azure Active Directory and Microsoft Intune.

The steps involved in a co-management transition (not necessarily in order) are as follows:

- Begin using the Windows as a Service model in Windows 10 and Office 365 ProPlus.
- Move from an on-premises Windows update solution, such as Windows Server Update Services, to the cloud-based Windows Update for Business.
- Transition from creating, maintaining, and deploying system images for Windows workstations to using Windows AutoPilot for cloud-based, zero-touch deployments.
- Stop using Group Policy to configure workstation settings in favor of the Microsoft Intune tool included with Enterprise Mobility + Security.

Although it is possible to undertake them separately, all these tasks are incorporated into a Microsoft 365 deployment.

## Windows as a Service

With the Windows 10 release, Microsoft changed the way in which they generate and release operating system updates. Dubbing the new system Windows as a Service (WaaS), it is designed to reduce the burden on users and administrators.

In the past, Microsoft released major version Windows upgrades every three to five years, large service packs in between those upgrades, and small updates every month. The version upgrades were a major undertaking both for administrators and for users. Administrators had to reinstall the operating system on all their workstations, and users were faced with a different interface and new features.

The Windows as a Service model eliminates the version upgrades. Instead, there are feature updates twice a year and quality updates at least every month. The quality updates address security and reliability issues, while the feature updates add new functionality. Because the feature updates are more frequent than the previous major version upgrades, they spread out the update deployment process for administrators and do not represent as profound an interface and feature change to the users.

Microsoft offers three servicing channels for Windows 10:

- **Semi-Annual Channel**  By default, Windows 10 installations use the Semi-Annual Channel.
- **Windows Insider Channel**  For users or organizations that want early access to updates for testing and the ability to provide feedback, there is the Windows Insider channel.

- **Long Term Servicing Channel**   For devices with specialized functions in which continuity is essential, such as medical equipment, point-of-sale systems, and kiosks, there is the Long Term Servicing Channel, which receives feature updates only every two to three years, which are then supported by Microsoft for ten years.

The semiannual feature update cycle begins with a development phase in which the update is first run by Microsoft engineers and then by a larger group of Microsoft internal users for six months, a process that Microsoft calls "dogfooding." Then, Microsoft releases the feature update to the members of the Windows Insider program, for testing and feedback. Finally, the update goes into general release, which in a large enterprise typically consists of a pilot or test deployment, followed by a general production deployment to all workstations, as shown in Figure 2-10. For most of the Windows 10 editions, Microsoft services each feature update for eighteen months after its general release. For the Windows 10 Enterprise and Education editions, the service period is 30 months.

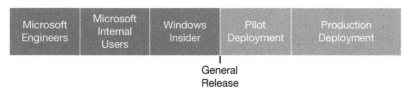

**FIGURE 2-10**  Phases of a Windows 10 feature update release

The monthly quality updates in the old model took the form of many individual patches, which enterprise administrators had to evaluate and deploy individually. Many administrators chose to deploy only essential security fixes, leaving their workstations in a fragmented state. It was only the infrequent service packs that incorporated all the previous patches and fully updated the workstations. Fragmented workstations made it difficult or impossible for Microsoft to accurately predict the result of future updates.

The WaaS quality updates take the form of cumulative monthly releases that include all the latest security and reliability fixes. This leaves workstations in a fully patched state each month. Therefore, Microsoft can test subsequent updates on a consistent platform, rather than having to be concerned whether all the previous patches have been applied.

One of the complaints made by many administrators responsible for update deployment is the size of the semiannual feature updates. A 3–4 GB download for every workstation in a large enterprise fleet of hundreds or thousands of computers can easily overwhelm even a robust Internet connection. In addition, because quality updates are cumulative, they grow larger each month after the most recent feature update, ultimately reaching 1 GB or slightly more.

Microsoft has addressed this issue with a feature called Express Updates, which generates differential downloads for workstations based the updates they already have installed. A differential download contains only the files that the workstation needs. Express Update can reduce a quality update to 150–200 MB on a computer that is already up to date. It is also possible to reduce the burden on Internet connections by using peer-to-peer features, such as BranchCache and Delivery Optimization.

# Using the Microsoft 365 portals

Because Microsoft 365 consists mostly of cloud-based services, administrators use web-based controls to manage them and users can use web-based portals to access them. The individual services that are included with Microsoft 365, such as Exchange Online and SharePoint Online, are also available as separate products, so they have their own administrative portals, called Admin Centers. However, the Microsoft 365 Admin Center is the main administrative portal for the product, and it provides access to all the individual portals as well.

## Using Microsoft 365 Admin Center

When you sign on to the Microsoft 365 Admin Center at *admin.microsoft.com*, you see the Home screen shown in Figure 2-11, with a navigation menu in the left pane and a series of cards containing essential controls on the right. Administrators can place their most frequently used controls on the Home page by dragging items from the navigation menu to the right pane to add more cards.

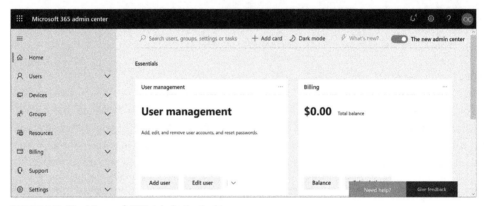

**FIGURE 2-11** The Microsoft 365 Admin Center Home screen

The navigation pane contains menus for control categories, with drop-down menus for specific control types. The categories are as follows:

- **Users** Enables administrators to create, manage, and delete user accounts. By assigning licenses to accounts, users will be granted access to Office 365 or other applications and services. Assigning administrative roles to users grants them privileges to access certain additional controls.

- **Devices** Enables administrators to add new devices, individually or in bulk, such as smartphones and tablets, create policies for securing the devices, and manage individual devices by resetting them, removing corporate data, or removing them entirely.

- **Groups** Enables administrators to create various types of groups, including Office 365, security, mail-enabled security, and distribution list groups, assign owners to them, and configure privacy settings. They can also create shared mailboxes for access by all members of a specific group.

- **Resources** Enables administrators to create and configure rooms and equipment for assignment to meetings and create SharePoint sites and collections. Full control over SharePoint is provided by the SharePoint Online Admin Center, but this interface can control site sharing and remove external users.

- **Billing** Enables administrators to purchase additional Microsoft applications and services, manage product subscriptions, monitor available product licenses, and manage invoices and payments.

- **Support** Enables administrators to find solutions to common Microsoft 365 problems and create and view requests for service from Microsoft technicians.

- **Settings** Enables administrators to configure service settings and add-ins for the entire enterprise, configure security settings, and monitor partner relationships.

- **Setup** Enables administrators to monitor their Microsoft products and manage the licenses for those products, purchase or add Internet domains, and migrate data from outside email providers into Microsoft 365 accounts.

- **Reports** Enables administrators to generate various reports, such as email activity, active users, and SharePoint site usage, over intervals ranging from 7 to 180 days. Reports like these can indicate who is using the Microsoft 365 services heavily, who is near to reaching storage quotas, and who might not need a license at all.

- **Health** Enables administrators to monitor the operational health of the various Microsoft 365 services, read any incident and advisory reports that have been generated, and receive messages about product update availability and other topics.

- **Admin Centers** Enables administrators to open new windows containing the admin centers for the other services provided in Microsoft 365, including Security, Compliance, Azure Active Directory, Exchange, SharePoint, and Teams.

---

*NOTE* **MICROSOFT 365 ADMIN CENTER**

Because the admin centers for the Microsoft 365 services are web-based, the product developers can easily modify them and add features as they become available without interrupting their users. Beginning in early 2019, Microsoft made a new design for the Microsoft 365 Admin Center the default setting and added a control in the upper-right corner that enables users to switch between the previous design and the new one at will. The figures of the admin center controls in this book are taken from the new design as it exists at the time of writing. Design and feature changes might have been introduced since the time of publication.

---

## Using the Office 365 portal

Once a user has been given a Microsoft 365 account, he or she has access to Office 365 ProPlus and can sign on to the user portal at *http://office.com*. After signing on using the email address created by the administrator as part of the user account, the Office 365 portal appears, as shown in Figure 2-12.

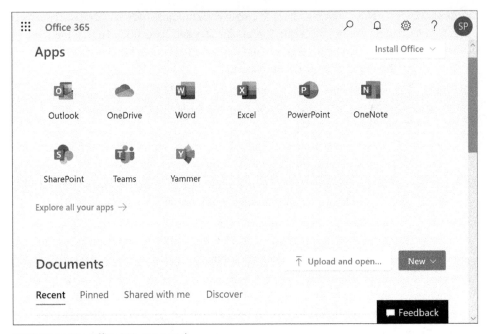

**FIGURE 2-12** The Office 365 user portal

The application icons on the portal's main page provide the user with access to the web-based versions of the Office productivity applications: Outlook, OneDrive, Word, Excel, and PowerPoint. Beneath the icons is a Documents area providing the user with access to recently used, pinned, and shared document files stored in the user's OneDrive cloud.

Along with the applications, additional icons provide access to the cloud-based services included with a Microsoft 365 license, including OneDrive, OneNote, SharePoint, Teams, and Yammer.

The SharePoint icon, by default, opens a new window containing the domain's main hub site. Adding users to groups can cause the icon to provide access to a team site instead. Clicking the **Teams** icon for the first time opens a page that invites the user to download the Teams app or use the web-based Teams client instead. After that, the web client appears by default. The **OneNote** icon opens the user's web-based note-taking client, and the **Yammer** icon opens the enterprise social networking website.

If the user has been granted global administrator privileges, an additional **Admin** icon appears in the portal, which provides the user with access to the Microsoft 365 Admin Center.

By default, Microsoft 365 permits the user to install the Office 365 productivity applications on up to five systems. Clicking **Install Office** and selecting **Office 365 Apps** opens the **My Installs** page, displaying interface shown in Figure 2-13.

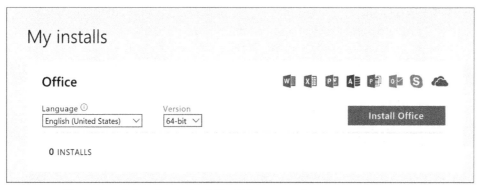

**FIGURE 2-13** The My Installs interface in the Office 365 user portal

The installation includes all of the on-premises Office applications, including Word, Excel, PowerPoint, Access, Publisher, Outlook, Skype for Business, and OneDrive for Business. This is the only way for an Office 365 user to run the Access and Publisher applications because there are no web-based versions of these.

## Understanding the Microsoft deployment and release model

As noted earlier, Microsoft 365 consists of three products: Windows 10 Enterprise, Office 365 ProPlus, and Enterprise Mobility + Security. However, the process of deploying Microsoft 365 is not just a matter of obtaining licenses for these three products and installing them. The ways in which the Microsoft 365 components work together to provide intelligent management, security, and collaboration require that the deployment be undertaken as an integrated process.

The complexity of a Microsoft 365 enterprise deployment depends on the size of the existing enterprise and the applications running on it. Microsoft has defined three Microsoft 365 deployment strategies:

- **FastTrack for Microsoft 365**   FastTrack is a benefit included as part of a Microsoft 365 Enterprise subscription that provides ongoing support from Microsoft personnel, including a FastTrack manager, an engineer, and a migration engineer. These specialists divide the subscriber's Microsoft 365 deployment into three stages, called Envision, Onboard, and Drive Value, enabling them to plan and deploy Microsoft 365 into the existing enterprise infrastructure, and then help the organization's people adapt their roles to the Microsoft 365 environment.

- **Third-party services**   Microsoft partners and consulting services can provide help with a Microsoft 365 deployment at many levels, ranging from complete control of the operation to occasional support.

- **Self-deployment** The Microsoft 365 Enterprise deployment guide defines a *foundation infrastructure* for the creation of a viable Microsoft 365 installation, which includes Windows 10 Enterprise and Office 365 ProPlus, after which the administrators can create workloads and scenarios, which include Exchange Online, SharePoint Online, and Microsoft Teams, as shown in Figure 2-14.

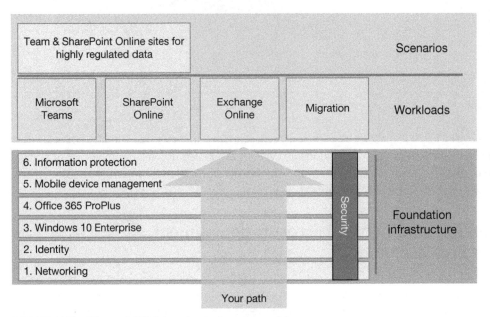

**FIGURE 2-14** The Microsoft 365 Enterprise deployment model

The Microsoft 365 Enterprise deployment guide breaks the foundation infrastructure—sometimes referred to as a *core deployment*—into six phases, as described in the following sections. Each phase is divided into steps and concludes with exit criteria that must be met before the foundation infrastructure deployment can be considered complete.

For a deployment in a relatively small or new organization that is just beginning to use Microsoft's cloud-based products, following the phases of the foundation infrastructure deployment in order will create a reliable structure for the workloads and scenarios to be deployed later. For an existing enterprise that is already using some of the Microsoft 365 components, some of the exit criteria might have already been met, and the six phases do not have to be followed in an unbroken sequence. Administrators can approach the phases in any order that they find practical, if they eventually meet the exit criteria for each phase.

---

*NEED MORE REVIEW*

For more detailed coverage of the steps in each of the foundation infrastructure deployment phases, as well as procedures for deploying Microsoft 365 workloads and scenarios, see the Deploy Microsoft 365 Enterprise documentation at *https://docs.microsoft.com/en-us/microsoft-365/enterprise/deploy-microsoft-365-enterprise.*

## Phase 1: Networking

The Networking phase is intended to ensure that all Microsoft 365 clients have sufficient Internet connectivity to access the cloud resources they require on a regular basis. This is not just a matter of bandwidth, however. The Microsoft Global Network provides endpoints to its cloud services all over the world, and for Microsoft 365 clients to function efficiently, they should have access to the closest possible endpoint.

Many enterprise networks were designed and constructed at a time when the proximity of the Internet connection was not a priority. It was common for Internet traffic at remote sites to be routed over a backbone network to a central location that provided the actual Internet access. This can result is a significant amount of network latency that can have a negative effect on Microsoft 365 performance.

Microsoft's DNS servers direct client traffic to the nearest endpoint based on their initial connection request. The clients should therefore also utilize a geographically local DNS server for their outbound Internet traffic.

For an enterprise that has a centralized Internet access infrastructure, the organization should take the steps necessary to reroute the Internet traffic so that each client is directed to the Microsoft endpoint that is geographically closest to its location. In a large enterprise with many remote sites, this can be a substantial undertaking, one that might play a role in the decision whether adopt Microsoft 365 in the first place.

Microsoft also recommends that enterprise networks avoid using protection mechanisms, such as proxy servers and packet inspection, for Microsoft 365 traffic. The DNS names and IP addresses used by the Microsoft 365 cloud services are well-known, and the services are already protected by Microsoft's own mechanisms. Duplicating this protection at the enterprise end can also have a negative effect on Microsoft 365 performance. To bypass these local protection mechanisms, it is necessary for browsers, firewalls, and other components to identify Microsoft 365 traffic and process it differently from other types of Internet traffic.

## Phase 2: Identity

In the Identity phase, administrators create the Azure AD accounts that will be needed for users to access Microsoft cloud services and applications. These accounts can be for the organization's internal users or for partners, vendors, and consultants outside the organization. For organizations without an on-premises infrastructure or for users that only require cloud services, administrators can create accounts directly in Azure AD. If the organization has an internal infrastructure based on Active Directory Domain Services, the administrators can synchronize the existing AD DS accounts to Azure AD.

Administrators should also plan how they are going to group users in the organization and how they are going to use the Office 365 groups for network administration. For example, Microsoft 365 supports group-based licensing, in which members of a group are automatically granted a license for Office 365 and/or Enterprise Mobility + Security. As with AD DS, it is also possible to assign permissions to groups, allowing the members access to SharePoint team sites and other resources. Azure AD also supports dynamic group membership, in which user accounts with specific properties, such as a department or country name, are automatically added to a group.

In this phase, administrators also configure protection for administrative accounts. Global administrator accounts, the most privileged in Microsoft 365, should be configured with the strongest passwords that are practical and also use multifactor authentication (MFA). In addition to the password, MFA can call for a biometric attribute, such as a fingerprint, or a verification code sent to a smartphone. Other administrator accounts, such as those for specific services, and even standard user accounts, might require a similar level of MFA protection.

When an organization has an existing AD DS infrastructure, administrators can conceivably create duplicate accounts in Azure AD, but they would have to manually make any future changes to both directories. A more streamlined solution is available in the creation of hybrid accounts. *Hybrid accounts* are AD DS accounts that are synchronized with Azure AD accounts, using a tool called Azure AD Connect. Running on an internal server, Azure AD Connect polls AD DS for changes in accounts and groups and replicates them to Azure AD, as shown in Figure 2-15.

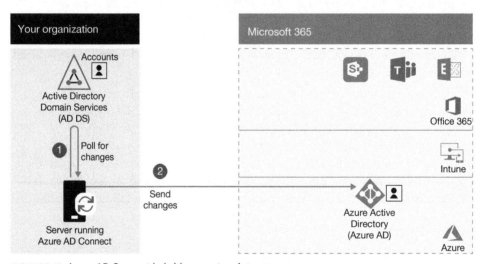

**FIGURE 2-15** Azure AD Connect hybrid account maintenance

When administrators create hybrid accounts using Azure AD Connect, they must select the authentication method that the hybrid identities will use. Cloud authentication uses either Azure AD password hash synchronization or Azure AD Pass-through Authentication. The other alternative, used when there are sign-in requirements needed that Azure AD does not support, is federated authentication, which uses a separate authentication service such as Active Directory Federation Services (AD FS).

Administrators can also configure Azure AD to support *password writeback*, a feature that enables hybrid users at remote locations and without access to the internal network to change their passwords in Azure AD, after which the passwords are automatically replicated to AD DS.

Password writeback is necessary to support the Azure AD Identity Protection feature that requires users to change their passwords when suspicious account activity is detected. With password writeback enabled, administrators can also enable self-service password reset (SSPR), which enables users to reset their passwords and unlock their accounts.

## Phase 3: Windows 10 Enterprise

The process of deploying Windows 10 Enterprise can vary depending on the current condition of the network and the tools administrators are using to manage the workstations. For an enterprise that has workstations already running Windows 7 or Windows 8.1, it is possible to perform an in-place upgrade to Windows 10 Enterprise and automate the process using System Center Configuration Manager.

The procedure for an SCCM in-place upgrade to Windows 10 Enterprise is as follows:

1. **Verify workstation readiness to run Windows 10**   The Upgrade Readiness tool in Windows Analytics, available through the Azure portal, collects information about computers, applications, and drivers and analyzes it for compatibility issues that could prevent a successful operating system upgrade. Administrators must also check that the workstations are running Windows 7 or 8.1 versions that are eligible for upgrade to Windows 10 Enterprise and prepare the SCCM environment by creating a System Management container.

2. **Add a Windows 10 image to SCCM**   In the SCCM Software Library, create an Operating System Upgrade Package by uploading a Windows 10 Enterprise image.

3. **Create a task sequence**   Create a task sequence that will function as the upgrade script by selecting **Upgrade An Operating System From Upgrade Package** and adding the image file you uploaded previously. Then, create a device collection for the task sequence, specifying the workstations that are to receive the upgrade. Then, create a deployment that associates the task sequence with the device collection.

4. **Start the task sequence on the workstations**   Run Software Center on each workstation, select the task sequence created earlier, and select **Install** to execute the task sequence and perform the upgrade. Optionally, the deployment can include settings that automate the upgrade process and schedule it to occur at a specified time.

For new Windows 10 workstations, administrators can use Windows AutoPilot to customize the workstation configuration, including changing the Windows 10 edition from Pro to Enterprise. To do this, the workstations must be running Windows 10, version 1703 or later.

To begin the process, administrators must first configure AutoPilot by creating a deployment profile and registering the workstations to be deployed. This can include modifying the Out of Box Experience (OOBE) with company branding and other specific installation settings as well as configuring enrollment of the workstations in Windows Intune. When AutoPilot is set up, workstation users can select the setup for an organization option in Windows 10 and sign on using their Microsoft 365 account credentials. AutoPilot then completes the rest of the process.

After Windows 10 Enterprise is deployed, administrators should ensure that security solutions are activated, such as Windows Defender Antivirus, Exploit Guard, and Advanced Threat Protection.

## Phase 4: Office 365 ProPlus

In a Microsoft 365 deployment, there are several ways to install Office 365 ProPlus, but they all should be preceded by a preliminary assessment and planning process. The assessment consists of a review of the target workstations with regard to the system requirements for Office 365, languages, licenses, and compatibility with other applications.

In the planning stage of the deployment, administrators must decide what deployment tool to use, what installation packages will be needed, where the source files will be located (cloud or local source), and which Office update channel the workstations should use, as shown in Figure 2-16. In some cases, these decisions will vary for different parts of the enterprise, depending on the workstation equipment used, the availability of Internet connectivity, and the administrative personnel available.

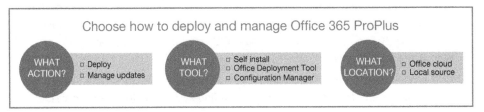

**FIGURE 2-16** Deploying Office 365 ProPlus

> **NOTE   CREATING A PILOT DEPLOYMENT**
>
> Microsoft's best practices recommendations call for the creation of two separate Office 365 deployment groups, a pilot group and a broad group, whichever deployment method an organization uses. This will call for the creation of two collections or two ODT scripts, depending on the method used. Administrators should deploy the pilot group first and test for compatibility before deploying the broad group.

With the deployment plan in place, administrators can proceed to use any of the following Office 365 deployment methods:

- **System Center Configuration Manager**   For organizations that already use SCCM, administrators can deploy Office 365 ProPlus as they would other applications, with no special modifications to the procedure. Administrators create collections representing groups of workstations with different installation requirements, then configure the Office 365 Installer with settings such as the update channel to use and whether to add language packs. Once the application is configured, administrators can schedule the deployment to occur at a specific time.

- **Office Deployment Tool (ODT) with cloud source**  The ODT is a command-line tool that uses an XML script file to specify Office installation settings. Administrators can modify the script manually, but Microsoft also provides an Office Customization Tool website, which uses a graphical interface to generate the XML code. The default Installation options setting—Office Content Delivery Network (CDN)—cause the ODT to use source files in the cloud to install Office 365, as shown in Figure 2-17. To perform the installation, run the ODT executable, naming the script file on the command line, as follows: **setup.exe /configure scriptfile.xml**.

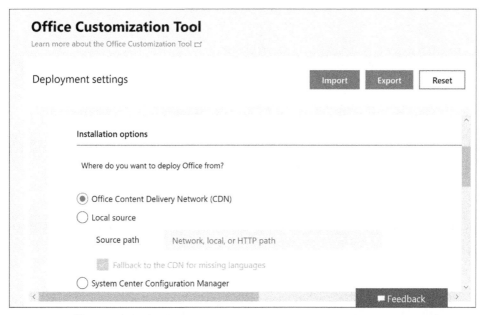

**FIGURE 2-17**  Office Customization Tool

- **Office Deployment Tool with local source**  The process for installing Office 365 using the ODT with a local source calls for administrators to create an XML script with the Local Source value in the Installation options setting and a path name to a network share. Running the ODT with the */download* switch—as in *setup.exe /download scriptfile .xml*—causes the program to download the Office 365 installation files to the path specified in the script. Once the download is complete, administrators can deploy Office 365 by running the ODT with the */configure* switch, using the same script.

- **Self-install using the Office portal**  The self-install method is typically used for workstations that are not connected to the internal network and which do not have access to installation tools, such as SCCM and ODT. Users install Office 365 themselves by signing on to the Office.com website using their Microsoft 365 accounts and clicking **Install Office**, as shown in Figure 2-18.

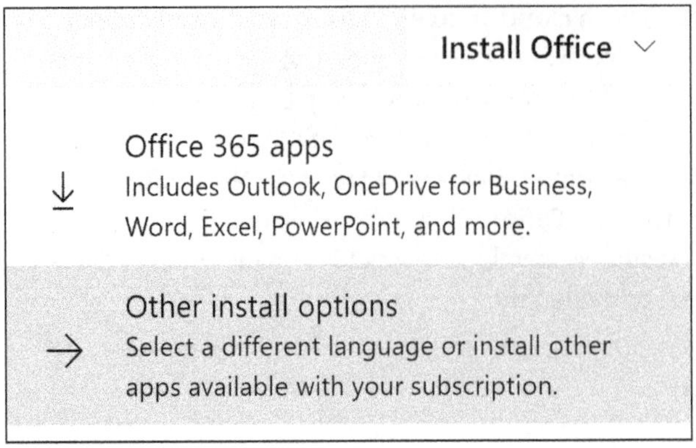

**FIGURE 2-18** Office portal installation controls

An important element of the Office 365 deployment process is the selection of the update channel the installed workstations will use. The update channel specifies how often the workstations will receive feature updates. Office 365 ProPlus supports four update channels, as follows:

- **Semi-annual Channel**   Provides Office workstations with new features every six months, in January and July. This is the default update channel for Office365 ProPlus, included in Microsoft 365.

- **Semi-annual Channel (Targeted)**   Provides Office workstations with new features every six months, in March and September, four months before the same features are released to the Semi-annual Channel. This option is intended for pilot deployments or test platforms, so that administrators can evaluate new features before they are released to the production workstations.

- **Monthly Channel**   Provides Office workstations with new features each month as they are available.

- **Monthly Channel (Targeted)**   Provides Office workstations with new features each month, approximately one week before the Monthly Channel release.

## Phase 5: Mobile Device Management

One of the most important features of Microsoft 365 is the capability to support mobile devices, such as laptops, smartphones, and tablets, even those running non-Microsoft operating systems, such as Android, iOS, and MacOS. The tool that administrators use to manage mobile devices is Microsoft Intune, which is included as part of the Enterprise Mobility + Security product.

Microsoft Intune provides two ways of managing mobile devices, as shown in Figure 2-19:

- **Mobile Device Management (MDM)**   In MDM, devices are enrolled in Intune and become managed devices. Administrators can install applications, assign password policies, and encrypt or remove any data on managed devices, as well as apply policies, rules, and settings. MDM essentially grants the organization complete control over the device, enabling administrators to ensure that the device is compliant with any required regulatory or other company policies.

- **Mobile Application Management (MAM)**  In MAM, Intune manages specific applications, but not the entire device. Administrators can impose policies on the managed applications, such as requiring a password to access Exchange, and can remove corporate data from the applications, but not any data on the system. MAM is more commonly used for organizations that support Bring Your Own Device (BYOD), in which users might not want to grant the organization full control over their property, and when the company does not have rigorous security compliance policies to maintain.

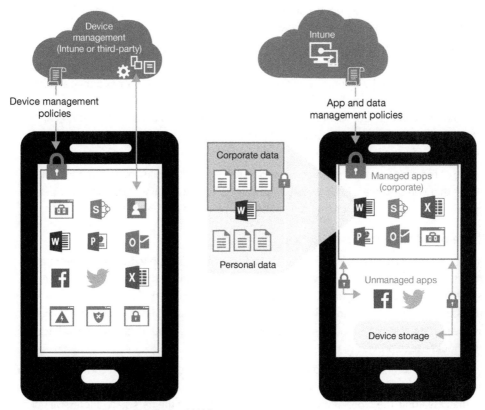

**FIGURE 2-19**  Microsoft Intune MDM or MAM

As part of the Intune planning process, administrators must decide whether to use MDM or MAM or both, and if the latter, which devices should use which management model. It is also possible to use Intune in a hybrid management environment along with another product, such as SCCM.

The process by which a device is added to Microsoft Intune for management is called enrollment. Before devices can be enrolled in Intune, administrators must create users and groups and assign Intune licenses to them. Administrators can create users and groups manually or synchronize the existing users from Azure AD or an on-premises AD DS installation. It might also be necessary to create additional groups specifically for Intune. For example, administrators might want to create individual groups for specific device types.

The enrollment process can take many forms, depending on the device platform and whether an administrator or user is enrolling the device. For BYOD devices, for example, users can download a portal app and perform the enrollment themselves. For devices owned by the organization, administrators can set up autoenrollment protocols and use the device enrollment manager (DEM), a special user account that enables the enrollment of up to 1,000 devices.

Once devices are enrolled, administrators can add applications to them through the Client apps page in the Microsoft Intune portal. The procedures for adding applications and the management tasks that are possible after the applications are added vary depending on the device platform and the type of application.

The most critical aspect of managing mobile devices with Microsoft Intune is protecting the organization's resources. One of the most powerful ways of doing this is by creating *compliance policies*, which specify the security conditions that a device must meet. For example, administrators can create and assign policies that require a minimum operating system version, or specify a required password length, or which prevent the use of devices that have been rooted or jailbroken. Based on a device's compliance with the assigned policies, administrators can restrict access to specific applications or to the entire device. This is called *conditional access*.

One of the most powerful management tools for use with mobile devices are the device profiles that you can create in Microsoft Intune, which enable administrators to apply a wide variety of features and settings that can enhance or restrict a device's capabilities.

## Phase 6: Information protection

The final phase of a foundation infrastructure deployment is to apply the various information protection tools included with Microsoft 365, to protect sensitive data from compromise. As with most of the deployments covered in this section, the first step is planning. This is the process of assessing the organization's data and creating classifications, which administrators can use to determine how much security is needed by various types of data and which tools they should use to provide it.

Microsoft recommends that organizations create at least three tiers of security protection, such as baseline, sensitive, and classified, and use them to categorize their data. Administrators can then assemble the types of protection needed for each of the tiers. Each successive tier will need more protection than the one below.

Some of the Microsoft 365 information protection tools that administrators can apply to the tiers, using different settings for each one, if necessary, are as follows:

- **Retention labels** These specify how long the organization must retain a particular document or document type and what should happen when the retention period expires. Some documents might have to be retained for a set number of years and then deleted, for example, while others might have to be retained indefinitely. Administrators can create retention labels with specific values in the Microsoft 365 Security Center and apply them manually or automatically to documents, folders, libraries, or sets.

- **Sensitivity labels** These identify documents as requiring specific types of security. Much like Azure Information Protection labels, administrators can create Microsoft 365 sensitivity labels that cause the documents to which they are applied to be watermarked, encrypted, restricted to specific applications or devices, and protected in other ways.

- **Threat management policies** Administrators can use threat management policies in Microsoft 365 Security Center to protect against phishing, malware attachments, malicious links, spam, and other hazards.

- **Windows Information Protection (WIP)** WIP provides administrators with the ability to separate company data from personal data on users' devices, selectively encrypt company data, wipe the corporate data from an MDM device while leaving the personal data intact, and audit user access to sensitive data.

- **Office 365 Data Loss Prevention** As with Exchange Online DLP, administrators can create policies that identify sensitive data by analyzing document contents and take action to protect them by limiting user access and preventing sharing.

- **Privileged access management** Enables administrators to create policies that help to prevent the compromise of privileged administrator accounts by requiring explicit approval for the performance of specific tasks.

## Workloads and scenarios

Whatever the order that the administrators complete the phases of the foundation infrastructure deployment, the exit criteria for all the phases must be met before the Microsoft 365 deployment can proceed. Once the foundation infrastructure is in place, administrators can then implement the workloads and scenarios that utilize the services provided by the foundation.

The workloads of Microsoft 365 are Microsoft Teams, Exchange Online, and SharePoint Online. The deployment process for each workload consists of three phases, as follows:

- **Envision** Assemble a team representing the business, IT, and user interests of the enterprise. Then, brainstorm and prioritize the scenarios in which the organization will make use of the capabilities the service provides.

- **Onboard** Prepare a detailed plan for the service rollout, including any account creation and data migration planning needed, as well as whether help from the Microsoft's FastTrack program will be needed. Then, create a pilot deployment, preferably including some or all the representatives involved in the Envision phase.

- **Drive value** Deploy the service to the rest of the enterprise, encourage its adoption as needed, and carefully monitor activity reports and user feedback to determine the success of the deployment.

Once the Microsoft 365 workload services are in place, administrators can begin to develop scenarios that utilize them, such as implementing data protection technologies, building team websites.

# Skill 2.4: Understand Office 365 ProPlus

Office 365 ProPlus is one of the three primary components of Microsoft 365; it is the one that is the most visible to users because it provides the applications they probably use every day.

For administrators, Office 365 ProPlus is a crucial part of the Microsoft 365 deployment process because its applications can make use of all the cloud-based services that are also included in the Microsoft 365 product.

Office 365 ProPlus is one of many versions of Office 365 that Microsoft offers for various types of users. For most of the Office 365 packages, the core applications are the same; the differences are the additional applications and services that are included in the bundle.

As a standalone product, Office 365 ProPlus includes the following elements:

- Word—Word processing
- Excel—Spreadsheets and charting
- PowerPoint—Presentation graphics
- Outlook—Email and scheduling
- Access—Database management
- Publisher—Desktop publishing
- OneDrive—Cloud storage
- OneNote—Cloud-based notetaking

Other business-oriented packages include various combinations of the Microsoft cloud services discussed earlier in this chapter. The Office 365 E5 package, for example, adds the following:

- **Exchange Online**   This is a cloud-based email and calendaring service that provides enterprise users with mailboxes and calendars that they can access and share using virtually any device.
- **SharePoint Online**   This is a cloud-based collaboration tool that enables administrators and users to create websites and maintain document libraries.
- **Teams**   This is a cloud-based collaboration package that enables groups of users to chat, place phone calls, and access shared documents, calendars, video, and other application resources.
- **Yammer**   This is a cloud-based enterprise social networking service.
- **Power BI**   This is a data mining and business analytics package that enables users to create dashboards, reports, and other visualizations of their data.
- **Stream**   This is a video streaming service that enables enterprise users to upload, view, and share video content.

The Microsoft 365 Enterprise E5 package includes all these elements, plus licenses for Windows 10 Enterprise and Enterprise Mobility + Security. The product is designed to enable all these components to work together in an intelligent manner and to provide users with advanced communication and collaboration capabilities.

The Office 365 ProPlus package included in the Microsoft 365 license includes access to both web-based and installed versions of the productivity applications, including Word, Excel, PowerPoint, and Outlook. There are also mobile versions of these applications for Android, iOS, and Windows devices. Installed versions of Access and Publisher are also included, but there are no web or mobile versions of these applications.

The Office applications for the web and mobile use are limited in their advanced features compared to the installed versions, but they enable users with a Microsoft 365 (or Office 365) license full access to their documents using any Internet-connected computer or mobile device with a web browser. Users can also save documents in their OneDrive cloud storage for access later.

**EXAM TIP**

The web-based versions of the Office applications are now officially designated by Microsoft as Office for the web. They were formerly known as Office Web Apps, and some older sources might still refer to them by that name.

## Comparing Office 365 ProPlus with on-premises Office

Office 365 is the subscription-based version of the on-premises Microsoft Office application suite that has been available for decades. Office was originally designed as an on-premises business productivity product that consisted of applications such as Word, Excel, and PowerPoint. All these applications were once standalone products, but by bundling them into the Office package, a single license gives a user unlimited access to all the applications. This simplifies the deployment and licensing process for IT purchasers and administrators.

The most recent release of the on-premises bundle is Microsoft Office 2019, but many corporate IT departments are still using the previous version, Microsoft Office 2016. The package includes desktop versions of Outlook, Word, Excel, PowerPoint, and OneNote for either Windows or Macintosh. The Office 2016 and 2019 products are purchased outright, so there is no ongoing subscription fee. Office 2016 and 2019 are both available in multiple editions, with varying contents. Enterprise administrators typically select Office Professional Plus 2016 or Office Professional Plus 2019, both of which are volume licensed.

Microsoft is clearly attempting to urge the Office market toward its subscription-based products. The list of features and benefits that are not included in the Office 2016 and 2019 packages, but which are available in Office 365, is a long one, including the following:

- **Automatic feature updates**   Microsoft 365 and Office 365 packages all receive regular feature, quality, and security updates at monthly or semiannual intervals determined by the enterprise administrator. Office 2016 and 2019, by default, automatically download quality and security updates every month from the Microsoft Content Delivery Network (CDN), but they do not receive feature updates at all. Major upgrades, such as from Office 2016 to Office 2019, require the purchase of a new license.

- **Licensed devices**   The Microsoft 365 and Office 365 licenses permit each user to install the Office applications on up to five devices. This means that a single license can be used for a user's office, laptop, and home computers, and even two smartphones or tablets. The Office 2016/2019 license only permits the installation of the applications on one Windows or Macintosh desktop computer.

- **Operating system support**   While Microsoft 365 includes Windows 10 Enterprise and requires that operating system for many of its collaboration features, the Office 365 ProPlus component can be installed on any system running Windows 7 with Service

Pack 1 or later. Office 2016 can also be installed on any system running Windows 7 with Service Pack 1 or later. Office 2019, however, requires Windows 10.

- **OneDrive cloud storage**   Any registered user can obtain OneDrive cloud storage, but Microsoft 365 subscribers receive 1 TB of storage. Unlicensed users and Office 2016/2019 licensees are only permitted 5 GB.

- **Technical support**   The Microsoft 365 and Office 365 business packages include 24/7 online and telephone support, as well as the FastTrack deployment service. The Office 2016/2019 licenses have more limited support options.

- **Email hosting and calendaring**   The Microsoft 365 package and many of the Office 365 packages include the Exchange Online cloud service, which provides email and calendaring. For Office 2016/2019 users, this service is only available as a separate subscription, for an additional fee. There is also an on-premises Exchange Server product that is sold separately.

- **Collaboration tools**   The Microsoft 365 package and many of the Office 365 packages include cloud-based collaboration services such as SharePoint Online and Teams. For Office 2016/2019 users, these services are only available as separate subscriptions, for additional fees. SharePoint is also available as an on-premises server, sold separately.

- **Reduced functionality mode**   With Microsoft 365 and Office 365, if a user's subscription lapses, if an administrator removes the user's license, or if the computer on which the Office applications are installed does not connect to the Internet at least once every 30 days, Office goes into reduced functionality mode and displays a message like the one shown in Figure 2-20. In reduced functionality mode, the user can open, view, and print existing documents, but all editing functions are disabled and the user cannot create new documents. Office 2016 and 2019 never revert to a reduced functionality mode and users are not required to connect to the Internet.

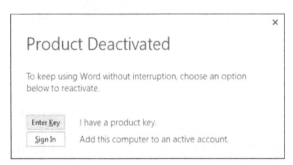

**FIGURE 2-20** Office 365 Reduced Functionality Mode warning

While individual users might see these omissions as considerable drawbacks to the Office 2016 and 2019 products, for enterprise administrators, this is not necessarily so. In some cases, administrators might prefer that the Office applications not receive feature updates, due to the additional support and training issues they might cause. In the enterprise, every new support issue is multiplied by hundreds or thousands of users, so the sudden appearance of substantial changes or new features in the Office applications can be more trouble than it's worth.

As to the additional cloud services provided in many of the Microsoft 365 and Office 365 packages, such as those providing email and collaboration, many organizations already have solutions for these services in place and do not want to pay for features they do not need or want. Microsoft technical support for individual users might also not be necessary, as enterprise administrators typically provide that support themselves. Many large organizations also obtain Office 2016 or 2019 by purchasing a volume license, which might include incident support, should it be needed.

## Deploying Office

The deployment process for Office 365 ProPlus in an enterprise environment is described earlier in this chapter in "Understanding the Microsoft deployment and release model." Because Office 365 is distributed using the Click-to-Run model, administrators can choose whether to use the Microsoft Office Deployment Tool (ODT) or System Center Configuration Manager (SCCM) to deploy Office 365, or they can allow users to install it for themselves from the self-service portal.

When deploying Office 365 using the ODT, administrators can modify the XML configuration file that contains the installation option settings manually, or they can use the Office Customization Tool (OCT) website to create the XML file using a graphical interface.

By default, Office 365 installs all the applications in the package, but the OCT enables administrators to selectively omit specific applications from the installation, as shown in Figure 2-21.

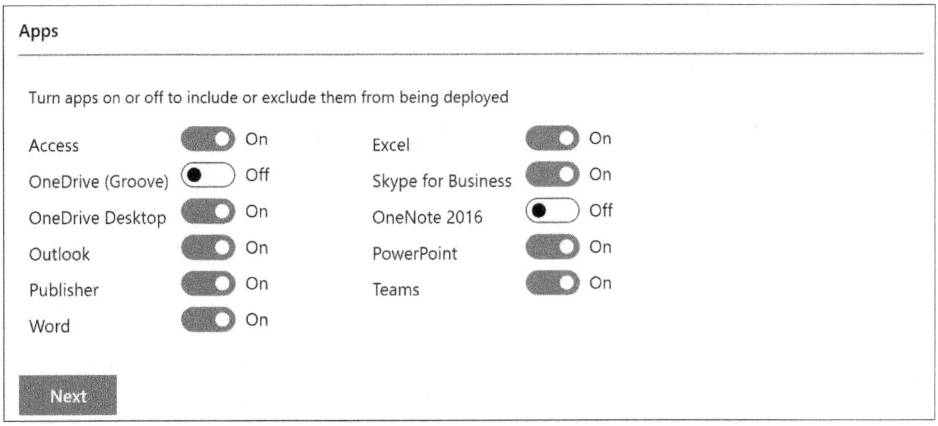

**FIGURE 2-21** Apps selectors in the Office Customization Tool

When you exclude applications using the OCT, the site creates an XML file that is modified to include an *ExcludeApp* code, as in the following sample that excludes the Publisher application.

```
<Add SourcePath="\\Server\share" Version="15.1.2.3" OfficeClientEdition="32">
    <Product ID="O365ProPlusRetail" >
      <Language ID="en-us" />
      <ExcludeApp ID="Publisher" />
    </Product>
</Add>
```

In addition to selecting the applications to install, OCT also provides controls for the following options:

- **Architecture**   32-bit or 64-bit
- **Products**   The specific Office 365 edition to be installed
- **Additional products**   Allows the addition of other Microsoft products to the installation, such as Project and Visio
- **Update channel**   Specifies which of the four available update channels the installation should use
- **Version**   Enables the selection of a specific product build release or just of the latest release
- **Language**   Specifies the primary language for the installation, plus additional languages and proofing tools
- **Installation**   Specifies the source of the Office 365 files (CDN, local disk, or SCCM) and configures installation options, such as whether the installation should be logged and visible to the user
- **Update and upgrade**   Specifies the source of future update files and whether to uninstall previous MSI installations
- **Licensing and activation**   For volume licensed installations, specifies the source of the product key (KMS or MAK)
- **General**   Enables the administrator to add the name of the organization and a description to the installation
- **Application preferences**   Enables the administrator to configure hundreds of policy settings, for Office as a whole and for the individual applications, as shown in Figure 2-22.

## Click-to-Run

*Click-to-Run* is a software delivery system that relies on the virtualization and streaming technologies developed for Microsoft Application Virtualization (App-V). During the installation process, a virtualized application space is created on the computer and the Office package is downloaded into it. Because the data is streamed from the Microsoft CDN in the cloud, the Office applications can start to run as the installation is proceeding. The basic functions are therefore operational while the more advanced features are still downloading in the background, as shown in Figure 2-23.

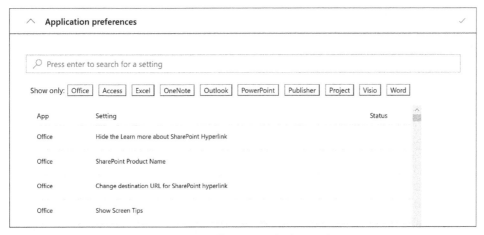

FIGURE 2-22 Application preferences in the Office Customization Tool

FIGURE 2-23 Background processing in a Click-to-Run Office 365 installation

Because the software runs within a virtualized environment, it doesn't conflict with other software on the system. For the most part, the only data that passes from the virtualized envelope to the local system is user data. Users can even install multiple versions of Office on one system without conflict, as long as they are all Click-to-Run installations.

Click-to-Run is also the basis for Office updates. Instead of releasing individual patch files containing updates, Microsoft releases a complete, new build of Office to the CDN. At regular intervals, a computer on which Office is installed executes a scheduled task and compares its installed version of Office with the latest one posted on the CDN. The system can then download only the new bits that it needs to update the installation. This reduces the amount of data that needs to be downloaded, and, as with the initial installation, the updates are streamed, so work can continue as they are downloading and installing.

The ODT is being positioned as the primary enterprise deployment tool for Office 365. While it is still possible to use SCCM to stage Office 365 deployments, they still use the Click-to-Run version of the installation package. Also, because of the virtualization inherent in the Click-to-Run delivery model, it is possible for administrators invested in App-V technology to create their own Office 365 packages and deploy them to users from a local source, as they would any other application package.

### Office 2016 and 2019 deployments

Office 2019 does not have a self-service portal, so administrators in an enterprise environment would be unlikely to have users install the product themselves. However, Office 2019 does use Click-to-Run, and therefore supports both ODT and SCCM for enterprise deployment.

When it was announced that Office 2019 could only be installed using Click-to-Run, a great many IT administrators were incensed. The previous on-premises version, Office 2016, was released at a time when the Click-to-Run installation model was used for home versions of Office, but volume licensees still used the traditional Windows Installer (MSI) deployment method. Sometime later, Click-to-Run was made available for all Office 2016 products, but the MSI installation model was retained for those administrators that preferred it.

The Windows Installer deployment method calls for the use of a package containing Office software in the MSI format. The Office product was only available in MSI format from the Microsoft Volume Licensing Center to organizations purchasing an Enterprise Agreement with Software Assurance. To manage the licenses, the organizations must either obtain Multiple Activation Keys (MAKs) or maintain a local Key Management Service (KMS) server. To deploy the MSI, administrators could use SCCM or other software delivery products.

The primary objection to the replacement of the MSI deployment model with Click-to-Run is a resistance to change. The Click-to-Run model offers many advantages: it's faster to install, the packages are smaller, and the software is always up to date. Click-to-Run is essentially the modern management deployment method, but there are still administrators that are loath to change to a new technology when the old one has been working well for years.

# Skill 2.5: Understand collaboration and mobility with Microsoft 365

At one time, it was common for workplaces to be divided into offices and cubicles. People worked alone, only coming together for meetings held in a separate conference room, away from their workspaces. Then, the open office design became popular; the cubicle walls came down, and workers were compelled to function as a team all day long. Both extremes tended to cause problems. Either it was difficult to get the team together for quality collaboration time, because their materials were mostly left back in their workspaces, or they felt cramped and stifled by being stuck together all the time. Achieving a balance between these two extremes can enhance both harmony and productivity. Workers who can collaborate when necessary and still spend some time concentrating on their own can often propel a project toward completion more efficiently.

Microsoft 365 is a product that is designed to provide workers with exactly this kind of flexibility. It might seem at first to be a simple bundle of an operating system, a suite of productivity applications, and a security package. However, the combination of Windows 10, Office 365, and Enterprise Mobility + Security is designed to be more than the sum of its parts.

Microsoft 365 includes both end-user applications and cloud services, all of which work together to create an environment that enables people to communicate and collaborate whenever they need to, from wherever they happen to be. Meetings can be held in which all the team members are located in their own workspaces: in the office, at home, or on the road. Messages can be exchanged by whatever medium best suits the team's purposes: chat, email, voice, or video conference. Documents can be stored in the cloud so that users can read, edit, or publish them from anywhere, using any device. Users can work individually, in pairs, or in groups of any size, in any combination, anywhere.

# Microsoft 365 collaboration tools

This section examines the collaboration capabilities built into the Microsoft 365 components, and then discusses how people can use them to enhance their workflows.

## Exchange Online

As the Microsoft email messaging server platform, Exchange is the most familiar collaboration tool for most users. Email provides rapid cross-platform communication, but it is often not immediate, and while emails can carry information between team members, their asynchronous nature prevents them from being the collaborative equivalent of a face-to-face conversation.

In addition to one-to-one email exchanges, Exchange Online also supports several other means for users to collaborate using email messaging, such as the following:

- **Distribution lists**   Also known as distribution groups, distribution lists enable users to send email messages to multiple recipients simultaneously. This collaboration tool has been available in Exchange for many years, but Office 365 groups now provide a more powerful alternative.

- **Dynamic distribution list**   This is a variation of a standard distribution list in which the membership is calculated each time a message is sent to the list, based on rules established by the administrator of the list. For example, the rules can specify that all users in a specific department or at a specific location be included as members of the list. Each time a message is sent to the list, only the users identified by the rules at that moment are included in the group.

- **Mail-enabled security groups**   Typically, security groups are used to assign permissions to resources, while distribution groups are used for emailing. However, it is possible to enable mail for a security group, so that the users possessing permissions to a protected resource can be notified by mail if there are issues pertaining to that resource. For example, if a printer is offline for maintenance or repairs, its users can be notified by email of its unavailability.

- **Shared mailboxes**   Typically, shared mailboxes are Exchange mailboxes with attached calendars that represent a role rather than an individual, which multiple users can access. For example, a technical support department can create a shared mailbox called **helpdesk@domain.com**, which is monitored by the team members who are on duty at any given time.

- **Public folders**   Exchange can maintain a hierarchy of folders that contain documents that are available to any user. Administrators can link a public folder to a distribution group so that mail sent to the group is automatically added to the folder.

While these mechanisms have their uses, and many administrators have been accustomed to using them for years, Office 365 groups offer a more comprehensive solution for collaboration that works across all the Office 365 applications and services.

In addition to mailboxes, Exchange Online provides each user with a calendar that provides scheduling, reminder, and sharing capabilities, as shown in Figure 2-24. Users can share their calendars with coworkers, enabling them to see their availability and plan meetings and appointments. Office 365 groups also have their own calendars, so that group members can share their scheduling information with the team and create meetings that don't conflict with anyone else's obligations.

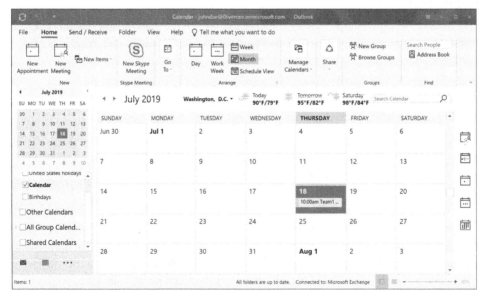

**FIGURE 2-24**  An Exchange Online calendar as displayed in Outlook

# Office 365 groups

Office 365 groups enable administrators to provide group members with access to resources that span the services that Microsoft provides. Creating an Office 365 group automatically creates the following resources, which are accessible to all group members:

- **Shared Exchange Online mailbox** This is an inbox displaying all the email messages sent to the group. Unlike a distribution list, the inbox is searchable and maintains a permanent record of the group's email communications. Users can display the contents of the group inbox separately in Outlook, as shown in Figure 2-25, or subscribe to the group, so that the messages appear in their personal inbox folders.

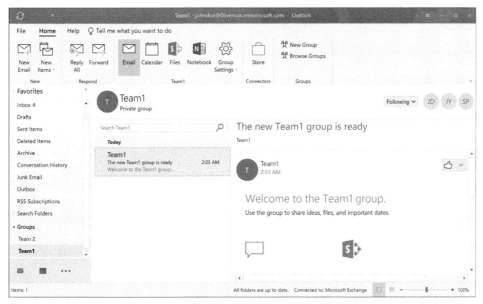

**FIGURE 2-25** Outlook displaying an Office 365 group inbox

- **Shared Exchange Online calendar** The group has a separate calendar that is shared, so that members are invited to all the events posted on that calendar. As with the inbox, users can configure Outlook to add the group calendar events to their personal calendars, or view them separately, as shown in Figure 2-26.

- **Shared SharePoint Online team site** Creating an Office 365 group also creates a dedicated team site for the group in SharePoint Online, as shown in Figure 2-27, which includes a library where members of the group can store, share, and collaborate on documents.

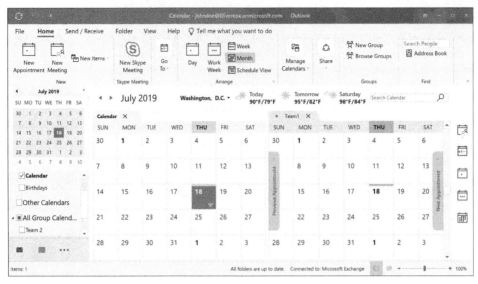

**FIGURE 2-26** An Outlook Calendar page with user and group calendars

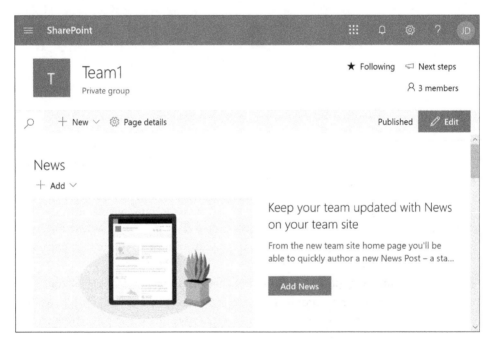

**FIGURE 2-27** Default SharePoint Online team site for an Office 365 group

- **Shared OneNote notebook** As part of the creation of the group's team site in SharePoint Online, a dedicated notebook is created, which members can access through the OneNote web client or the desktop application, as shown in Figure 2-28.

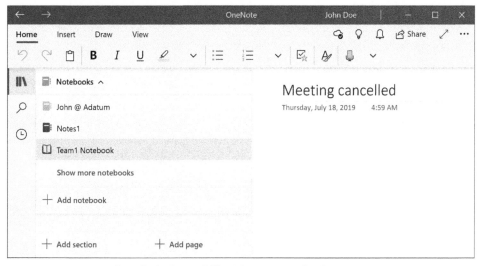

**FIGURE 2-28** OneNote client displaying an Office 365 group notebook

Because of their usefulness in so many of the applications and services, there are methods for creating Office 365 groups in many different Microsoft 365 tools, some of which create the group directly and others indirectly, including the following:

- **Microsoft 365 Admin Center** On the Groups page, clicking **Add A Group** displays the interface shown in Figure 2-29, with which you can create an Office 365 group, as well as a distribution list, security, or mail-enabled security group.

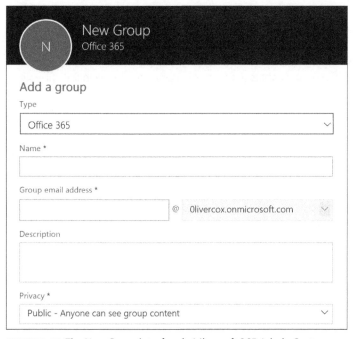

**FIGURE 2-29** The New Group interface in Microsoft 365 Admin Center

- **Azure Active Directory Admin Center** On the **All Groups** page, clicking **New Group** opens an interface in which you can create an Office 365 group or a security group.

- **Exchange Online Admin Center** On the **Recipients** page, selecting the **Groups** tab and clicking **New Office 365 Group** opens a new window containing an interface for the creation of a new group.

- **SharePoint Online Admin Center** When you create a new team site in the SharePoint Online Admin Center, using the interface shown in Figure 2-30, an Office 365 group is automatically created, which is associated with the site and uses the same name.

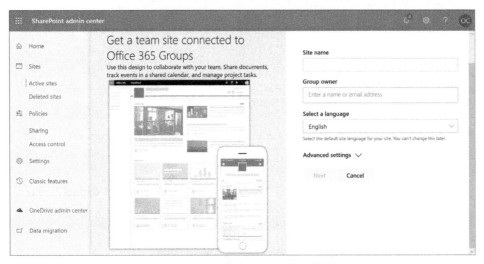

**FIGURE 2-30** The team site creation interface in SharePoint Online Admin Center

- **Outlook** Office 365 groups can be created by users as well as administrators. The **New Group** button on the home tab enables the Outlook user to create a public or private group and add members to it.

- **Yammer** Creating an Office 365 group in Yammer by selecting **Create A Group** in the navigation pane enables you to specify whether you want to create an internal or external group, as shown in Figure 2-31. Internal groups enable members to collaborate only with people inside the organization, while members of external groups can collaborate with people outside the organization.

- **Planner** When a user creates a new plan in Planner, the tool creates an Office 365 group for it by default. Users can also opt to create a plan and associate it with an Office 365 group that already exists.

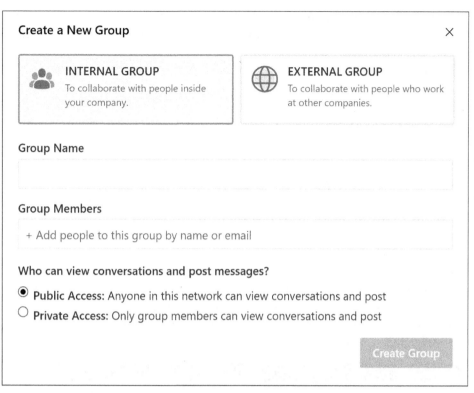

**FIGURE 2-31** The Create A New Group interface in Yammer

These interfaces have different appearances, but most of them require the same information, including the following:

- **Group Name**   Specifies the name by which the group will be listed in all Microsoft 365 tools.
- **Group Email Address**   Specifies an email address in the enterprise domain for the Exchange mailbox that is created along with the group.
- **Public or Private**   This setting specifies whether anyone can see group content or only group members can see group content.
- **Owner Name**   Specifies the user who will function as the owner of the group and receive full administrative access to its properties.

## SharePoint Online

As noted earlier in this chapter, SharePoint Online is a service that hosts intranet hub, communication, and team websites that enable users to store libraries of documents and also collaborate on documents by editing them simultaneously. In the Microsoft 365 collection of cloud services, SharePoint Online occupies an interesting position in that it can both function as an end destination for users and provide file storage to other services, such as Microsoft Teams.

Administrators can easily create separate SharePoint Online team sites for each project that a group of users works on and populate the sites with not only libraries containing the documents and files the users will need, but also with lists, news items, apps, and links to other web pages, among other things.

Access to the team site is controlled by the Office 365 group that is automatically created with the team site. Adding users to the group grants them the permissions they need. Users can access a team site from the SharePoint home page using any browser, or they can use the SharePoint mobile apps. Users can also access the files on a team site using OneDrive for Business.

SharePoint Online team sites can also be integrated into a Microsoft Teams interface, along with elements provided by other Microsoft 365 services, such as Exchange Online mailboxes, OneDrive files, Stream videos, and Yammer groups.

## Microsoft Yammer

Yammer is designed to be a cloud-based social networking service for an enterprise, enabling users all over the organization to communicate and collaborate using the other Microsoft 365 services. Yammer users can communicate much in the way they do in Facebook and other social networking applications, as shown in Figure 2-32, except that the service is local to the enterprise. Administrators can admit outside users, but only on an invitation basis.

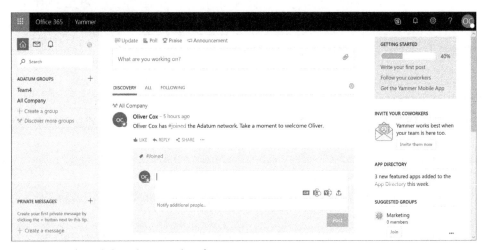

**FIGURE 2-32** The web-based Yammer interface

Much like Teams, Yammer enables users to access the other Microsoft 365 services available to them within the Yammer interface. For example, users can open a video call, schedule a meeting in Outlook, access files stored in OneDrive, or collaborate on a document from a SharePoint library, all from within a Yammer conversation.

In the Microsoft 365 collaboration model, Yammer is placed in what is referred to as the outer loop, the broader audience within the enterprise. These are people that a user might not work with every day. While Yammer can provide group-based collaboration, many organizations use it to provide an alternative, company-wide communications channel, enabling users who rarely see each other because they work in different departments or different cities to build a corporate identity.

While Yammer is often referred to as a social networking tool, the fact that its scope is restricted to the enterprise means that its communication need not be strictly social. Yammer users might not all be on the same project team, working toward a definite goal, but they can still exchange valuable information among themselves about best practices or the corporate culture—information that can build a sense of community that can't exist on an Internet service with thousands of utter strangers.

## OneDrive for Business

Every user that registers a personal Microsoft account for use with Windows 10 or other applications receives a free OneDrive account for storing personal files in the cloud. OneDrive for Business is an equivalent service that is provided with Microsoft 365. OneDrive and OneDrive for Business are nearly identical in their functionality. Users can access their OneDrive files from any device with access to the cloud and sync their files to a local disk.

The primary difference between OneDrive and OneDrive for Business is that the latter is administered as part of Microsoft 365. Office 365 users receive 1 TB of cloud storage space in a personal OneDrive account. However, in OneDrive for Business, the amount of space allocated to each user and the access permissions granted to that space are controlled by Microsoft 365 administrators.

OneDrive for Business serves as a storage medium for other Microsoft 365 services. Office 365 uses it for general cloud storage, and Microsoft Teams uses it to store user files, as well as files shared in private chats. Files shared in a Teams channel, however, are stored in a SharePoint Online library associated with a team site. Users can also access documents stored in SharePoint Online libraries using the OneDrive client.

## Microsoft Stream

Microsoft Stream is a video storage and distribution service that enables browser clients to stream video and that also provides video content to other Microsoft 365 services, including Office 365, Exchange Online, SharePoint Online, Teams, and Yammer. The Stream service includes its own Azure-based storage and therefore has its own storage quotas.

In addition to accepting preexisting video content uploaded by users, as shown in Figure 2-33, Microsoft Stream can process live events created in Teams, Yammer, or Stream itself and provide them as streamed video to real-time users or later as on-demand video content.

Stream can also enhance the video content by generating speech-to-text transcripts and closed captioning, as well as by identifying and indexing the faces of the people speaking in the video. This enables users to locate specific footage in a video searching for spoken terms or by locating a particular speaker. Stream has also introduced a "blur" feature that makes it possible to defocus the background in a video, to eliminate distractions and unwanted artifacts and concentrate the viewer's attention on the speaker.

**FIGURE 2-33** The Microsoft Stream home page interface

## Microsoft Planner

Microsoft Planner is a simple project management tool that enables users to create plans and populate them with tasks, events, and other elements from various Microsoft 365 services. The default view of a plan consists of vertical columns called buckets, each of which consists of tasks, as shown in Figure 2-34. Tasks can contain graphics, links, and files hosted by SharePoint Online.

**FIGURE 2-34** A plan created in Microsoft Planner

When a user creates a plan, an Office 365 group is automatically created, the members of which are those to whom the plan applies. The opposite is true as well; when a user or administrator creates an Office 365 group, a plan is created for it. As with all Office 365 groups, there is a group mailbox and calendar associated with it also, which the users of the plan can employ to schedule appointments and events and receive email notifications.

A Planner plan can also be integrated into Microsoft Teams by adding a new tab to a team's General page. Users can therefore work with planned tasks while in contact with other team members via chat or call.

## Microsoft Teams

If Yammer is part of the outer loop in the Microsoft 365 collaboration model, Microsoft Teams is in the inner loop, the people that see each other and work together every day. Teams is another collaboration tool that can host elements provided by other Microsoft 365 services. The primary function that is actually built into Teams is its chat and voice/video calling capabilities.

The tool is therefore designed around groups that are actively working in real-time and must communicate continuously and immediately, without the latency delays inherent in other media such as email. As noted earlier, this is exactly the kind of collaborative tool that can enable team members to function in their native workspaces and still remain in constant communication with their colleagues, even when they are miles apart and using different devices.

**EXAM TIP**

**Office 365 previously relied on Skype for Business for voice calling and video conferencing. These capabilities have now been incorporated into Microsoft Teams. Microsoft is deprecating the Skype for Business product and urging organizations currently using Skype for Business to plan on migrating to Teams. Candidates for the MS-900 exam should be aware that many older Microsoft 365 and Office 365 sources still reference Skype for Business.**

Apart from the chat and calls that provide basic communication, the other components that the group members might need are provided by other Microsoft 365 services, such as the following:

- Office 365 groups
- Exchange user and group mailboxes and calendars
- SharePoint Online team sites
- OneDrive for Business storage
- Stream meeting recordings and video content
- Planner task lists
- OneNote notebook sharing

One of the primary benefits of Teams is that all these elements can be combined into a single unified interface, preventing users from having to constantly switch between applications. Administrators can add tabs to a channel page in the Teams interface that use connectors to link to other Microsoft 365 applications, such as an Excel spreadsheet or a Planner plan. This is especially advantageous for users working on mobile devices with smaller screens, such as smartphones and tablets. The Teams environment is, of course, stored in the cloud, and users can access it through a web-based interface, by using a desktop application, or with apps for all the major mobile platforms.

When you create a team in Teams, it consists of a single channel, called General. For groups working on multiple projects, it is also possible to create additional channels, which have their own separate chat conversations, email addresses, and SharePoint folders. For groups whose members span countries or cultures, the chat capability in Teams also includes the ability to translate messages in over forty languages.

# Collaborating in Microsoft 365

As should be clear from the preceding sections, Microsoft 365 provides a wide array of collaboration tools and capabilities. For some administrators, it might even be too wide, requiring a great deal of testing and evaluation even to determine which of the many forms of collaboration available are best suited to their users.

For a worldwide enterprise network with tens or hundreds of thousands of users, there might be sufficient cause to roll out all of the Microsoft 365 components and make use of them in a variety of different ways, but for smaller organizations, a selective deployment might be the better option. How then can administrators determine which services are most suitable for their users, and how can users determine which of the many forms of collaboration are best for them?

Collaboration in a Microsoft 365 environment depends on the specific needs of the group or team. To determine what collaboration tools are best, consider questions like the following:

- How many people are in the group or team?
- How timely are the team communication requirements?
- Where are the group or team members located?
- Do the team members have to share and edit documents?
- What other media are required for the team's workflow?

Answers to questions such as these can help administrators to determine which components can best benefit the users in their collaboration environment. Take, for example, a project team that at one time would work together in the same room, brainstorming the project and generating reports together. Now, however, the team members are located in several different cities and some are traveling frequently.

The team's basic communication could conceivably be via email, especially if they used a group mailbox like one supplied by an Office 365 group. This would provide everyone with access to all the email messages generated by the members. However, in a team environment, it can be difficult to maintain a true conversation in email. Responses can be delayed, and users might end up not replying to the latest post. A chat environment, such as that provided by Microsoft Teams, might suit the group better.

For the document processing requirements, a SharePoint Online team site can enable multiple users to work on the same document, emulating the type of collaboration that can occur in a single room. Documents stored in a SharePoint site can easily be integrated into a Microsoft Teams environment.

Microsoft Planner can serve in a project management capacity, allocating tasks to specific users, maintaining a schedule for the group, and generating calendar appointments and email notifications. The Planner information can also be integrated into Teams.

As team members are working, whether by themselves or in chat, notetaking can be an important means of maintaining a record of activities. Microsoft OneNote enables users to maintain notebooks in the cloud and share them with the other group members. The notebooks can also be integrated into the Teams environment.

While chat can provide a steady and immediate conversation stream, video conference calls or presentations might also be necessary at regular intervals. Teams can provide calling capability, and Microsoft Streams can maintain a video record of the calls, generating transcripts and facial indexes for future reference. This, while an administrator might decide that Microsoft Teams is the preferable tool to create a unified collaboration environment for this particular group, the actual solution might involve several other Microsoft 365 services as well.

This example is based on Teams, but for a group project that doesn't require the chat capabilities that Teams provides, many of the same services can be integrated into a SharePoint Online team site. Administrators that are familiar with SharePoint might prefer to stick to the tools they know rather than adopt new ones. However, for administrators, the most efficient use of the Microsoft 365 cloud services would be to think of the overall product as a toolbox and, after familiarizing themselves with all the tools available, to choose the correct ones for each particular job.

Microsoft thinks of its collaboration tools in terms of the roles they can fulfill in an organization. Much like a diagram of a solar system, the Microsoft 365 collaboration model consists of outer and inner loops and a central core, as shown in Figure 2-35.

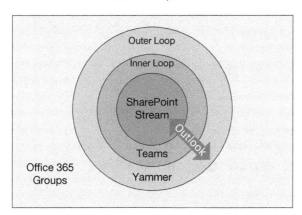

**FIGURE 2-35** The Microsoft 365 system of collaboration tools

The outer loop, representing the largest group of users in the enterprise, is serviced by Yammer, which provides a communication medium that spans the enterprise. The inner loop, representing the people that users know and work with daily, is serviced by Teams. Services like SharePoint and Stream, at the center of the system, provides services to both loops, just as Outlook provides communication between both. Underlying the entire model is Office 365 groups, which provides identity services for the entire organization.

The interrelationships between the Microsoft 365 services can be extremely complex, with some components feeding content to many of the others. For example, as shown in Figure 2-36, the Microsoft Stream service can supply video content to SharePoint Online sites, Yammer groups, and send video directly to Exchange Online user or group mailboxes. Microsoft Teams can then receive that same video from the SharePoint Online team sites. Stream can also record video of Microsoft Teams meetings and furnish that video to other services, creating a web of content supply and delivery that is further enhanced by the exchange of files and email messages.

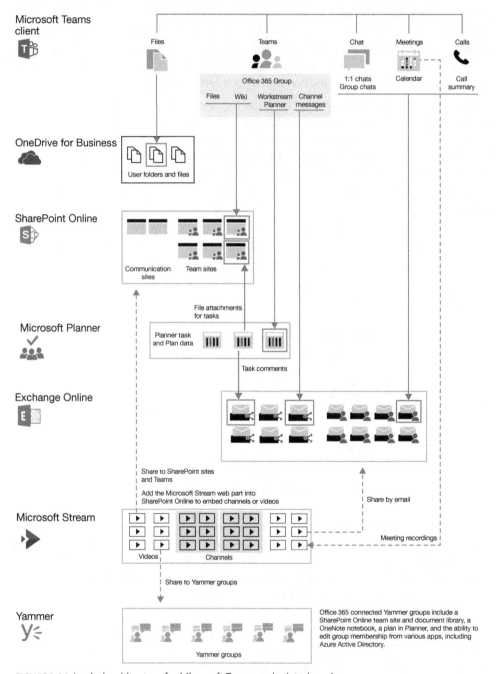

FIGURE 2-36 Logical architecture for Microsoft Teams and related services

## Microsoft Graph

Collaboration in Microsoft 365 can therefore be a matter of cloud-based services that provide content to each other, integrating the functions of multiple services into one interface. However, there is more to Microsoft 365 collaboration than simply placing Stream content next to SharePoint Online content in a Teams window. Microsoft Graph is a developer API that enables Office 365 applications to make intelligent suggestions about how users might take advantage of the content available to them.

For example, when editing a Word document stored on a SharePoint team site, a user can use @*mentions* to communicate with other team members. Pressing the **@** key in a comment causes a list of team members to appear, as shown in Figure 2-37. After selecting a user from the list and typing a message, pressing the **Send** button generates an email containing the message to the selected user.

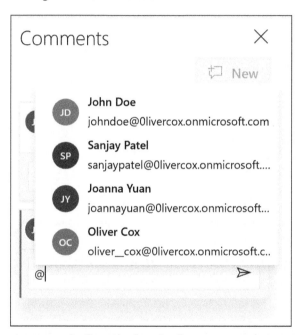

**FIGURE 2-37** An @mention insertion list

Another function of the @mention capability is for users to insert notes to themselves by selecting **To-do** from the @ list. Graph interprets the contents of the note and, if there are references to other documents in the SharePoint library, for example, displays an **Insert From File** pane containing suggested files.

Microsoft Graph can also evaluate the data in a document and suggest possible actions. For example, in an Excel spreadsheet that contains a list of countries, clicking the **Geography** button on the **Data** tab adds an information icon to each cell. Clicking the icon in one cell displays information about the country found on the Internet, as shown in Figure 2-38.

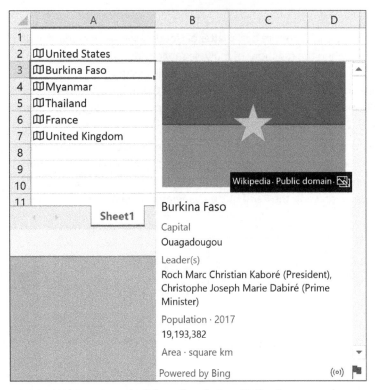

**FIGURE 2-38** Internet country information displayed in Excel

Selecting the list of countries and clicking the **Insert Data** button displays a list of statistical properties, as shown in Figure 2-39. Selecting one of the properties, such as **Population**, inserts the appropriate datum for each country in the adjacent cell.

Selecting the newly added **Population** figures and clicking the **Quick Analysis** button displays the menu of options shown in Figure 2-40, which enables you to select formatting options and add chart types and totals to the spreadsheet.

Microsoft 365 administrators and developers can also enhance collaboration processes by using Microsoft Flow to automate workflows that incorporate Graph functions and other services. For example, when users discover a malfunctioning device, they can send a photograph of it to a mailbox associated with a flow. The flow can use Graph to identify the device in the photograph, search for a replacement in an inventory, and generate a shipping order that has the part shipped out to the user that reported the problem. The same type of process can automate technical support services, generate sales leads based on users' Internet presence, and perform any number of other tasks without user intervention.

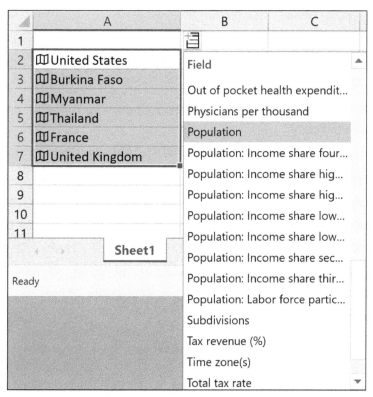

**FIGURE 2-39** Insert Data options for selected countries in Excel

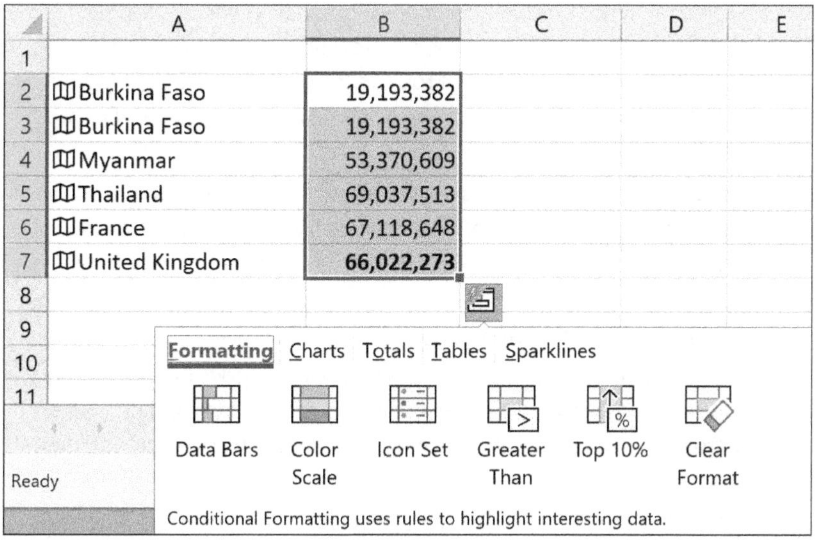

| | A | B | C | D | E |
|---|---|---|---|---|---|
| 1 | | | | | |
| 2 | 🗺 Burkina Faso | 19,193,382 | | | |
| 3 | 🗺 Burkina Faso | 19,193,382 | | | |
| 4 | 🗺 Myanmar | 53,370,609 | | | |
| 5 | 🗺 Thailand | 69,037,513 | | | |
| 6 | 🗺 France | 67,118,648 | | | |
| 7 | 🗺 United Kingdom | **66,022,273** | | | |
| 8 | | | | | |
| 9 | | | | | |
| 10 | | | | | |
| 11 | | | | | |

**Formatting** Charts T<u>o</u>tals Tables Sparklines

Data Bars | Color Scale | Icon Set | Greater Than | Top 10% | Clear Format

Conditional Formatting uses rules to highlight interesting data.

**FIGURE 2-40** Quick Analysis options for Excel data

# Enterprise mobility

As noted earlier in this chapter, the modern workplace is no longer restricted to a single office, or building, or even city, and even if it was, typical workers have multiple devices that they have come to expect they can use to access enterprise resources. Mobility has become a critical element of modern management, and Microsoft 365 includes the tools needed to enable users with smartphones, tablets, laptops, and home computers to access the enterprise files, applications, and services they need.

The first obstacle to mobility is access to data, but fortunately, Microsoft 365 enables users, applications, and services to store their data in the cloud, thus making it available to any device that has an Internet connection. It is for this reason that all Microsoft 365 users receive One-Drive for Business cloud storage and SharePoint Online uses cloud storage as well.

The second issue is access to the various Microsoft 365 applications and services. The traditional Office product required users to install the productivity applications, such as Word, Excel, and PowerPoint, on a desktop computer or laptop. The back-end services, such as Exchange and SharePoint, had to be installed on local servers. Users on site could access their email and SharePoint sites, but for users who were traveling or working from home, special arrangements were needed, such as remote access or virtual private network connections.

With Microsoft 365, users still have the ability to install the Office applications on their computers, but the product also includes the Office on the web applications, which enable users to work with Word, Excel, and PowerPoint documents online, using any device with a web browser and Internet access. The Microsoft 365 back-end services are all installed in the cloud, which provide users with access to their email and other services without a special connection to the company data center. Here again, only an Internet connection is needed.

In addition to the traditional Office productivity applications, new clients such as those for Teams and Yammer are available as Web-based apps also, requiring no special preparation. Microsoft 365 also includes downloadable desktop clients for many of its applications, available in versions for all the major mobile platforms, including Android, iOS, MacOS, and Windows.

The third and arguably most critical mobility issue concerns the mobile devices themselves. In the early days of cellular connectivity, organizations provided their users with mobile devices. The devices were relatively limited in their capabilities, and administrators retained full control over them.

Today's mobile culture is radically different, however, with smartphones having become ubiquitous and functioning as a personal status symbol as much as a work tool. Some organizations do provide mobile devices, but administrators now also must accommodate workers who want to use their personal devices to access enterprise resources, which raises complex issues of security and support.

It was Microsoft's task to develop clients that mobile workers can use to access their enterprise data, applications, and services. However, providing mobile devices with client access is only half of the picture. The other half is ensuring that sensitive enterprise resources are protected against loss, theft, and attack. Microsoft provides tools that make this possible, but it is up to the enterprise administrators to implement them in a manner that is suitable both for the worker's usability needs and the sensitivity of the data.

## Enterprise Mobility + Security

The Microsoft 365 component concerned with the management of mobile devices and their protection is Enterprise Mobility + Security (EMS). The primary tools that compose EMS and the functions they provide for mobile devices are as follows:

- **Azure Active Directory**   Contains the accounts that provide users with single-sign on capability for all the Microsoft 386 applications and services. Administrators can configure user accounts to require multifactor authentication to enhance the security of mobile devices.

- **Microsoft Intune**   Enrolls mobile devices and associates them with particular users or groups, as shown in Figure 2-41. Using Intune, administrators can specify whether to use Mobile Device Management (MDM) or Mobile Application Management (MAM), specify device compliance policies, create device configuration policies.

- **Azure Information Protection**   Provides document-level security by applying labels that classify the sensitivity of the information files contain and applying protection to specific documents, in the form of encryption, user restrictions, and other means.

- **Microsoft Advanced Threat Analytics**   Gathers information from many Microsoft 365 enterprise sources and analyzes it to anticipate, detect, and react to attacks and other security threats.

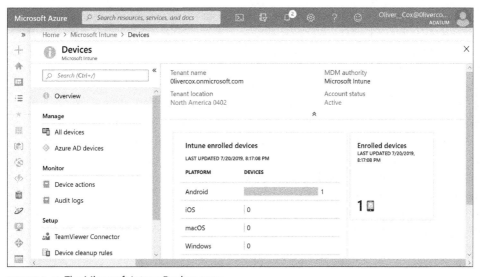

**FIGURE 2-41**  The Microsoft Intune Devices page

## Microsoft Intune

Microsoft Intune is the tool that administrators use to enable the enrollment of users' personal devices into Microsoft 365 and regulate their capabilities. Mobile Device Management (MDM) enables administrators to take nearly complete control over enrolled devices, even to the point of issuing remote commands that erase all company data on the device.

For users who do not like the idea of the organization exercising that kind of control over their personal property, Mobile Application Management (MAM) provides devices only with managed applications, leaving the rest of the device unrestricted. Which option administrators choose must depend on the sensitivity of the data that might be stored on the device and any security compliance terms that the organization must meet.

Device compliance policies are rules that specify how a device must be configured for it to access Microsoft 365 services. For example, a policy can require that mobile devices must have an unlock password, rather than a simple swipe, as shown in Figure 2-42, that data be stored on the device in encrypted form, and that the operating system on the mobile device be updated to a specific level. A device that does not meet the compliance policy settings cannot be enrolled, and even when it is successfully enrolled, it must be checked for compliance at regular intervals to maintain its access to the Microsoft 365 cloud services.

Typically, protecting enterprise data on mobile devices is a matter of restricting what the user of the device can do. In some cases, administrators might want to prevent the users from endangering sensitive data. Another security issue is the possibility of data theft or destruction when a mobile device is lost or stolen. Administrators can control the capabilities of mobile devices by creating device configuration profiles in Microsoft Intune for the various platforms and enabling or disabling device functions, as shown in Figure 2-43.

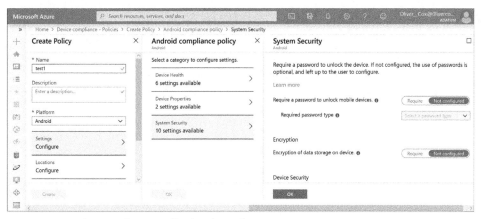

**FIGURE 2-42** Device compliance profiles in Microsoft Intune

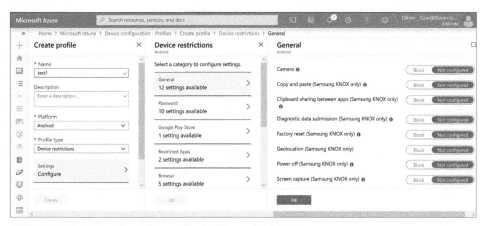

**FIGURE 2-43** Device configuration profiles in Microsoft Intune

Administrators can further specify which applications mobile devices are permitted to run and also explicitly block them from running certain applications. Clearly, mobility is not just a matter of allowing devices to connect to a Microsoft 365 domain; their capabilities also must be restricted.

# Skill 2.6: Describe analytics capabilities in Microsoft 365

As mentioned elsewhere, Microsoft 365 is not just a bundle of applications and services. The product includes a variety of analytical tools that gather information from components all across the Microsoft 365 environment. These tools—called analytics—can detect existing and potential security breaches, track usage of the Office 365 applications, and even examine the production and collaboration patterns of users and groups.

# Microsoft Advanced Threat Analytics

*Microsoft Advanced Threat Analytics (ATA)* is an on-premises service that collects traffic from Active Directory domain controllers and event logs and uses deep packet inspection to detect suspicious activity on the network and generate reports such as the one shown in Figure 2-44. A license for Microsoft ATA is included as part of the Enterprise Mobility + Security package in Microsoft 365.

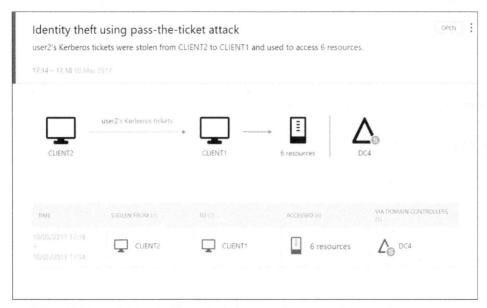

**FIGURE 2-44** A Microsoft Advanced Threat Analysis report of a pass-the-ticket attack

Some of the known attack types that ATA can detect from the captured traffic include the following:

- **Pass-the-Ticket (PtT)** This is an attempt to use a Kerberos Ticket Granting Ticket on multiple systems to request Kerberos service tickets that provide access to other resources.

- **Pass-the-Hash (PtH)** This is an attempt to bypass the NTLM authentication process by supplying a captured password hash instead of a cleartext password.

- **Overpass-the-Hash** This is a variant on the Pass-the-Hash attack used to penetrate Kerberos authentication, in which the intruder attempts to substitute a key instead of a hash.

- **Forged PAC** This is an attempt to penetrate a Kerberos authentication using an unauthorized Privileged Attribute Certificate (PAC).

- **Golden Ticket** This is an attempt to gain unrestricted access to an entire Active Directory domain by taking control of its Key Distribution Service (KDS).

- **Malicious replications** This is an attempt to trigger an Active Directory replication process by a computer that is not a domain controller.

- **Reconnaissance**   This is an attempt to discover user accounts in an Active Directory domain using DNS, SAM-R, or Kerberos queries.
- **Brute Force**   This is an attack that tries to penetrate a system by repeated authentication attempts until the correct credentials are discovered.
- **Remote execution**   This is an attempt to use compromised credentials to execute remote commands on a domain controller.

ATA bases its analysis on the typical phases of an attacker's infiltration of the network and attempts to detect the activities that commonly used during these phases. By understanding the types of information attackers attempt to gather during the initial phases of an infiltration, ATA can often detect an attack while it is imminent and before the actual data loss or other damage is underway. The phases are as follows:

- **Reconnaissance**   This is the phase in which attackers gather information about the network infrastructure, such as account names and IP addresses
- **Lateral movement**   This is the phase in which attackers attempt to use the knowledge gathered during the reconnaissance phase to widen the attack surface to other resources and other computers
- **Persistence**   This is the phase in which attackers capture additional information that will permit them to continue the attack after the initial detection, using other entry points and user credentials

While ATA is capable of deterministic detection of known threats, it can also report on suspicious activity that does not conform to any known threat signature, but which appears to be dangerous nonetheless, using a technique called Abnormal Behavior Machine Learning.

Some of the abnormal behavior types and typical examples of them are as follows:

- **Anomalous logins**   Authentication traffic for a specific account on computers where the account has never been used before
- **Password sharing**   Multiple authentications on different computers at nearly the same time or at remote locations
- **Lateral movement**   Similar authentication patterns discovered on multiple computers
- **Group modification**   Unusual or frequent additions of users to sensitive groups, such as those with administrative permissions

For ATA to function effectively, it must capture the authentication traffic of on-premises Active Directory Domain Services domain controllers. To do this, it requires an ATA Gateway, which is a service that uses a procedure called port mirroring to duplicate the traffic running to and from the network's domain controllers, as shown in Figure 2-45. One copy of the traffic is sent to the ATA Center for analysis, while the other copy travels on to its original destination. As an alternative, administrators can install the ATA Lightweight Gateway on the domain controllers themselves.

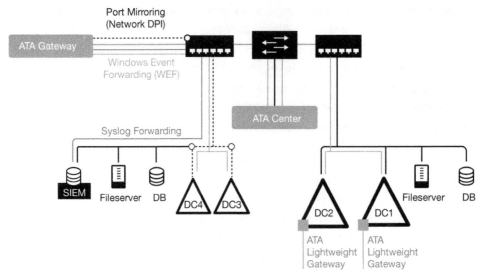

**FIGURE 2-45** The Microsoft Advanced Threat Analytics architecture

Before installing the ATA Center or any ATA Gateways, administrators must download and run the ATA Sizing Tool. This is a tool that measures the network traffic levels by counting the number of packets. After running for 24 hours, the tool generates a spreadsheet like the one shown in Figure 2-46. By matching the values in the spreadsheet to a published table, administrators can determine what hardware configuration is needed for the ATA Center and ATA Gateway or ATA Lightweight Gateway computers.

| Number of DCs | 4 |
|---|---|
| Number of Samples | 69 |
| Overall Start Time UTC | 2016-07-21 10:41:54 |
| Overall End Time UTC | 2016-07-21 10:43:09 |
| Display DC Times as UTC/Local | Universal Time (UTC) |

| Center | Max Packets/sec | Avg Packets/sec | Busy Packets/sec | Busy Packets/sec Start UTC | Busy Packets/sec End UTC |
|---|---|---|---|---|---|
| Grand Total | 1,616 | 1,184 | 1,184 | 10:41:55 | 10:43:08 |

| DC | Max Packets/sec | Avg Packets/sec | Busy Packets/sec | Busy Packets/sec Start Time | Busy Packets/sec End Time |
|---|---|---|---|---|---|
| DC1 | 644 | 457 | 457 | 10:41:54 | 10:43:08 |
| DC3 | 334 | 234 | 234 | 10:41:54 | 10:43:08 |
| DC4 | 408 | 249 | 249 | 10:41:54 | 10:43:08 |
| DC2 | 405 | 244 | 244 | 10:41:54 | 10:43:08 |
| Total | 1,792 | 1,184 | 1,184 | | |

**FIGURE 2-46** Spreadsheet output of the ATA Sizing Tool

Once computers with appropriate hardware are available, administrators can install the ATA Center, connect it to Active Directory, and then install and configure the ATA Gateway or ATA Lightweight Gateway. In addition to the Active Directory traffic, ATA can utilize event information from other systems, which is gathered by Windows Event Forwarding and sent to the gateway.

With the components in place, the flow information proceeds as shown in Figure 2-47. Domain controller traffic and Windows events are resolved in the ATA gateway and transmitted to the ATA Center, where they are analyzed and stored in a MongoDB database.

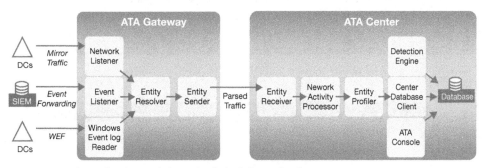

**FIGURE 2-47** Microsoft Advanced Threat Analytics information flow

As ATA gathers information, it uses behavioral algorithms to establish a usage baseline for specific accounts and computers. Once the baseline is in place, a sudden burst of activity that differs substantially from the norm is then considered to be anomalous and deemed suspicious. The activity might not be associated with the known pattern of a specific attack type, but the very fact that it is out of the ordinary is enough for ATA to flag it as a sign of a potential attack.

The ATA Center computer also provides administrators with access to the ATA Console, as shown in Figure 2-48, which displays the most recent activities that ATA has classified as suspicious. Administrators can also configure ATA to advise them of suspicious activity by generating system notifications, emails, or log entries.

**FIGURE 2-48** The Microsoft Advanced Threat Analytics console

# Microsoft 365 Usage Analytics

The Reports/Usage page in Microsoft 365 Admin Center can display information about activity levels in the various Microsoft 365 services in chart form, as shown in Figure 2-49. Administrators can modify the charts to display 7, 30, 90, or 180 days of information. Microsoft 365 Usage Analytics is a service within the Power BI business analytics tool to track how workers are using the various Microsoft 365 components over the previous 12 months in much greater detail.

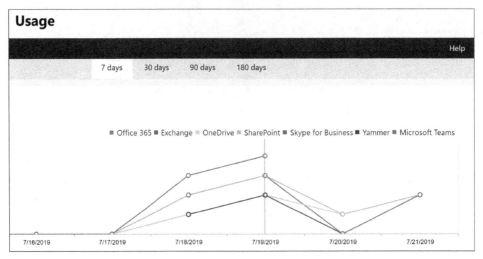

**FIGURE 2-49** A service usage chart in Microsoft 365 Admin Center

Administrators can use the Power BI–based service to determine what tools workers are using to perform specific types of tasks, which Microsoft 365 components are over- or under used, and which might be seldom adopted at all. This type of information can enable administrators to determine whether workers might need training to make better use of specific tools that are available to them.

For example, there might be users who complain that it is difficult for them to communicate on a company-wide basis, because they usually spend most of their time with their immediate team members. These users might not be aware that Yammer exists or know how to use it. A brief tutorial might resolve these users' problem, as well as increase cross-communication across the enterprise.

To use Microsoft 365 Usage Analytics, an administrator must open the Microsoft 365 Admin Center, browse to the Reports/Usage page, and, on the Microsoft 365 Usage Analytics card, shown in Figure 2-50, click **Get Started** to instantiate the data collection process, which can take up to 48 hours.

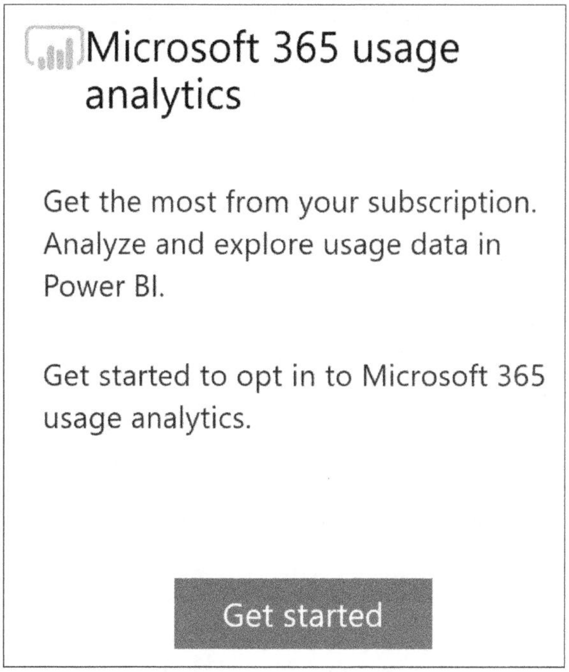

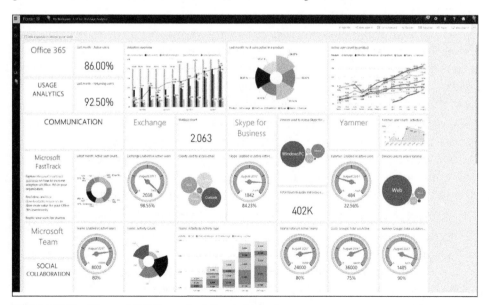

## Microsoft 365 usage analytics

Get the most from your subscription. Analyze and explore usage data in Power BI.

Get started to opt in to Microsoft 365 usage analytics.

Get started

**FIGURE 2-50**  The Microsoft 365 Usage Analytics card in the Microsoft 365 Admin Center

When the data collection process is complete, the administrator can add the Microsoft 365 Usage Analytics service to the Power BI application, authenticate the enterprise's tenancy, and generate a dashboard of chart-based data, as shown in Figure 2-51.

**FIGURE 2-51**  The Microsoft 365 Usage Analytics dashboard

By clicking individual charts, administrators can see more detailed information about specific usage factors, including the following:

- **Office activation** Specifies the number and types of devices on which users have installed their five copies of Office 365, as permitted by their license.

- **Adoption** Specifies how many Office 365 licenses have been assigned to users each month, how many are actually in use, and how many people are using Office 365 for the first time

- **Collaboration** Indicates how often users collaborate by accessing the documents of other users stored in SharePoint Online libraries or in OneDrive for Business

- **Communication** Specifies which Microsoft 365 tools workers prefer to use to communicate with each other in the enterprise, such as Exchange email, Teams, Yammer, or Skype

- **Product usage** Tracks the usage of specific activities within each Microsoft 365 service

- **Storage use** Tracks per-user cloud storage for SharePoint sites, OneDrive for business, and Exchange mailboxes

- **Access from anywhere** Specifies which clients and devices workers are using to connect to email, Teams, Yammer, or Skype

- **Individual service usage** Provides activity reports for individual Microsoft 365 services, including Exchange, Teams, and Yammer

Power BI is also customizable, enabling administrators to create their own reports and even to add their own additional data sources.

## MyAnalytics

Referred to by Microsoft as "the fitness tracker for work," MyAnalytics is a personal productivity recordkeeping tool that enables users to review how they spend their work time and who they spend it with. Available to all Office 365 users, MyAnalytics consists of a dashboard that is available in the list of Office 365 apps and a plug-in for Microsoft Outlook that displays MyAnalytics information as a separate pane in the standard Outlook interface.

MyAnalytics gathers information from a users Exchange Online calendars and mailboxes, Teams chat and call histories, Skype for Business activities, and optionally, Windows 10 application activities. The information is stored in each user's Exchange mailbox store. By compiling the information and displaying it in a series of charts, MyAnalytics attempts to advise users on how well they are managing their productivity and their leisure time.

The MyAnalytics dashboard, shown in Figure 2-52, consists of four panes, as follows:

- **Focus** Compares the amount of work time the user has left to concentrate on individual effort, as compared to the work time spent collaborating with team members. Based on these relative times, MyAnalytics can help the user book one to two hours per day for focused individual work and suppress incoming communications during those hours.

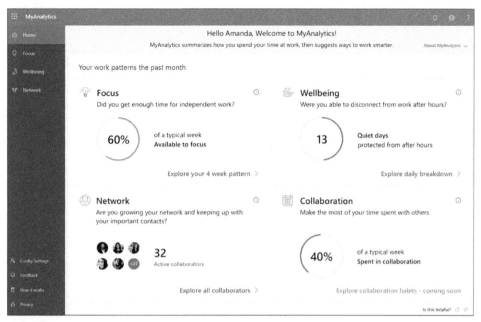

**FIGURE 2-52** The MyAnalytics dashboard

- **Wellbeing**   Based on Exchange calendar data and communication activities, MyAnalytics analyzes the user's time outside of normal working hours and tracks the time spent doing work-related activities then. Days in which the user spends less than two hours of outside time on work activities are designated as quiet days. When a user has insufficient quiet days, MyAnalytics makes recommendations for improving the quality of the user's leisure time.

- **Network**   Based on scheduled meetings, chats, calls, and emails, MyAnalytics tracks the amount of time that the user spends with his or her closest coworkers and team members during the previous month. Based on the data gathered, MyAnalytics can then make suggestions to improve the user's communication with the people designated as important, such as recommendations to schedule extra meetings and reminders to respond to calls and emails.

- **Collaboration**   Evaluates the user's time spent in collaboration with team members, as compared to time spent on other activities. Based on the results, MyAnalytics might recommend that a user spend less time answering email and phone calls and more time working with close colleagues.

There are also separate pages for the panes, in which MyAnalytics displays more detailed information and suggestions, as shown in Figure 2-53.

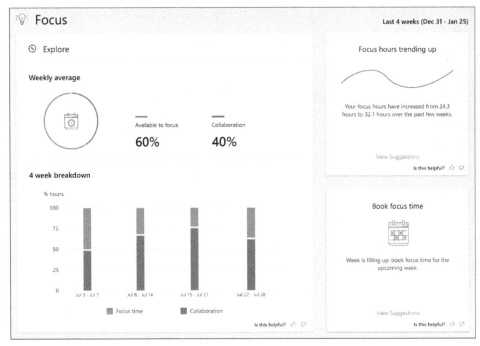

**FIGURE 2-53** The Focus page of the MyAnalytics tool

MyAnalytics is designed to be a personal self-improvement tool for individual users. It is not intended to be used by employers to monitor or track workers' productivity, nor does it provide users with personal information about their coworkers.

## Workplace Analytics

Workplace Analytics is similar to MyAnalytics, except that it compiles information for the entire enterprise rather than just one person. Like MyAnalytics, the primary motivation for Workplace Analytics is to provide management with insight into how workers are spending their time and whom they are spending it with.

Workplace Analytics begins with the same sources as MyAnalytics, such as Exchange email and calendaring data and Teams chat and calling histories. However, administrators can also incorporate additional information into the analysis, such as human resources data about employees, including job titles, management levels, and geographical locations. With this information, the analysis can calculate factors that are not realizable with the service data alone.

Based on this analysis, Workplace Analytics generates metrics in the following areas:

- **Week in the life** Calculates the average number of hours employees devote to collaboration in a selected week. The collaboration time is broken down into hours spent in meetings and hours answering emails.

- **Management and coaching**   Calculates the average time employees spend in meetings with their manager present, specifying also how many hours they spend in one-on-one meetings with managers.

- **Internal networks**   Specifies the network size and the network breadth of employees' collaboration. Network size is the number of people employees collaborate with in meetings or emails, while network breadth is the number of different departments or divisions with which the employees collaborate.

- **Teams collaboration**   Calculates the employees' usage of Microsoft Teams communication, including the number of calls and chat messages, as well as the amount of time spent in calls and chat sessions.

- **External collaboration**   Calculates several statistics quantifying workers' collaboration with people outside of the company, such as the percentage of employees engaged in external collaboration and the percentage of their time they spend in external collaboration.

- **Meetings overview**   Quantifies the amount of time employees spend in meetings and specifies the nature of the meetings in which they are engaged.

As an example of the tool's analytics capabilities, the Meetings overview page can use Exchange calendar information to calculate how much time workers spend in meetings, as shown in Figure 2-54; also, Meetings can quantify meetings of different lengths. However, Workplace Analytics can also use the workers' geographical locations (from the Human Resources information) to determine how much travel time they expend getting to the meetings.

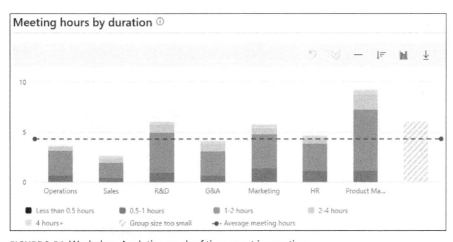

**FIGURE 2-54** Workplace Analytics graph of time spent in meetings

The analysis can also identify how much of the meeting total consists of low-quality time, as shown in Figure 2-55, is defined as meeting hours during which a worker is playing a redundant role, is scheduled to attend another meeting at the same time, or is multitasking by answering email in the meeting. Workplace Analytics can then explain the significance of these statistics and suggest of ways to improve the allocation of meeting time by reducing these negative factors.

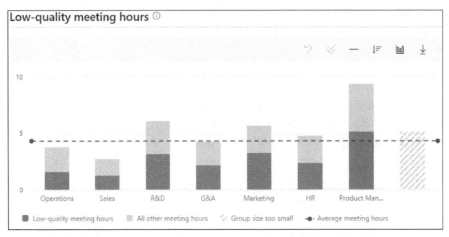

**FIGURE 2-55** Workplace Analytics graph of low-quality time spent in meetings

In addition to these predefined statistics, Workplace Analytics also enables administrators to create their own queries that use the data to answer questions about specific users, groups of users, and activities. There are four query types supported, as shown in Figure 2-56:

- **Person** Provides individual, itemized time-utilization information for a (deidentified) group of employees

- **Meeting** Provides insight into the relationship between meeting properties, such as size, duration, subject, and organizer

- **Group-to-group** Quantifies the time two teams or groups of employees spent interacting

- **Person-to-group** Quantifies the time that an individual spent interacting with a specific team or group

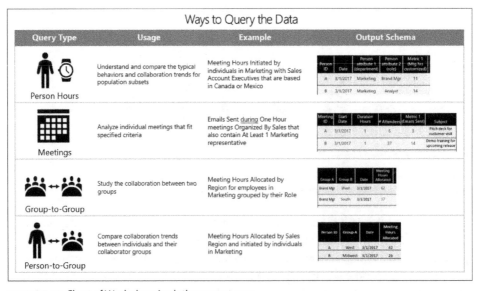

**FIGURE 2-56** Chart of Workplace Analytics query types

For example, if the Meetings overview metric indicates that an abnormally large number of low-quality meetings are occurring, an administrator can create a query to try to identify which teams or groups of workers are most frequently involved in these meetings and attempt to ascertain why, in the hope of discovering a means of addressing the problem.

## Summary

- Microsoft 365 consists of three main components: Windows 10, Office 365, and Enterprise Mobility + Security. Office 365 includes additional services, including Exchange Online, SharePoint Online, and Microsoft Teams. Enterprise Mobility + Security includes Azure Active Directory Premium, Microsoft Intune, Azure Information Protection, and Advanced Threat Analytics.

- Some of the Microsoft 365 components are available as on-premises applications and services. The incentives to use cloud-based rather than on-premises software include reduced initial cost outlays, more frequent feature updates, and high availability.

- Modern management is an evolution of the traditional IT deployment and support models to emphasize client mobility and cloud-based services and administration.

- Office 365 ProPlus includes the traditional, installable Office productivity applications, including Word, Excel, and PowerPoint, as well as cloud-based services, such as Exchange Online, SharePoint Online, Microsoft Teams, and Yammer. Compared to the on-premises products, Office 2016 and Office 2019, Office 365 offers many advantages, including more frequent updates, licenses for up to five devices, mobile device support, and cloud-based email and collaboration services.

- Microsoft 365 is designed to provide users with the ability to work anywhere, using any device. By supplying cloud-based collaboration tools and enabling administrators to manage users' Bring Your Own Device hardware, Microsoft 365 supports a more modern productivity model.

- Microsoft 365 includes analytics tools that can gather information from applications and services across the enterprise and use to anticipate threats and improve worker productivity.

## Thought experiment

In this thought experiment, demonstrate your skills and knowledge of the topics covered in this chapter. You can find answers to this thought experiment in the next section.

Alice is planning an Office deployment for her company's new branch office in Chicago and is comparing the advantages and disadvantages of Office 365 and Office 2019. The branch office is expected to ramp up to a maximum of 120 new users within a year, and Alice is trying both to anticipate the needs of the users and stay within her initial outlay budget, which is relatively limited.

Alice wants to create as stable a working user environment as possible, to minimize technical support and training issues. She is concerned about the possibility of monthly feature updates in Office 365, which might generate too many support issues and require additional training for both users and support personnel. She knows that Office 2019 does not receive feature updates.

The branch office is connected to the Internet through a connection with a local Internet service provider. The company's main office has on-premises Exchange and SharePoint servers, which are accessible through the Internet. Alice is wondering whether it would be more efficient for the users to access their mail and document libraries on the main office servers or for her to use the cloud-based Exchange Online and SharePoint Online services. A third option would be for her to install on-premises Exchange and SharePoint servers at the branch office. She is also concerned about Exchange and SharePoint administration because she would prefer that her onsite staff manage the new user onboarding and maintenance processes.

Alice is also concerned about identity management for the branch office users and the Active Directory authentication traffic that they will generate. The New York office has Active Directory Domain Services domain controllers installed, but Alice has not as yet planned to install domain controllers in the branch office. She is aware that Azure Active Directory can provide cloud-based identity management, but she is concerned that the branch office users might at times require access to resources stored on New York servers.

After careful consideration of all these factors, Alice has decided to choose Office 365 and its cloud services for the branch office deployment. List five reasons why her selection is justified.

## Thought experiment answer

Alice can address all her concerns by deploying Office 365 and using cloud-based Exchange Online and SharePoint Online services for the following reasons:

- Office 365 can be configured to receive feature updates only twice a year, which would reduce the potential training and support issues, when compared to monthly updates.
- Because it is subscription-based, Office 365 has a much smaller initial cost outlay than Office 2019, which must be paid for in full during the initial deployment.
- The cloud-based services available with Office 365 provide users with access to Exchange and SharePoint through a nearby Microsoft Global Network endpoint. Requiring users to access Exchange and SharePoint servers in New York would be likely to generate additional network latency and therefore reduce user efficiency.
- Exchange Online and SharePoint Online are administered through web-based tools that can be accessed directly by the branch office support staff. Onboarding new users on the New York servers would require remote access or participation of the New York staff to complete the onboarding processes.
- Azure Active Directory would enable the branch office support staff to manage the user accounts themselves and would lessen the network latency that authenticating through the New York domain controllers would cause. Azure AD can also be configured to synchronize with the New York domain controllers, enabling branch office users to receive authenticated access to resources on New York servers.

# CHAPTER 3

# Understand security, compliance, privacy, and trust in Microsoft 365

Microsoft 365 was originally conceived as a product that would present users with familiar tools—such as the Office productivity applications—and enable them to collaborate in new ways, more easily, more efficiently, and using any device at any location. This is a wonderful aspiration, but the product's designers soon realized that this idea of universal collaboration raised security, compliance, privacy, and trust issues that had to be addressed before the ideal could be realized.

Typically, these issues are the main impediment to the full adoption of Microsoft 365 for many IT professionals. The idea of storing sensitive data in the cloud and allowing workers to use their own devices to access that data is terrifying to administrators for whom security is becoming a greater issue every day. However, the Microsoft 365 designers have taken great pains to address these issues, and they have created a product that, when used correctly, should satisfy the concerns of even the most skittish IT directors.

## Skills in this chapter:

- Understand security and compliance concepts with Microsoft 365
- Understand identity protection and management
- Understand the need for unified endpoint management, security usage scenarios and services
- Understand the Service Trust Portal and Compliance Manager

## Skill 3.1: Understand security and compliance concepts with Microsoft 365

At one time, enterprise security could be thought of as a perimeter surrounding an organization. Data remained largely within the organization's sites and could be protected from unauthorized access by firewalls and physical barriers. Even when data began to be accessible beyond the organization using Internet websites and portable devices, these potential attack vectors were still owned and managed by the company.

The assets that an organization needs to protect, now referred to as its *digital estate*, have grown enormously in recent years and so have the enterprise's means of ingress and egress. This digital estate certainly includes the company's data, but it also includes the users who access the data and the systems and devices by which they access the data. All three of these assets are potential weak points in an enterprise security system, as shown in Figure 3-1. All three need protection.

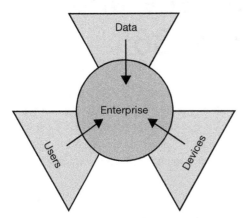

**FIGURE 3-1** The enterprise asset types needing protection

The commitment to the cloud required by adopters of Microsoft 365 creates a new attack vector. However, to fully protect the company's data, IT administrators now have to be concerned with the cloud, and they must be concerned with security for devices that are not directly owned by the organization, not located within the organization, and, in some cases, owned by users who are not even employees of the organization.

Therefore, the primary storage for an organization's data can be located in the cloud or on servers kept on-premises. In many cases, the data is split between the two. That means administrators must be responsible for the security of both. However, in addition to the primary storage locations, the devices that workers use to access the data are potential attack vectors as well. The increasing adoption of the Bring Your Own Device (BYOD) paradigm complicates the process of securing data that might be stored in someone's pocket on a device that might not be fully manageable by the enterprise administrators.

The security problem also extends beyond the logical extremities of the enterprise to the partners, clients, and consultants with which employees share data. These people use their own systems and devices that are even farther out of reach of the enterprise administrators. All these attack vectors can provide intruders with a way into the enterprise network, and once sophisticated intruders are inside, they often manage to stay there and extend their influence.

While there are always a certain number of casual cybercriminals who are relatively easy to repulse, the serious, professional penetration attempts that often afflict large enterprises can be incredibly sophisticated and take place over long periods of time. Microsoft 365 includes a powerful array of security tools that make it possible for administrators to implement various types of protection over the company's data and the devices that access it, but these tools are not simple turnkey solutions. Enterprise administrators must design a security plan that prioritizes the sensitivity of the company's data, assesses the vulnerability of the systems and devices on which the data is stored, identifies the users and their data needs, and specifies how the Microsoft 365 tools will be used.

## Risk management

Typically, information is the most valuable resource a business possesses. When considering security measures for an enterprise network, the ultimate end of these measures is to protect the information. Protection against unauthorized users or devices is really just a means of protecting the data that those users can access and store on those devices. Computers and other hardware devices have monetary value, but the physical security measures of a data center—for example, the electronic door locks, the security guards, and the fire suppression systems—are there primarily to protect the information stored on the hardware and not so much the hardware itself.

The process of creating a security plan for an enterprise is known as *risk management*, which is the act of identifying the assets that need protection, determining the potential dangers to those assets, assessing the impact of those dangers to the organization, and implementing protective measures appropriate to the assets and the threats. Microsoft 365 includes a large collection of tools that can help with all phases of this process. The security technologies in Microsoft 365 are divided into four areas, as follows:

- Security management
- Identity-based protection
- Information protection
- Threat protection

The technologies in each of these areas are shown in Figure 3-2. An organization that is seeking to secure its enterprise network is unlikely to need all these technologies. Consider these to be a toolkit from which administrators can select the right tool for each task. Microsoft's Core Services and Engineering Operations (CSEO) group has chosen the technologies protruding from the wheel shown in Figure 3-2.

Therefore, the first step of the risk management plan is to identify the types of information the organization possesses and determine the value of each information type to the business.

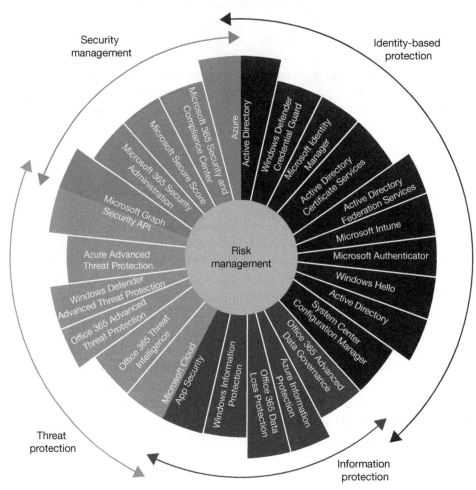

Microsoft 365 technologies and their associated security areas

**FIGURE 3-2** Microsoft 365 security technologies used by the Microsoft CSEO group

## Identifying and valuing information assets

Companies often generate vast amounts of data, which conform to various levels of sensitivity. It is usually not practical for an organization to implement the ultimate level of security over all their data, so it is necessary to classify the information according to its function and value. Therefore, the risk management process should begin with an inventory of the organization's information assets and a determination of each asset's value to the company, taking into account its need for confidentiality, integrity, and availability. The factors to consider when compiling such an inventory are shown in Table 3-1.

**TABLE 3-1** Risk factors for asset inventory

| RISK FACTOR | DESCRIPTION | EXAMPLE |
|---|---|---|
| Confidentiality | Access and disclosure of sensitive information by unauthorized persons | What if users' passwords or Social Security numbers were stolen? |
| Integrity | Modification or damage of sensitive information by unauthorized persons | What if the company's payroll information or product designs were changed? |
| Availability | Prevention of access to sensitive information by authorized users | What if the company's client list or website was rendered inaccessible? |

The definitions used for information types will be specific to the nature of the business, as will their value to the business. For example, in the case of a company that uses its website to provide support information to customers, an attack that renders the site unavailable for several days would be an inconvenience. For a company that sells its products exclusively on the web, however, the unavailability of its e-commerce website for several days could be disastrous.

For a large enterprise, this type of asset inventory is typically not the exclusive province of the IT department. It will likely require the involvement of personnel from various departments and at various levels of the organization, including management, legal, accounting, and even clients and partners outside the company.

The value of an information resource might not necessarily be expressed in monetary terms. The result of a data threat might be lost productivity, the creation of additional work to restore or re-create the data, fines or penalties to government or regulating agencies, or even more intangible effects, such as bad public relations or lost customer confidence.

To quantify the inventoried assets, the best practice is to create a graduated scale that considers all the risk factors particular to the business. A general numerical scale from 1 to 3 or a risk gradation of low, medium, or high would work, with a larger number of grades if the security measures the administrators choose to implement warrant it.

The value or sensitivity of a data asset will determine the nature of the security mechanisms administrators use to protect it. Some types of data might be subject to legal or contractual compliance specifications, which impose strict limits on where and how they are stored and who can access them. The security requirements for this most sensitive data might define the highest value on the risk scale, which can call for extreme security measures such as on-premises storage in a secured data center, data encryption and redundancy, and highly restricted access permissions.

Other types of sensitive data might not even be subject to broadly categorical security mechanisms, such as those applied to file folders or specific file types. Microsoft 365 includes the Azure Information Protection (AIP) tool that can apply labels to documents containing sensitive information. Administrators can configure the labels to trigger various types of security, such as watermarks, encryption, and limited access. While users and administrators can manually apply the labels to documents, AIP is also capable of detecting sensitive information in documents and automatically applying labels to them. For example, when a user creates a

Word document, administrators can configure AIP to detect values that appear to be credit card numbers, as shown in Figure 3-3, and apply a label to the file that calls for a specified degree of protection.

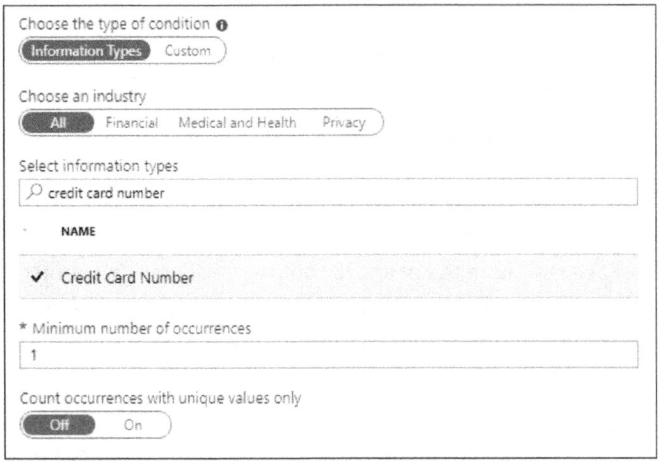

**FIGURE 3-3** AIP configuration

Data that does not greatly threaten confidentiality, integrity, and availability is at the low end of the risk scale. This data will require some protection, but the security at the low end of the scale might be limited just to file system access permissions.

## Inventorying hardware

Once the data sensitivity and the value of the data has been assessed, the next step of the risk management plan design process is to consider the technology used to store, access, transmit, and process that data. This includes the servers or cloud services where the data is stored when at rest, the client systems and devices used to access the data, the network components that carry the data between the various systems, and the applications that process the data.

In the same way that the data itself is inventoried in the previous phase, there should be an inventory of all the hardware involved in the storage of the data. This information can be used to locate the precise source of a security breach and to help prevent unauthorized devices from accessing secured company resources.

The primary storage locations for all sensitive company information should be servers located in a secured environment, such as a data center or server closet, or a cloud service, which should have its own security policies detailed in the service contract. However, the process of compiling an inventory of client systems and devices can be significantly more complicated. Workstations located at the enterprise sites are presumably already inventoried, but home computers and employees' mobile devices, such as smartphones and tablets, need to be considered. Also, computers and devices belonging to people outside the organization, such as partners, consultants, temporary workers, and customers, need to be considered.

Administrators should document every device that comes into contact with company data. The inventory should include information such as the following:

- **Make**   The manufacturer of the device
- **Model**   The manufacturer's model name and number for the device
- **Serial number**   The manufacturer's serial number for the device
- **Owner**   The person or organization that is the owner of the device
- **User**   The person or persons who use the device to access company data
- **Location**   The place where the device is installed or if mobile, the location of the person responsible for it
- **Service ID**   The owner organization's assigned ID number, if applicable
- **Operating system**   The operating system installed on the device
- **OS version**   The version and build of the operating system running on the device
- **Network provider**   The provider used by the device to access the Internet or the company network
- **Applications**   The applications on the device that are used to access company data
- **Information used**   The specific types of company data that the device can access

For workstations owned by the organization, this information is typically compiled during the system's deployment process and can probably be imported into the inventory. For systems and devices owned by employees, the information-gathering process should be required before any access to sensitive company data is permitted.

Verification of the inventory information can be difficult for users who are frequent travelers or home computer users, but in the modern management model implemented by Microsoft 365, tight control of hardware devices is an essential element of enterprise security. For devices owned by people who are not employees of the organization, such as customers, the diplomatic aspects of enforcing these policies can be even more difficult, but administrators might be able to mitigate them by creating a risk level that provides these users with access only to a limited class of information that is not extremely sensitive.

In addition to the systems and devices that access company data, networking technology can also present an element of risk. The most obvious potential attack vector is wireless network devices, which are vulnerable to outside attacks in a variety of ways. Microsoft 365 includes Microsoft Intune, which enables administrators to create Wi-Fi network profiles that contain preshared keys and other security measures that prevent unauthorized devices from connecting to a company wireless network. There are also some extremely sensitive data types that can require special handling even for wired networks, such as compliance regulations that require network cables to be enclosed in sealed conduits for protection against wiretapping. Hardware-based security devices, such as firewalls, should also be included in the inventory.

When hardware that accesses sensitive information is compromised, the data is presumed to be compromised as well. Administrators can use the hardware inventory to ensure that the operating systems and applications on the devices are kept up to date with security patches and that antivirus and other security tools are updated. Administrators can also use Microsoft 365 tools to create compliance policies so that devices cannot access network resources unless they meet specific requirements, including up-to-date software.

The hardware security elements of a risk management plan can go beyond the capabilities of the tools in Microsoft 365. Protecting the hardware can include other mechanisms, including the following:

- **Physical security**   Software-based security measures cannot fully protect the data stored on a computer if intruders have physical access to the machine. Even if the intruders can't compromise the data, they can always destroy it, which can be just as damaging to the organization. Physical measures, even those as simple as a locked door, are basic elements of any risk management plan. For mobile devices, which are always vulnerable to loss or theft, administrators can use Microsoft Intune mobile device management to implement the ultimate hardware solution: remotely erasing the data from the device.

- **High availability**   In addition to malicious or criminal intrusion, hardware devices are also liable to failures from wear and tear or destruction from natural disasters, such as fires, earthquakes, and extreme weather. High-availability measures, such as RAID arrays, redundant servers, and duplicate data centers, can preserve data against loss and ensure that the data remains available to users. For Microsoft 365 data stored in the cloud, the Microsoft Global Network maintains data centers at locations throughout the world, as shown in Figure 3-4, providing subscribers with a 99.9 percent availability rate.

- **Disaster recovery**   Data backups and cloud synchronization can enable sensitive data to be restored, even after an attack or a disaster renders the original data or the hardware on which it is stored unusable.

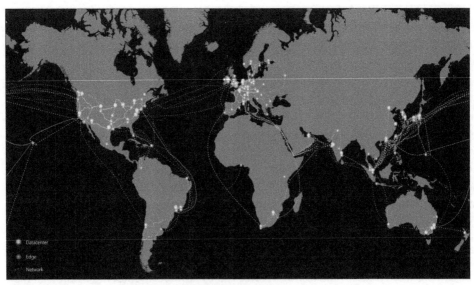

**FIGURE 3-4** Microsoft Global Network data center locations

## Classifying users

The third element of the digital estate that must be considered when creating a risk management plan is the people who actually access the data. Users, whether deliberately or inadvertently, are a constant vulnerability—if not an actual threat—to the organization's data. After quantifying the organization's information assets and their value and after inventorying the hardware used to store, access, transmit, and process the information, the next step is to list the people who have access to the information.

The people with access to the organization's information certainly include employees who are authorized to create, view, and modify the data. However, a risk management team must consider the possibility of other individuals accessing the data as well. Anyone with physical access to computers on which data is stored or from which it is accessible is a potential threat. This includes cleaning and maintenance staff, repair people, and even security guards. Even if an individual doesn't have the credentials needed to sign on to a computer, it is still possible for a person to steal or destroy the computer or remove a hard drive from it.

A risk management plan should include a list of everyone who has access to sensitive information and what exact information they can access. Access control policies should be designed to provide users with permissions only for the data they need and no more. Within the organization, administrators often do this by defining roles, granting the roles access to the required data, and then assigning individuals to those roles. This simplifies the process of authorizing new users, moving users to other jobs, and deauthorizing departing users. Administrators can then create an orderly lifecycle for each individual user's identity, as shown in Figure 3-5.

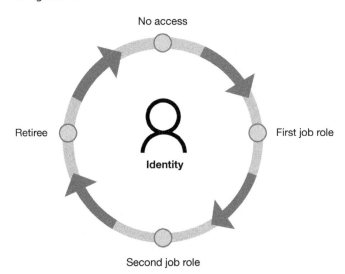

**FIGURE 3-5** Identity lifecycle for an individual user

Every person who is granted access to company data should have an individual user account, including people who are working on-site temporarily. Any convenience that might be realized by creating generic guest accounts and assigning them to temporary users as needed will be nullified by the difficulty these accounts can cause when investigating an incident involving data loss or unauthorized access.

The plan must also include the means of ensuring that the individuals signing on to computers are actually the people they purport to be. Password policies can ensure that users create passwords that are sufficiently long and complex and change them regularly. Microsoft 365 also includes several enhanced authentication mechanisms, including multifactor authentication options calling for a fingerprint scan or a code sent to a mobile phone in addition to a password.

Users with administrative privileges present a greater potential threat to company data. The risk management plan should include policies that require administrators to use standard user accounts for all typical work functions and administrator accounts only for tasks that require the additional privileges. This not only helps to protect the company data from accidental damage or deletion, but it also reduces the possibility of unauthorized software installation, whether intentional or not. Privileged access user accounts should have their own lifecycle policies with more stringent monitoring and control, as shown in Figure 3-6.

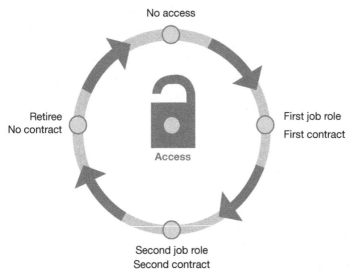

**FIGURE 3-6** Lifecycle for a privileged access user account

Of course, even authorized users can be a threat, and the risk management plan should define the specific means by which new employees are vetted, which should include national (or international) background checks, credit histories, and confirmation of degrees and other credentials. For organizations working with data that is extremely sensitive, more extensive investigation of new hires might be in order.

Internal users are a major source of security incidents, although the incidents can be unintentional as well as deliberate. Disgruntled workers and industrial espionage are certainly legitimate causes of data theft or loss, but simple slips, such as leaving a signed-on computer unattended, can be equally dangerous. In addition to addressing malicious threats, a risk management plan should devote sufficient attention to accidental threats.

## Anticipating threats

Arguably, the most difficult part of the risk management planning process is trying to anticipate all the possible threats that could afflict the company data in the future. The three basic risk factors for the data—confidentiality, integrity, and availability—can be exploited in any number of specific ways, but the general threat categories are listed in Table 3-2.

**TABLE 3-2** Risk management threat possibilities

| CONFIDENTIALITY | INTEGRITY | AVAILABILITY |
| --- | --- | --- |
| Theft of data by internal employee | Accidental alteration of data by internal user | Accidental damage or destruction of data by internal user |
| Theft of data by external intruder | Intentional alteration of data by internal employee | Intentional damage or destruction of data by internal user |
| Inadvertent disclosure of data | Intentional alteration of data by external intruder | Intentional damage or destruction of data by external intruder |
| | | Damage or destruction of data by natural disaster |

The core of the risk management process is to anticipate potential threats in detail and use the information gathered earlier in the data, hardware, and user inventories to estimate the severity and likelihood of each threat. For example, the threat of the company's client sales figures being disclosed when a travelling user misplaces his smartphone is far more likely than the threat of a competitor breaking into the company headquarters at night and hacking into a workstation to steal the same information. The severity of the threat in the two scenarios is the same, but the loss of a smartphone is the more likely occurrence, so administrators should expend a greater effort at mitigating that possibility.

In another example, a competitor's burglary attempt might result in the theft of those same client sales figures; in another scenario, this same burglary attempt might cause deliberate damage to the company's web servers, taking the company's e-commerce site down for several days. The likelihood of these scenarios is roughly the same, but the web server damage is the far more severe threat because it interrupts the company's income stream. Therefore, the more severe threat warrants a greater attempt at prevention.

Microsoft 365 provides tools that administrators can use to predict, detect, and respond to security threats. However, a comprehensive risk management plan goes beyond these types of tools and incorporates policies and includes purchasing policies, hiring policies, building policies, and administration policies.

## Updating the plan

Risk management is not a one-time event; it must be a continual process to be effective. Security threats continue to evolve at a rapid rate, so the protection against them must evolve as well. At least once a year, the risk management team should repeat the entire assessment process, updating the inventories of all the organization's information, hardware, and human assets to ensure that no changes have occurred without the company's knowledge. The team must update the threat severity and likelihood matrix as well. New or updated threats will require new security tools, procedures, and policies to provide protection against them.

In addition to the internal updates of the risk management plan, an organization might want to engage outside contractors to perform a vulnerability assessment, which is an evaluation of the threats in an organization's security infrastructure. Depending on the size of the organization and the current nature of its possible threats, a vulnerability assessment can be a minor and relatively inexpensive procedure or an elaborate and costly undertaking.

Some of the specific types of vulnerability assessments are as follows:

- **Network scan**   Identifies avenues of possible threats through internal network and Internet connections, including router, firewall, and virtual private network (VPN) configurations
- **Wireless network scan**   Evaluates the organization's Wi-Fi networks for vulnerabilities, including improper configuration, antenna placement, and rogue access points
- **Host scan**   Identifies vulnerabilities in servers, workstations, and other network hosts, including port and service scans, configuration settings, and update histories
- **Application scan**   Examines web servers and other Internet-accessible servers for software vulnerabilities and configuration issues
- **Database scan**   Identifies database-specific threats in database servers and the databases themselves

Another possible method of assessing security vulnerabilities in an organization's risk management system is to have a penetration test performed. A penetration test is a procedure in which an outside contractor is engaged to attempt an attack on the company's systems to ascertain whether the potential vulnerabilities identified in the risk management process are actual vulnerabilities and to assess the organization's response procedures.

## Key security pillars

Microsoft 365 provides a variety of security tools and services that enterprise administrators can use to protect the various elements of their organizations. Based on the information gathered during risk management planning, the team can establish priorities that dictate the degree of security required and the specific elements that require priority attention. A comprehensive security implementation must distribute protection among the four primary pillars supporting the enterprise infrastructure, as shown in Figure 3-7.

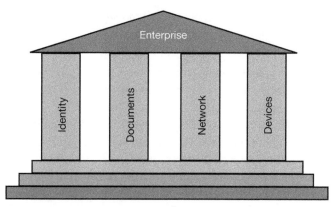

**FIGURE 3-7** The four key security pillars

These pillars are as follows:

- **Identity**   The process by which a user is authenticated and then authorized to access protected resources

- **Documents**   The functions by which the organization's data resources are protected from unauthorized access

- **Network**   The wired and wireless media that carry data signals, the components that provide Internet connectivity, and the protocols used to encode the signals, all of which are potentially vulnerable to attack

- **Devices**   The computers, smartphones, and other devices that access documents and other data via the network

These four elements function together to enable users to access the data they need, and Microsoft 365 includes tools that can provide protection in each of these areas. Depending on the needs of the organization and the possible threats identified, administrators can modify the degree of protection applied at each of these pillars. The tools and procedures that Microsoft 365 provides for these four main security areas are described in the following sections.

## Identity

It's easy to build a perfectly secure house; just omit all the windows and doors. Your possessions will be safe, but you won't be able to get at them. In the same way, it would be easy to build a perfectly secure network by establishing a formidable perimeter around the sensitive resources and not letting anyone at all through it. This would be pointless, of course. Workers need access to those sensitive resources, and identities are the basis of that access. In enterprise networking, an *identity* is a collection of attributes that uniquely describe a *security principal*, that is, a specific individual and the resources that individual is permitted to access.

For data to be secure, the most fundamental types of protection are ensuring that the individuals accessing the data really are who they claim to be and that the individuals have been granted appropriate levels of access to the data they need. The process of confirming a user's identity on the network is called *authentication*, and the process of granting a user access to specific data or services is *authorization*. Securing the identities of the network's users is the process of making these procedures as safe and impenetrable as they can be.

The identities of an organization's users are the prime target for cybercriminals because stealing a user's name and credentials enables the attacker to access everything that the user knows about the company. News stories regularly report thefts of large blocks of identities from major companies, which endanger not just the companies' sensitive data but their employees' personal lives as well. For example, the theft of the names, addresses, and Social Security numbers that are part of any organization's human resources records leave users open to credit fraud and numerous other criminal intrusions. For the organization, identity theft can be catastrophic in many ways, resulting in data theft, damage, or destruction that can prevent the company from doing business and cost it vast amounts of money.

The attacks that attempt to steal user identities can be extremely simple or incredibly sophisticated. A major security breach for an organization can begin with one intruder calling an unsuspecting user on the phone and claiming to be Jack Somebody from account maintenance in the IT department and talking the employee into disclosing the user's login name and password. Once the intruder has one user's credentials, it becomes easier for the intruder to gain others. This sort of lateral movement within the organization's security infrastructure can be a slow and methodical process that eventually yields access to an identity with high-level access to the network and leads to a major security event. This is why administrators should take pains to protect all the organization's identities, not just the ones with elevated privileges.

In Microsoft 365, *Azure Active Directory (Azure AD)* allows administrators to create user identities and performs the authentication and authorization processes, as shown in Figure 3-8. Azure AD is a directory service that is a cloud-based alternative to *Active Directory Domain Services (AD DS)*, which has been the on-premises directory service for Windows networks since 1999. The primary objective in creating Azure AD is the ability to service identities and perform authentications and authorizations for cloud-based resources. This is an essential element of administering Microsoft 365.

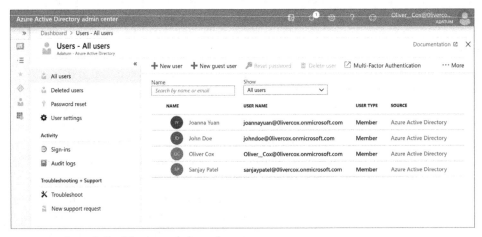

**FIGURE 3-8** Azure Active Directory admin center

An Azure-based Active Directory implementation is necessary for Microsoft 365 because AD DS is limited to providing on-premises security functions. Users must have access to the on-premises network to sign in to their organization's AD DS domain controllers. The only way a remote user can authenticate to the company network using AD DS is to establish a connection to an on-premises server, such as a virtual private network (VPN) connection. Azure AD is strictly cloud-based and enables users working anywhere and with any device to sign in to the organization's Microsoft 365 network and gain access to its services. Another advantage of a cloud-based directory service is that administrators can create identities for people outside the organization, such as partners, clients, vendors, or consultants, who need occasional or restricted access to company resources.

> **NOTE   USING AZURE AD WITH AD DS**
>
> Azure Active Directory and Active Directory Domain Services are not mutually exclusive. For an organization that already has an AD DS infrastructure in place, it is possible to deploy Azure AD and create hybrid identities by synchronizing the two directory services. For more information, see "Understand identity protection and management," later in this chapter.

Creating an identity in Microsoft 365 is a simple matter of supplying name values in a form like the one from the Azure Active Directory Admin Center shown in Figure 3-9. The Microsoft 365 Admin Center contains a similar form that also enables the creator of the identity to assign product licenses, such as a Microsoft 365 license, to the user. While creating identities is a quick and easy process, securing them can be considerably more complicated.

**FIGURE 3-9**  Creating an Azure AD user account

The traditional means of authenticating a user's identity is for the individual to supply an account name and a password. In Microsoft 365, administrators can create password policies that compel users to create long and complex passwords and change them frequently.

However, passwords are always subject to potential weaknesses that make them an unwieldy authentication mechanism, including the following:

- Users might have difficulty remembering long or complex passwords and write them down in unsecured locations.
- Users might share their passwords with coworkers for the sake of convenience.
- Users with dedicated accounts that have elevated privileges might overuse their administrative passwords for everyday tasks.
- Users might supply the same passwords for multiple services or resources, compounding the damage if a password on one server is compromised.
- Users might be tricked into supplying their passwords by phishing or social engineering attacks.
- Users' identities might be compromised when their passwords are subjected to replay attacks, in which an intruder retransmits a captured password to gain access to a protected resource.
- Users' passwords might be compromised by malware that captures keystrokes and transmits them to an intruder.
- Some users can be relentlessly clever in discovering ways to evade the password policies imposed on them.

Because some of the weaknesses of password-based authentication are caused by human failings rather than technological failings, the process of strengthening user passwords is often an educational one. Administrators can devise policies to mitigate some password weaknesses, though urging users to abide by them can be difficult.

For example, a 20-character, randomly generated, administrator-assigned password would be extremely difficult for attackers to compromise, but it might be equally difficult to put down the outright insurrection that could result from the users forced to use them. Because of the complications inherent in the use of passwords, Microsoft 365 supports other types of authentication mechanisms that administrators can use instead of (or along with) passwords.

Windows Hello for Business is a desktop authentication mechanism that can replace passwords with certificate or key pair authentication using a PIN or a biometric credential, such as a fingerprint scan or an infrared facial recognition process. Microsoft Authenticator is a mobile device app that enables users to sign in to a Microsoft account using a combination of authentication mechanisms, including PINs, biometrics, and one-time-passcodes (OTPs).

> **NOTE IDENTITY PROTECTION**
>
> For more information on protecting identities, see "Understand identity protection and management," later in this chapter.

## Documents

As noted earlier in this chapter, virtually all the security mechanisms in Microsoft 365 are ultimately intended to protect the enterprise's information, and documents are one of the primary containers for that information. The traditional method for securing documents is to apply access control permissions to them. Permissions take the form of access control lists that are stored as attributes of individual files and folders. An *access control list (ACL)* consists of multiple *access control entries (ACEs)*, each of which specifies a security principal, such as a user or group, and the permissions that grant the principal certain types of access to the file or folder.

Permissions specify who can access documents and what actions users can perform. For example, a user might be able to read a document but not modify it, while another user might not even be able to see that the document exists. Permissions have been around for decades, and they enable users and administrators to restrict access to particular documents, but they must be applied manually and are difficult to manage for a large document collection. Someone also must keep track of which documents contain sensitive information that requires additional protection.

Microsoft 365 therefore includes security mechanisms, such as Azure Information Protection (AIP) and Data Loss Prevention (DLP), which can protect documents in other ways. The process of identifying documents containing sensitive data and securing them consists of the following four steps:

- **Discovery**   The location of documents containing sensitive information, either by automatic detection based on established data patterns or by prompting users to apply classification labels
- **Classification**   The application of labels to documents containing sensitive information that indicate what types of protection should be applied to them
- **Protection**   The implementation of specific security mechanisms to documents based on the classification labels that have been applied to them
- **Monitoring**   The process of tracking document access trends, activities, and events and taking action when necessary

The process of discovering documents containing sensitive information is highly dependent on the nature of the organization, the types of businesses it is engaged in, and the policies or regulations with which it must comply. Tools like Data Loss Prevention have preconfigured sensitive information types that enable the automated discovery of documents that contain common data patterns, such as credit card and Social Security numbers. Also, administrators can create customized sensitive information types that can discover documents that contain specific industry-based keywords and data patterns.

Like a physical label, the sensitivity labels provided by tools like AIP and DLP can warn users that a document contains sensitive information and recommend that certain actions be taken. The labels persist with the documents as they travel to different systems and are opened in other Office applications—even those on other computing platforms. However, AIP and DLP labels can also be configured to apply various types of protection, like those shown in Figure 3-10. The labels can cause documents to be encrypted, both at rest and in transit; limited to use with specific applications; restricted to specific users or devices; or configured to expire and even be deleted after a specified lifespan.

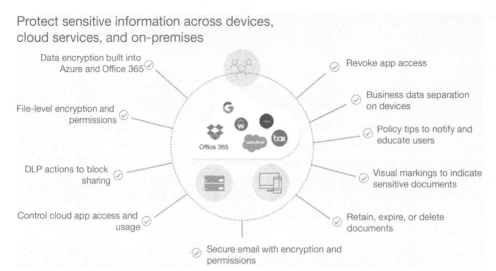

Protect sensitive information across devices, cloud services, and on-premises

Data encryption built into Azure and Office 365

File-level encryption and permissions

DLP actions to block sharing

Control cloud app access and usage

Secure email with encryption and permissions

Revoke app access

Business data separation on devices

Policy tips to notify and educate users

Visual markings to indicate sensitive documents

Retain, expire, or delete documents

**FIGURE 3-10** Microsoft 365 document protection mechanisms

Once the document classification and protection phases are complete, it is still the responsibility of administrators to monitor the reports and alerts that are generated by the security tools. For example, repeated attempts to access or share protected documents by the same user or device can indicate the presence of a security breach, even if the attempts fail. The monitoring process should include remediation as well so that an administrator who notices anomalous behavior can intervene by revoking document access privileges or quarantining files.

## Network

The traditional network security model calls for the construction of a perimeter surrounding the enterprise premises; this traditional model has servers, workstations, and users all located inside the perimeter and firewalls protecting them by filtering out unwanted traffic. Remote users could connect to enterprise resources only by establishing a secured connection to a remote access server located in a DMZ on the perimeter network. A Microsoft 365 installation places substantial and potentially vulnerable resources outside the perimeter in the cloud, requiring a revised network security model.

Remote users might still connect to on-premises servers for some functions, but others will connect directly to cloud services. Also, the new emphasis on mobile devices means that users will be accessing enterprise resources from a wider variety of locations, including public locations, such as hotels and coffee shops, over which the company has no control.

The Microsoft 365 deployment process begins with an assessment and possibly a redesign of the network to ensure that Internet bandwidth and proximity to the nearest Microsoft cloud endpoint is optimized. Also, adapting the security model to a network infrastructure that includes cloud services requires a shift in emphasis from perimeter security to endpoint security, in which the focus is placed more on securing the locations of the data and the locations of the users accessing the data than on the network medium connecting them.

While the security perimeter around the existing data center must remain in force, the load on the firewalls might be substantially decreased by the migration to cloud services. In some cases, firewall barriers might have to be weakened deliberately to enable Office 365 traffic to reach the cloud. However, this does not mean that the standard means of protecting the firewalls themselves, such as changing their administrative login names and passwords on a regular basis, can be abandoned.

Endpoint network security means that the protective features built into the Microsoft 365 cloud services take on a more prominent role in the enterprise security strategy. Microsoft 365 administrators do not have control over the network traffic reaching the cloud services, nor can they erect a perimeter around every remote or mobile device that accesses the enterprise services. Therefore, instead of trying to block malicious traffic with firewalls, security comes from mechanisms such as multifactor authentication, Data Loss Prevention, and Cloud App Security.

This does not mean that the networks themselves cease to be vulnerable or that they can be left unprotected. Administrators must be wary of the threats that have always afflicted networks, including unauthorized packet captures, unprotected Wi-Fi networks, and rogue access points. For example, if an enterprise allows both managed and unmanaged devices to access company resources—regardless of the policies they use to control that access—it is still a good idea to keep the managed devices on a separate wireless network from the unmanaged ones. Also, internal Wi-Fi networks must still be protected by appropriate security and encryption protocols, and their administrative passwords and preshared keys must be modified on a regular basis.

## Devices

If one of the two main innovations of Microsoft 365 is the use of cloud-based services, the other is the ability of users to access those services using many different types of devices that run on various computing platforms and work at any location that has Internet access. As noted earlier, VPN connections have long enabled remote users to access the company network from home or while traveling, using a laptop or desktop. VPNs use a technique called *tunneling* to protect the data as it is transmitted over the Internet. In subsequent years, there were a few mobile devices—nearly always supplied to users by the company—that were able to access a remote network, but with limited utility, such as email only. Today, Microsoft 365 enables remote users working with desktops, laptops, tablets, and smartphones to access virtually any enterprise service or resource that they could access using an on-premises workstation. The trick, however, is not just to make this access possible, but to make it secure as well.

Device security in Microsoft 365 therefore must address two relatively new issues:

- Mobile devices that frequently operate outside of the organization's protective perimeter
- The increasing use of mobile devices that are not selected and owned by the company

Because mobile devices can access any and all sensitive information maintained by the enterprise, it is essential that there be some means to protect that information from the threats to which all mobile devices are subject, including loss, theft, and misuse.

While administrators can still use traditional access-control measures, such as file system permissions, to regulate who is able to work with the organization's sensitive data, it is the Azure Active Directory and Microsoft Intune services that are primarily responsible for ensuring that the devices used to access that data are safe. Microsoft 365 supports a large number of mobile computing platforms, including the following:

- Windows 10
- Android
- Android enterprise
- iOS
- macOS

The interaction between mobile devices and the Microsoft 365 cloud services is a complex one, as shown in Figure 3-11; however, as you can see in the diagram, Microsoft Intune functions as a clearing house for many of these services and uses Azure AD for authentication and authorization.

Even though the organization might support a BYOD (Bring Your Own Device) policy for its users, it is essential that those devices be subject to some form of enterprise endpoint security. This is the primary function of Microsoft Intune, which is Microsoft 365's endpoint management tool; administrators use Intune to enroll users' devices and exercise some degree of management on them. By creating health compliance policies using Intune, enrolled devices can be checked for adherence to those policies before Azure AD authorizes them to access enterprise services and information. This is known as *conditional access*. Because Azure AD and Intune both operate in the cloud, they can function outside of the enterprise's premises perimeter, just like the mobile devices, and they can control access to the other Microsoft 365 services from any location.

The process of securing devices begins with their enrollment using Microsoft Intune, at which time an administrator must decide what type of management will be imposed on the device. Mobile Device Management (MDM) grants the organization nearly complete control over the device, requiring the user to comply with all the enterprise policies. MDM even allows an administrator to perform a remote wipe of the entire device if it should be lost or stolen, which ensures that any sensitive data is not compromised further.

MDM is intended primarily for use on company-owned devices; it can be problematic to some users who might not like the idea of granting the organization such comprehensive control over their personal property. For example, MDM policies might require smartphone users to sign on with a password or use another authentication mechanism every time they use their phones—something which users might find to be inconvenient.

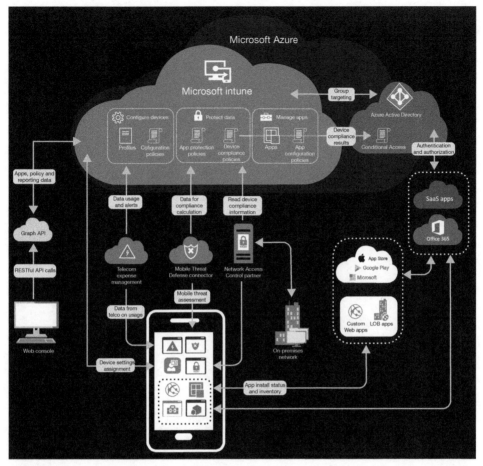

**FIGURE 3-11** Microsoft Intune service architecture

The alternative is Mobile Application Management (MAM), which provides administrators with control over specific applications running on a device, but it does not provide control over the entire device itself. For example, a similar policy in MAM might require the users to sign in when using Microsoft Exchange to access their email, but they don't have to sign in every time they turn on their phones. MAM also enables administrators to wipe company data from the phone, but only the data associated with the managed applications can be wiped.

Cloud App Security is another Microsoft 365 tool for mobile and other devices; Cloud App Security is a cloud access security broker application that scans network resources to detect the cloud applications that users are running, and it detects unauthorized Infrastructure as a Service (IaaS) and Platform as a Service (PaaS) products that might be in use. The object here is to detect "shadow IT"—that is, cloud applications that have not been approved by the IT department and which could be a threat to enterprise network security.

Cloud Discovery is the process by which Cloud App Security examines traffic logs from firewalls and proxy servers and compares the information to Microsoft's cloud app catalog, which contains more than 16,000 cloud applications. The catalog includes an assessment of each application as a potential threat, and scores are based on more than 70 risk factors.

Once Cloud App Security has compiled a report of the cloud applications being used, administrators can then sanction the applications they want employees to use and unsanction those they do not want them to use. For the sanctioned applications, Cloud App Security supports the use of APIs supplied by the cloud application providers. These APIs enable Cloud App Security to function as an intermediary between cloud applications and the enterprise's users, as shown in Figure 3-12, by accessing activity logs, user accounts, and data sources. Cloud App Security can then use this information to monitor usage, enforce policies, and detect threats.

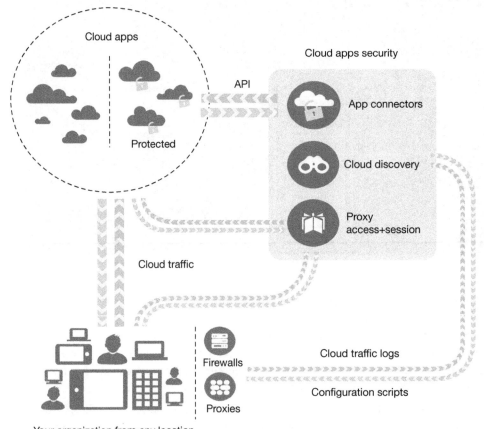

**FIGURE 3-12** Interactions of Cloud App Security with an enterprise network and cloud applications

# Skill 3.2: Understand identity protection and management

Identities are the fundamental security issue in Microsoft 365 or any network environment. Identities are the doors and windows that provide ingress and egress to the enterprise network environment. They are essential if anyone is going to be able to actually use the information stored by the enterprise services. Therefore, protecting those identities from improper use is a major priority in the design, implementation, and maintenance of an enterprise network.

An identity is a logical representation of a user in a network environment. To users, an identity is a name that they type to sign in to the network, along with a password or some other means of authentication. To administrators, an identity is a collection of attributes associated with a particular individual, as shown in Figure 3-13. The sign-in name is one of those attributes, but there can be many others, including personal information, such as a home address, telephone number, job title, and so on.

An identity also typically includes a list of the groups to which the individual is a member. Administrators use groups to assign rights and permissions to individuals. When a group is assigned rights and permissions to access network resources, all the group's members automatically inherit those rights and permissions. This is an efficient alternative to assigning multiple rights and permissions to each user identity individually.

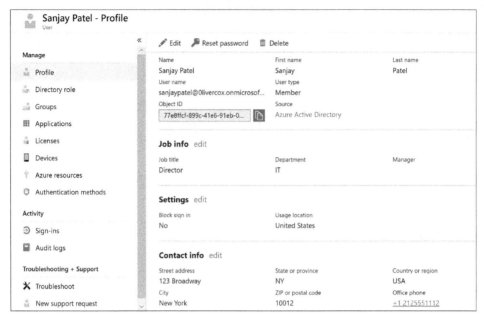

**FIGURE 3-13** User attributes in the Azure Active Directory Admin Center

# Identities

Every computer or mobile device has the capability to maintain a user's identity and employ it to protect the device from being accessed by anyone else. However, when a user wants to access applications, services, or data from his or her company's network, another identity is needed; this identity is created and maintained by the network's administrators and stored on the network itself, not on the user's computer or other device.

## On-premises identities

Beginning with the Windows 2000 Server release, enterprise identities were stored in Active Directory, which is an on-premises directory service that is still a part of the Windows 2019 Server product, although it is now called Active Directory Domain Services (AD DS). Installing the AD DS role on a computer running Windows Server enables it to function as a domain controller, which contains an object-oriented database of user identities and other network resources, including groups, computers, and applications. AD DS is a domain-based hierarchical database that uses container and organizational unit objects to separate users and other resources into logical collections, which usually represent the departmental or geographic divisions of the company.

Typically, enterprise networks have multiple domain controllers, which administrators configure to synchronize the contents of their AD DS databases with each other, for fault tolerance and high availability purposes. AD DS uses multiple master replication, which means administrators can create or modify users and other objects on any domain controller, and the changes will be replicated to all of the other domain controllers, as shown in Figure 3-14.

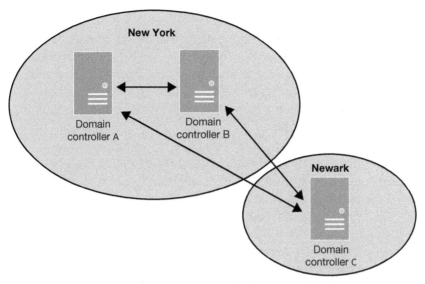

**FIGURE 3-14** Active Directory Domain Services multiple master replication

Administrators can create AD DS user objects using graphical tools, such as Active Directory Users and Computers, as shown in Figure 3-15, or command-line tools, such as the *New-ADUser* cmdlet in Windows PowerShell. The user objects in AD DS are strictly *on-premises identities*. Domain controllers must be located within the network perimeter and are not directly accessible from the Internet. When users access on-premises resources, their identities are authenticated and authorized by the nearest domain controller, which uses a protocol called Kerberos to perform a complicated ticket-based authentication procedure. Users outside the network perimeter can only perform an AD DS sign in to the network by establishing a VPN connection to a remote access server. This provides users with a presence on the internal network, which enables them to access internal resources.

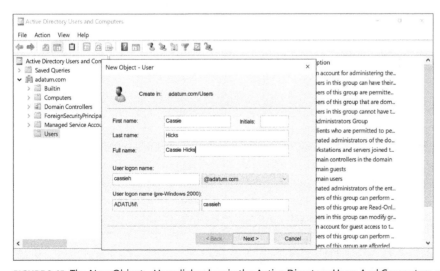

**FIGURE 3-15** The New Object – User dialog box in the Active Directory Users And Computers console

## Cloud identities

Because AD DS can only perform its functions when both the user and the resources to be accessed are located on-premises, it is not a viable solution for cloud-based applications and services. Therefore, Microsoft had to devise an alternative authentication and authorization solution for its cloud-based products, such as Microsoft 365. This solution is Azure Active Directory (Azure AD), a cloud-based directory service alternative (or companion) to AD DS in which administrators create *cloud identities*.

Microsoft 365 relies on the Azure Active Directory service for its identity management, and all the Microsoft 365 services use Azure AD for authentication and authorization. Microsoft 365 subscribers (as well as Office 365 and Windows Azure subscribers) become Azure AD tenants automatically. When a user accesses an Office 365 application in the cloud, as shown in Figure 3-16, Azure AD is the invisible intermediary that confirms the user's identity with the authentication mechanisms the Microsoft 365 administrators have selected. In the same way, Azure AD authorizes the user's access to the application and to the files the user opens in the application.

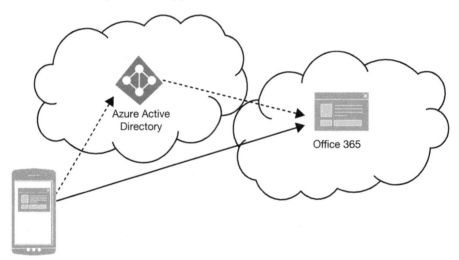

**FIGURE 3-16** Azure Active Directory provides authentication and authorization services for Microsoft 365 applications and services

Unlike AD DS, it is not necessary for administrators to install multiple domain controllers for Azure AD or configure directory replication. An Azure AD tenancy is automatically replicated to multiple data centers in the Microsoft Global Network. Also, unlike AD DS, Azure AD uses a single master replication model. There is only one primary replica of an Azure AD tenant, and all new users and account modifications are written to that primary replica. The changes are then automatically replicated to multiple secondary replicas at different data centers, as shown in Figure 3-17. All incoming read requests are handled by the secondary replicas, using the replica closest to the requesting user, application, or service. Because there are many secondary replicas, the Azure AD service is always available. Because there is only one primary replica, it works differently by using a deterministic failover procedure.

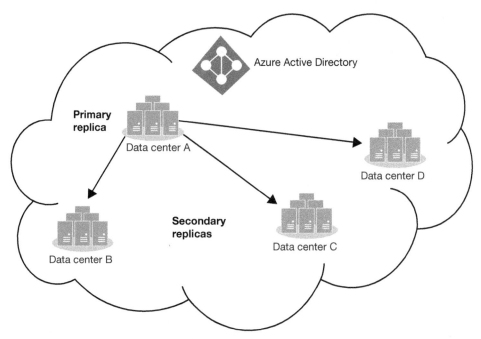

**FIGURE 3-17** Azure Active Directory single master replication

To create users in Azure AD, administrators can use several different tools, including the Microsoft 365 Admin Center and the Azure Active Directory Admin Center. Azure ID's authentication and authorization are also token-based, but the protocols and procedures that Azure AD uses are different from those that AD DS uses. Instead of Kerberos, Azure AD uses OAuth 2.0 or OpenID Connect.

## Hybrid identities

It is important to understand that Azure Active Directory is not intended to be a replacement for Active Directory Domain Services, nor are the two interchangeable. If an organization has internal servers and an on-premises AD DS implementation, they should not expect to be able to migrate their user identities from AD DS to Azure AD and then deprecate their AD DS domain controllers. It is equally important to understand that Microsoft 365 requires Azure AD; it is not possible to use AD DS identities to authenticate and authorize users for Microsoft 365 applications and services. The converse is also true; it is not possible to use Azure AD identities to provide authentication and authorization services for on-premises resources.

It is, however, possible to use Azure AD and AD DS together, creating what are known as hybrid identities. A *hybrid identity* is a user account that exists in both the Azure AD and AD DS directories with the same set of attributes. The usual scenario for the use of hybrid identities is an organization that has an existing AD DS infrastructure, but which is considering an expansion into the cloud by using Software as a Service (SaaS) products, such as Office 365. The organization might have hundreds or thousands of on-premises identities, but the prospect of having to re-create them in Azure AD and then maintain two identities for each user could be a deciding factor in the organization choosing not to use cloud services.

Hybrid identities are a solution to this problem. Because the assumption is that the AD DS identities already exist, creating hybrid identities is a matter of synchronizing them from AD DS to Azure AD. To do this, administrators must install a tool called Azure AD Connect on the on-premises network, which accesses the AD DS directory on a domain controller and replicates all the user accounts it finds to Azure AD (along with their passwords and other attributes).

> ***NOTE*** **FIRST SYNCHRONIZATION**
>
> When Azure AD Connect synchronizes on-premises AD DS identities to Azure AD for the first time, new cloud identities for the users are created, but product licenses are not automatically assigned to them. Therefore, in a new Microsoft 365 hybrid identity deployment, administrators must add Microsoft 365 licenses to the users in Azure AD after the first synchronization is complete. The administrators can add licenses to Azure AD users individually, but the process can also be performed dynamically by making the license assignment a result of group membership.

Passwords in AD DS are stored as a hash (a one-way mathematical algorithm that cannot be reversed to extract the password), and by default, Azure AD Connect applies another hash algorithm to the AD DS hash. Thus, the password transmitted by Azure AD Connect to the cloud is secured by it being a hash of a hash. The passwords in Azure AD are never stored in plain text, nor are they ever encrypted using a reversible algorithm.

After the initial synchronization, Azure AD Connect continues to detect changes made to the AD DS identities and replicates those changes to the corresponding Azure AD identities in the cloud, as shown in Figure 3-18. Therefore, administrators managing hybrid identities must use the AD DS tools, such as Active Directory Users and Computers, to make changes to the on-premises user accounts. Because the identity replication flows in only one direction—from AD DS to Azure AD—no one should make changes directly to the cloud identities using the Microsoft 365 tools.

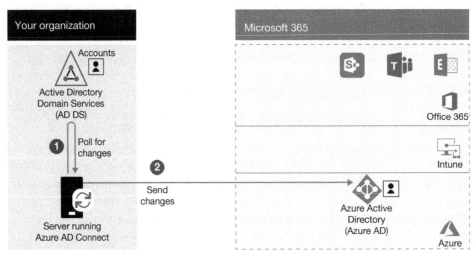

**FIGURE 3-18** Azure AD Connect identity synchronization

Hybrid identities can simplify the identity management process for administrators, but they can also simplify the user experience as well. For administrators who are adding cloud services to an existing on-premises infrastructure, the main objective should be to make user access to the cloud applications as invisible as possible. One way to do this is to implement *single sign-on (SSO)* so that users can authenticate with their familiar AD DS credentials and receive access to the cloud services without having to sign in again, either at the Azure AD level or in the individual applications. Another option, called *seamless single sign-on*, enables users connected to the enterprise network to be automatically signed in without any interactive authentication. Seamless sign-on is compatible with the password hash synchronization and pass-through authentication methods, but it is not compatible with the federated authentication method.

During the process of installing Azure AD Connect, an administrator must select the authentication method that Azure AD will use to provide the users with access to cloud resources. There are three options to choose from, as follows:

- **Azure AD Password Hash Synchronization**   The simplest form of the Azure AD Connect authentication methods, which requires no additional infrastructure to implement. Azure AD Connect creates a hash of each user's AD DS password hash and applies it to the corresponding Azure ID identity. This enables users to access both on-premises and cloud resources using the same password, as shown in Figure 3-19. Azure AD Connect updates the cloud identity passwords every two minutes without interrupting a session in progress when a password change occurs. Because the password hash synchronization model is fully implemented in the cloud, it shares the high availability of the other Microsoft cloud services. To ensure continuous operation, Microsoft recommends the installation of Azure AD Connect on two or more servers as a standby, preferably at different locations.

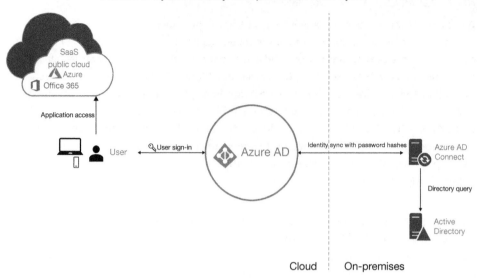

Azure AD hybrid identity with password hash sync

**FIGURE 3-19** Azure AD password hash synchronization

- **Azure AD Pass-Through Authentication** Avoids all cloud-based password validation by using a lightweight pass-through authentication agent installed on on-premises
  servers. (Microsoft recommends three.) When users sign in to Azure AD, their requests
  are forwarded to the agent, which forwards them in turn (in encrypted form) to a
  domain controller for validation of the users against their on-premises identities in AD
  DS, as shown in Figure 3-20. The agents require only outbound access to the Internet
  and access to an AD DS domain controller, so they cannot be located on a perimeter
  network. The end result is the same user experience as password hash synchronization, but this method avoids the storage of user passwords in the cloud in any form and
  enables administrators to enforce on-premises Active Directory security policies, such as
  disabled or expired accounts, and it allows sign-in hours and complies with contracted
  security requirements. It is also possible to deploy password hash synchronization in
  addition to pass-through authentication to function as a backup in the event of an on-
  premises failure that prevents the agents from functioning.

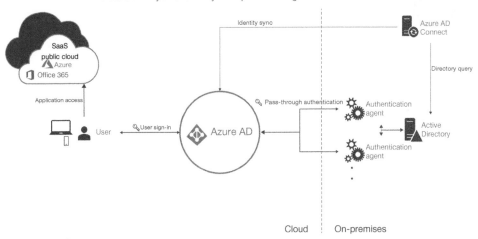

**FIGURE 3-20** Azure AD pass-through authentication

- **Federated Authentication** Offloads the authentication process to an external solution that the organization trusts, such as Microsoft Active Directory Federation Services (AD FS). The configuration and management of the authentication process—as well as the user experience—are the responsibility of the federated system; Azure AD is not involved. Depending on the security requirements of the organization, the sign-in process with the federated system might be simpler or more complicated than that of Azure AD. The federated system typically consists of a load-balanced cluster of servers—called a farm—for high availability and fault-tolerance purposes. Because the federation servers require access to both Azure AD and AD DS domain controllers, the servers themselves (or proxy intermediaries) must be located in the DMZ of an on-premises perimeter network, as shown in Figure 3-21. Organizations typically opt for the federated authentication option because they want to (or are compelled to) use an authentication method that Azure AD does not support, such as certificates or smart cards. The additional hardware, software, and administrative infrastructure that the federated authentication method requires can be a significant extra expense; in many cases, organizations that choose this option do so because they have already invested in the infrastructure. It is also possible to deploy password hash synchronization in addition to federated authentication, so that it functions as a backup in the event of an on-premises failure that prevents federation servers or their proxies from functioning.

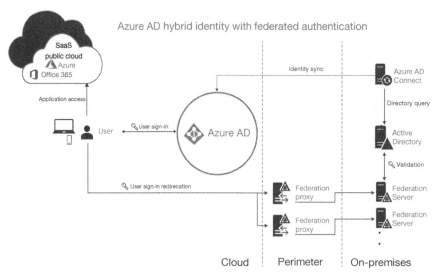

FIGURE 3-21 Federated authentication

# Authentication

If identities are the doors and windows in the enterprise network environment, authentications are the locks that keep them secure. An administrator can grant a specific user the permissions needed to access a file, an application, or a service, but this means nothing unless there is some way to ensure that the individual using those permissions is really the person to whom they were assigned. Authentication is how individuals actually prove their identities.

There are three basic means of authenticating an individual's identity. The individual must supply one or more of the following:

- **Something you know**   A piece of information that only the individual possesses, such as a password or PIN
- **Something you are**   A characteristic that is unique to the individual, such as a fingerprint or a facial scan
- **Something you have**   A unique item that the individual possesses, such as an ID card or a smart phone

# Password authentication

A password is *something you know*, and this has been the standard means of authenticating users' identities for many years. Password authentication costs nothing to implement, and it can be relatively secure. However, there are many possible flaws in the password authentication model. For example, passwords can be forgotten, shared, written down, easily guessed, or overly simple.

To prevent users from creating passwords that provide too little security, there are policies that specify rules for the creation and maintenance of passwords. Operating systems and directory services, such as Azure AD and AD DS, include tools that administrators can use to create and enforce such policies.

In Azure AD, user accounts are subject to the following password policies:

- **Characters allowed**    Specifies the characters that users are permitted to use when creating passwords, including upper- and lowercase alphabetical characters, numbers, blank spaces, and most symbols.

- **Password restrictions**    Specifies that passwords must have from 8 to 256 characters and must contain three of the following four character types: uppercase, lowercase, number, and symbol.

- **Passwords expiry duration**    Specifies that passwords expire in 90 days by default. The value can be modified using the *Set-MsolUser* PowerShell cmdlet.

- **Password expiry notification**    Specifies that the user will receive a password expiration notification 14 days before the password is set to expire. The value can be modified using the *Set-MsolPasswordPolicy* PowerShell cmdlet.

- **Password expiry**    Specifies a default value of False, indicating that the password will expire after the Passwords expiry duration interval. The value can be modified using the *Set-MsolUser* PowerShell cmdlet.

- **Password change history**    Specifies that  users cannot reuse the same password when changing passwords.

- **Password reset history**    Specifies that users can reuse the same password when resetting a forgotten password.

- **Account lockout**    Causes users to be locked out of their accounts for one minute after 10 unsuccessful but unique sign-in attempts. Additional unsuccessful attempts result in longer lockout intervals.

In AD DS, administrators can configure password settings using Group Policy. The available settings have slightly different names, but their functions are essentially the same.

These password policies are designed to prevent users from creating passwords that are overly simple for the sake of convenience, but password security is difficult for administrators to enforce. Users can still create passwords that would be easy for attackers to guess by using their children's names and birthdays, for example. There is also no software setting that can prevent users from writing their passwords down or sharing them with their coworkers.

As threats to network security become ever more severe, administrators have sought for ways to enhance the security of the authentication process. There have been alternative authentication methods available for many years, which could conceivably augment or replace passwords, but until relatively recently, these technologies were too expensive or inconvenient to be practical for the average user base. The increased need for identity protection has brought these authentication technologies to a wider market, however, resulting in lower prices, and the need is increasing constantly. Microsoft 365 includes the ability to enhance the security of the authentication process in a variety of ways.

## Multifactor authentication

Multifactor authentication is a procedure in which users prove their identities in two or more ways. Typically, in addition to a password—*something you know*—they supply a different authentication factor: *something you are* or *something you have.*

### SOMETHING YOU ARE

The *something you are* is usually some type of biometric scan. The Windows Hello for Business feature in Windows 10 supports multifactor authentication with biometric scans as one of the factors. It is also possible to use the Microsoft Authenticator app for mobile devices as a biometric scanner that enables users to access Microsoft 365 resources with no password.

Fingerprint readers are inexpensive and are becoming an increasingly common feature on laptops and other mobile devices. There are also aftermarket keyboards for desktop computers with integrated fingerprint readers as well. Fingerprint scans do not provide impenetrable security; fingerprints can conceivably be duplicated, and a scan of a finger would presumably still work, even if it was not attached to its owner. However, in combination with a password, fingerprint scans provide a multifactor authentication solution that could not be penetrated casually.

Facial recognition is another type of biometric scan that Windows Hello can use for multifactor authentication. Cameras are all but ubiquitous in modern society, so it would seem that the hardware costs of a facial recognition system are minimal. This is not the case, however, at least with Microsoft's facial recognition products. Facial recognition raises questions both of security and of privacy. If a computer can recognize a person's face as a security factor, what would stop an intruder from holding up a picture of the person to the camera? And where is the image of the user's face being sent to accomplish the authentication?

Microsoft has answers to both questions. Windows Hello for Business supports the use of facial recognition for user authentication, but it requires a camera with a separate infrared light source and near infrared sensor. The main problem with facial recognition systems on personal devices is that people might use them in any kind of lighting. Near infrared imaging provides a consistent image regardless of the visible light conditions. Windows Hello also does not store images of the user's face and never transmits them to other locations for authentication. When a user first enrolls in Windows Hello, the Windows Biometric Framework processes a facial image within the device and stores it as an enrollment profile. In subsequent authentication attempts, the system performs the same process and compares the results to the profile.

## SOMETHING YOU HAVE

While the *something you have* in multifactor authentication can be a smart card or some other form of identification, in Microsoft 365, it is usually a cell phone. This is a more practical option because most people today carry cell phones with them, while card readers far less common.

It has already become common for Internet websites to require a secondary authentication factor, usually in the form of a code (called a one-time password or OTP) sent to the user's cell phone as a call or SMS text. The user supplies the code in the website and authorization is granted. Microsoft 365 supports this method for multifactor authentication of users' Azure AD identities, among others.

The cell phone-based options for Azure AD Multifactor Authentication (MFA) are as follows:

- **SMS Text Of OTP Code To Mobile Phone**   After the user completes the password authentication, Azure AD sends a text message containing an OTP code to the user's preconfigured telephone number. The user types the code into the sign-in screen to complete the authentication.

- **Automated Voice Call To Mobile Phone**   After the user completes the password authentication, Azure AD generates an automated voice call to the user's preconfigured telephone number. The user answers the call and presses the phone's # key to complete the authentication.

- **Notification To Mobile App**   After the user completes the password authentication, Azure AD sends a notification to the Microsoft Authenticator app on the user's smartphone. The user taps the Verify button in the app to complete the authentication.

- **Verification Code In Mobile App**   The Microsoft Authenticator app generates a new OATH verification code every 30 seconds. After the user completes the password authentication, the user types the current verification code from the Microsoft Authenticator app into the sign-in screen to complete the authentication.

Of course, cell phones can be lost, stolen, or destroyed, so any authentication method that relies on them is not going to be completely secure, but in combination with a password, they provide a significant barrier against the standard attacker. Multifactor authentication is not required for Microsoft 365, but it is rapidly becoming a *de facto* standard for network security, largely because many administrators are finding that they have reached the limit of password authentication, as far as users' tolerance is concerned.

Administrators can enable multifactor authentication for specific users using the Azure Active Directory Admin Center. When the users next sign on, a screen informs them that more information is required. Another screen, shown in Figure 3-22, then enables them to enter a phone number and specify whether the initial contact to a user should be through a code sent to the user's cell phone or through a mobile app, such as Microsoft Authenticator.

**Additional security verification**

Secure your account by adding phone verification to your password. View video to know how to secure your account

**Step 1: How should we contact you?**

Authentication phone

Select your country or region

Method
- ● Send me a code by text message

Next

Your phone numbers will only be used for account security. Standard telephone and SMS charges will apply.

**FIGURE 3-22** The initial Multifactor Authentication configuration interface

After the initial successful multifactor authentication, another screen appears, as shown in Figure 3-23, on which the users can select from among the cell phone–based authentication options listed earlier and configure a phone number or the Authenticator app.

**Additional security verification**  App Passwords

When you sign in with your password, you are also required to respond from a registered device. This makes it harder for a hacker to sign in with just a stolen password. View video to know how to secure your account

what's your preferred option?

We'll use this verification option by default.

Text code to my authentication phone
Notify me through app
Use verification code from app or token
how would you like to respond?

Set up one or more of these options. Learn more

☑ Authentication phone     United States (+1)     7175555555

☐ Authenticator app or Token     Set up Authenticator app

Save     cancel

**FIGURE 3-23** The second Additional Security Verification - App Passwords screen

## Identity protection

All identities are a potential source of risk for the entire network, no matter what level of privileges they possess. Once attackers compromise one identity, it becomes relatively easy for them to spread laterally within the enterprise and compromise others. For that reason, administrators should make every effort to protect all identities, not just the ones with administrative privileges.

One of the key innovations of Microsoft 365 is the greater emphasis on proactive threat detection and remediation. Azure AD can provide this type of security for user accounts with a feature called Azure AD Identity Protection. Identity Protection works by evaluating the sign-in activities of individual user accounts and assigning them risk levels that increment when multiple negative events occur. There are two risk levels associated with each identity, as follows:

- **Sign-in risk**   The probability that an unauthorized individual is attempting to authenticate with another person's identity

- **User risk**   An accumulated probability that a specific identity has been compromised

Azure AD Identity Protection recognizes the following risk events and modifies an identity's two risk levels based on the order and frequency in which they occur:

- **Atypical travel**   The user signs in from a location that is not typical for the user or that is geographically impossible, based on the user's other recent sign ins. Azure AD takes into account the travel time between the locations and gradually develops its own profile of the user's habits, which helps to prevent the occurrence of false positives (that is, conclusions of risk from sign-in patterns that are common for that user).

- **Anonymous IP address**   The user signs in from a browser that suppresses the user's IP address, such as Tor or a virtual private network (VPN) client. The user signing on might or might not be the owner of the identity, but Azure AD considers the anonymity itself to be suspicious.

- **Unfamiliar sign-in properties**   The user signs in from a client that has unfamiliar properties, such as a new location or an unusual IP address or autonomous system number (ASNs), based on the user's previous activities. For new identities, there is a period of information gathering that lasts at least five days, during which Azure AD makes no risk assessments using this criterion.

- **Malware linked IP address**   An identity is associated with an IP address that has previously been used to contact a known bot server on the Internet. The system is then assumed to be infected with malware and considered to be a risk.

- **Leaked credentials**   An identity is determined to use credentials that are known to have been compromised. Microsoft gathers information about such credentials from numerous sources, including law enforcement agencies, security consultants, and illicit websites.

When these events occur, Azure AD evaluates them and modifies the behavior of the authentication process according to criteria established by administrators. There are obviously many possible combinations of behaviors that Azure AD might have to take into account when evaluating the risk levels of an identity. For example, if the same risk events occur repeatedly, the risk levels will continue to rise until a drastic reaction might be required, such as blocking all access to the identity.

The basic Azure AD Identity Protection process is illustrated in Figure 3-24.

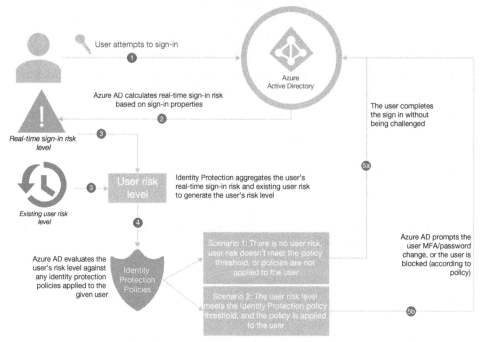

**FIGURE 3-24** The Azure AD Identity Protection risk evaluation process

As an example, when a user attempts to sign in with a simple password from an anonymous IP address, Azure AD determines that it is a risk and assigns it a sign-in risk level of medium. This risk level causes Azure AD to implement a Conditional Access policy that imposes a specific action, such as requiring multifactor authentication during the sign-in process. If the user successfully completes the multifactor authentication, the user risk level remains unchanged.

However, if the user fails to complete the multifactor authentication, Azure AD considers this to be a possible indication that the identity has been compromised and raises the user risk level. The next time the user attempts to sign on, the process might proceed completely normally, with no sign-in risk detected; however, the user risk level associated with the identity persists, and Azure AD might be configured to prompt the user to change the password as a result.

Azure AD Identity Protection is included only with the Azure Active Directory Premium P2 plan, which is supplied with the Microsoft 365 Enterprise P2 edition.

 **EXAM TIP**

The additional security provided by Azure AD Identity Protection is applicable only to cloud-based identities, not to the on-premises identities in Active Directory Domain Services. Microsoft's increased emphasis on cloud-based solutions, such as Office 365 and now Microsoft 365, means that the latest innovations in security and other areas are not being ported to the traditional on-premises versions. It is for this reason that Microsoft is recommending that enterprise networks shift more of their applications and services away from on-premises servers and into the cloud. When preparing for the MS-900 examination, candidates should be conscious of this emphasis on the cloud and be careful to distinguish Microsoft's cloud-based products from its on-premises products.

# Protecting documents

The fundamental purpose of identities is to protect documents and other data. When protecting identities, the threat of lateral penetration forces administrators to apply equal protection to all of them, regardless of their privileges. When protecting documents, however, the security can and should be more selective. While an enterprise might have hundreds or thousands of identities to protect, it might easily have hundreds of thousands or millions of documents, and this makes applying equal protection to them all impractical. Therefore, it is important for administrators to identify the documents containing sensitive data, which require more protection.

As discussed earlier in this chapter, Azure Information Protection (AIP) and Office 365 Data Loss Prevention (DLP) are tools that enable administrators and users to apply classification labels to documents and specify security measures that are applied to the documents based on those labels. While these tools can, in some cases, detect sensitive data within documents based on criteria that administrators specify, there are many other cases in which it is up to the users to apply the labels correctly to their own documents.

> **NOTE  INFORMATION PROTECTION AND DATA LOSS PREVENTION**
>
> For more information on Azure Information Protection and Office 365 Data Loss Prevention, see the "Documents" section, earlier in this chapter.

The technological aspects of implementing tools such as AIP and DLP are relatively straightforward; however, the administrative, cultural, and educational aspects of the implementation can be more troublesome, especially in a large enterprise. For these tools to function effectively, the classification labels representing the various levels of data sensitivity must be understood by everyone involved and applied consistently throughout the organization.

When the intention is to create a single classification label taxonomy that the entire enterprise will use, it makes sense for representatives from all areas and all levels of the enterprise to have a say in the design of that taxonomy. Unless the terms used for the labels mean the same thing to everyone, there is a chance that documents could be labeled incorrectly, or worse, not labeled at all when they should be.

With the labeling taxonomy agreed on and in place, the next step in the deployment—as with all new programs—should be a pilot deployment. With a small group of representative users applying labels to their documents, and with DLP configured to classify a subset of the company's documents automatically, careful monitoring of the labeling process and evaluation of the classified documents will almost certainly disclose some incorrect labeling, requiring modifications to the tools themselves or to the users' procedures. Successive iterations of the taxonomy and the DLP algorithms will likely be needed before the system is completely reliable.

The final phase of the deployment—and arguably the most difficult one—will be educating all the users in the organization in what the labeling system is, how it works, and why it is necessary. This is particularly true for users that are not involved in the technology behind the system. Document protection is not a problem that administrators can solve with technology only; the human factor is also a critical part.

> ## Quick check
>
> - Which of the following elements is responsible for creating hybrid identities by replicating on-premises identities to the cloud?
>   - Azure AD
>   - Azure AD Connect
>   - Password hash synchronization
>   - AD DS

> ## Quick check answer
>
> - Azure AD Connect is a software tool that runs on the on-premises network and replicates Active Directory domain Services identities to Azure Active Directory in the cloud, creating hybrid identities.

## Skill 3.3: Understand the need for unified endpoint management, security usage scenarios and services

At one time, enterprise network security consisted of company-owned computers, deployed and managed internally, and protected using password policies, firewalls, antivirus software, and, for a few remote users, dial-up and virtual private network connections. Network administrators controlled all the equipment, and a generation of *Client Management Tools (CMTs)* appeared, such as Microsoft's *System Center Configuration Manager (SCCM)*. SCCM provides a unified management solution that enables administrators to inventory hardware, deploy operating systems and applications, update software, manage licenses, and remotely control computers all over the enterprise.

Unfortunately, management platforms like SCCM are designed for use with on-premises computers only, and they communicate over local area networks (LANs). As mobile computing devices became increasingly common, a new management platform was needed, one that could function through the cloud. *Mobile Device Management (MDM)* was the first iteration of that new platform. MDM products typically exercise complete control over the mobile devices they manage, and as a result, it became common for organizations using the products to own the devices as well.

However, workers often had problems with the usability constraints imposed on them by company-owned, company-managed devices. These problems only became more severe as people began to purchase their own smartphones and find them easier to work with than their MDM-managed company devices. This eventually resulted in the BYOD (Bring Your Own Device) concept, which certainly pleased users but made the lives of administrators more difficult.

To provide adequate security on devices the company does not own, a new evolutionary step in the management products was needed, and *enterprise mobility management (EMM)* tools, such as Microsoft Intune, were the result. Using Intune, administrators can enroll, configure, and manage mobile devices on several different operating system platforms, wherever the devices happen to be. Administrators can even intervene when a threat to security occurs, by blocking a device's access to the company network and erasing any sensitive information stored on it.

However, despite the advances in mobile computing and mobile device management, on-premises devices, applications, and services have not gone away, and they still need to be managed. CMTs and EMMs are different types of management platforms in many fundamental ways. Both require administrators to have a significant amount of training and experience, but the two generally do not overlap. A need arose for a management platform that could work with both on-premises and cloud-based devices, as shown in Figure 3-25; this management platform also needs to be extendable to include new technologies as they develop, such as wearables and the Internet of Things (IoT). This new platform has come to be known as *unified endpoint management (UEM)*.

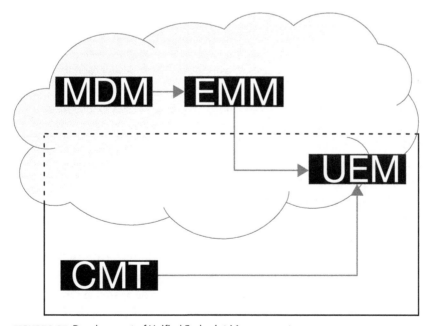

**FIGURE 3-25** Development of Unified Endpoint Management

The term *endpoint* has come to be used to refer to any user device, including desktop computers, laptops, printers, tablets, smartphones, as well as newer technologies, such as wearables and Internet of Things devices. The object of unified endpoint management is to eliminate the need for separate management tools for on-premises and mobile devices. An ideal UEM solution is a "single-pane" administration platform that can manage the applications, identities, resources, updates, security, and policy compliance for all the endpoints in the enterprise, regardless of their locations, device types, or operating systems.

> **NOTE  INTERNET OF THINGS**
>
> As mobile networking moves beyond the now ubiquitous smartphone, the next evolution appears to be the Internet of Things (IoT), in which mobile computing devices are embedded in various types of tools, appliances, and systems. Home and building automation is a growing market for IoT devices, including thermostats, light switches, and refrigerators, as well as large-scale industrial and utility systems.
>
> In the health care industry, IoT devices can monitor patients' conditions both inside and outside hospitals, including heart rate, blood pressure, and blood glucose monitors; also, they can control implanted devices, such as pacemakers and defibrillators. Automobiles and other vehicles are also common applications for IoT, which can provide location monitoring, toll collection, and traffic control services.
>
> All these device types require management by network administrators and could conceivably be as much of a security threat as any of the other mobile computing devices in use today. One can only imagine the chaos that could result if an attacker managed to penetrate a hospital network or a city's power grid, for example.

In Microsoft 365, UEM is implemented in the Enterprise Mobility + Security (EMS) product, which includes a suite of tools that can work together to provide a comprehensive management solution for both on-premises and cloud-based endpoints. The relevant tools in EMS include the following:

- **Azure Active Directory Premium**  The cloud-based directory service that manages identities and provides authentication and authorization for all the Microsoft 365 applications and services, including all the EMS management tools

- **Azure AD Connect**  An on-premises tool that replicates user identities on AD DS domain controllers to Azure AD identities stored in the cloud so that users can sign in through the cloud and administrators can take advantage of the Azure AD identity security features

- **Microsoft Intune**  A cloud-based enterprise mobility management (EMM) service that enables administrators to enroll mobile devices, deploy apps, and enforce security policies

- **System Center Configuration Manager (SCCM)**  An on-premises CMT that administrators can use to inventory computer hardware, deploy operating system images on internal workstations, manage applications, apply software updates, and enforce device compliance policies

- **Azure Information Protection (AIP)**  A cloud-based tool that enables users and administrators to apply classification labels to documents and implement various types of protection based on the labels, such as access restrictions and data encryption
- **Microsoft Advanced Threat Analytics (ATA)**  An on-premises platform that captures network traffic and log information and analyzes it to identify suspicious behaviors related to multiple phases of the attack process
- **Cloud App Security**  A cloud-based service that analyzes traffic logs and proxy scripts to identify the apps that users are accessing—including unauthorized apps—and enables administrators to sanction or unsanction individual apps and connect to APIs supplied by cloud app providers to perform Cloud App Security analyses
- **Azure Advanced Threat Protection**  A cloud-based threat prevention, detection, and remediation engine that uses machine intelligence look for security threats unique to the Azure environment by analyzing user behavior and comparing it to known attack patterns

> *NOTE*  **MICROSOFT ATA**
>
> For more information on Microsoft Advanced Threat Analytics, see the "Describe analytics capabilities in Microsoft 365" section in Chapter 2, "Understand core Microsoft 365 services and concepts."

# Microsoft 365 and Directory Services

A directory service is a software product that stores information about network resources for the purpose of unifying them into a single, manageable entity. For example, the Domain Name System (DNS) is a directory service that associates the names of network resources with their corresponding network addresses.

As noted in the "Identity" section, earlier in this chapter, Azure Active Directory (Azure AD) and Active Directory Domain Services (AD DS) are the directory services that store and manage user identities for the various Microsoft 365 components. Azure AD stores its directory information in the Microsoft Azure cloud, and AD DS is stored on computers running Windows Server that have been configured to operate as domain controllers.

## Azure Active Directory

Azure AD is available in three plans, as shown in Table 3-3. All the Microsoft 365 products include either the Premium P1 or Premium P2 plan.

**TABLE 3-3**  Azure Active Directory licenses

| AZURE ACTIVE DIRECTORY LICENSE | INCLUDED WITH |
| --- | --- |
| Azure Active Directory Free | Office 365 or Microsoft Azure subscriptions |
| Azure Active Directory Premium P1 | Microsoft 365 Enterprise E3 and Microsoft 365 Business |
| Azure Active Directory Premium P2 | Microsoft 365 Enterprise E5 |

The Azure Active Directory Premium P1 plan supports the following features and services:

- **Unlimited directory objects**  Enables administrators to create cloud identities for an unlimited number of users.

- **User and group management**  Enables administrators to create and manage user and group identities using cloud-based tools, such as the Azure AD admin center and the Microsoft 365 Admin Center.

- **Cloud authentication**  Enables users to sign on to the network using hybrid identities stored in the cloud and with password hash synchronization or pass-through authentication.

- **Synchronization with AD DS using Azure AD Connect**  After installing the Azure AD Connect tool on an AD DS domain controller or on-premises server, on-premises identities can be replicated to the Azure AD directory in the cloud. This creates hybrid identities that enable users to access both cloud-based and on-premises resources with a single sign-on.

- **Seamless single sign-on**  Enables users with hybrid identities that are connected to the on-premises network to sign in with no interactive authentication procedure.

- **Support for federated authentication**  Enables administrators to offload the Azure AD authentication process to a federated service, such as Active Directory Federation Services.

- **Multifactor authentication using phone, SMS, or app**  Enables administrators to require that users supply two or more forms of identification when signing in with an Azure AD identity, such as a password plus a biometric scan or a one-time code sent to the user's smartphone.

- **Support for hybrid user access to cloud and on-premises resources**  Enables users with hybrid identities to access both cloud-based and on-premises resources after a single Azure AD authentication.

- **Self-Service Password Reset**  Enables users with cloud-based identities to modify their passwords without administrator assistance.

- **Device write-back from Azure AD to AD DS identities**  Enables devices registered in Azure AD and modified cloud identity passwords to be copied to an AD DS container. Ordinarily, Azure AD Connect only synchronizes data from AD DS to Azure AD.

- **Application Proxy**  Enables cloud-based remote users to access internal web applications by forwarding their requests to a connector running on an on-premises server.

- **Dynamic groups**  Enables administrators to create rules specifying the attributes a user account must possess to be automatically added to a group.

- **Group naming policies**  Enables administrators to create policies that specify a format for group names. For example, group names can be required to specify a function, a department, or a geographic location.

- **Conditional access**  Enables administrators to specify conditions that mobile devices must meet before they are granted access to cloud-based resources, such as sign-in risk, client app in use, the state of the mobile device, and the location of the device.

- **Microsoft Identity Manager** Provides identity and access management, including synchronization of users, groups, and other objects for AD DS and Azure AD, as well as third-party directory services.
- **Azure Information Protection Premium P1** Enables users and administrators to classify and label documents based on the sensitivity of the data they contain.
- **Security and activity reporting** Provides administrators with reports that list potential threats, including risky sign-ins and audit logs that document user activities.

With these features and services, the Azure Active Directory Premium P1 plan enables administrators to manage an organization's cloud-based resources, as well as identify, predict, detect, and remediate a wide variety of security threats. However, the Azure Active Directory Premium P2 plan supports everything included in the P1 plan and also provides the following additional security features:

- **Azure AD Identity Protection** Evaluates users' sign-in activities, quantifies their risk levels, and takes action based on those levels.
- **Privileged Identity Management** Enables administrators to regulate access to sensitive resources by granting temporary privileges to specific users, requiring additional security measures, and receiving notifications when the resources are accessed. The objective is to prevent users with administrative privileges from using them unnecessarily.
- **Cloud App Security** A cloud-based service that analyzes traffic logs and proxy scripts to identify and monitor the apps that users are accessing.
- **Azure Information Protection Premium P2** Expands on the capabilities of the Premium P1 plan by automating the process of identifying, classifying, and labeling documents.

Azure Information Protection is included in all the Microsoft 365 plans, but it is also available with other Microsoft products in a free version with limited functionality and as a separate subscription in two plans of its own, called Premium P1 and Premium P2. Each subscription level adds features, as shown in Table 3-4, and includes all the features of the lower subscription levels.

**TABLE 3-4** Azure Information Protection subscriptions

| PLAN | INCLUDED WITH | DESCRIPTION |
|---|---|---|
| Free | No purchase necessary | Allows consumption of AIP-protected content by users with accounts that are not associated with Azure identities |
| Azure Information Protection for Office 365 | Office 365 Enterprise E3 and above | Provides protection for Office 365 services using custom templates and supporting Office 365 Message Encryption |
| Azure Information Protection Premium P1 | Microsoft 365 Business Microsoft 365 Enterprise E3 Microsoft Enterprise Mobility + Security E3 | Provides the ability to use on-premises connectors, track and revoke documents, and manually classify and label documents |
| Azure Information Protection Premium P2 | Microsoft 365 Enterprise E5 Microsoft Enterprise Mobility + Security E5 | Provides support for policy-based rules and automated classification, labeling, and protection of documents |

## Active Directory Domain Services

Active Directory Domain Services (AD DS) is an object-oriented, hierarchical directory service that functions as an internal authentication and authorization provider for Windows networks. Because it is not located in the cloud like Azure AD, the primary source of protection for AD DS is the firewall and other perimeter protection surrounding the on-premises network. AD DS domain controllers are Windows servers that are located inside the network perimeter; they must not be deployed in a DMZ or in any other way that leaves them open to access from the Internet.

Also, unlike Azure AD, an AD DS directory must be designed, deployed, and maintained by the network administrators. The service is provided as a role in the Windows Server operating system, which administrators must add after the installation of the operating system itself. An AD DS directory does not include any of the built-in maintenance and fault tolerance found in Microsoft's cloud services.

Typically, AD DS domain controllers perform no other function other than acting as DNS servers. For example, it is not considered secure to use domain controllers as application or file servers. To ensure fault tolerance and high availability, administrators must install multiple domain controllers, preferably at different sites. The domain controllers replicate the contents of the directory among each other on a regular basis.

Unlike Azure AD, AD DS is a hierarchical directory service that enables administrators to create a directory that emulates their company's departmental or geographical infrastructure, as shown in Figure 3-26.

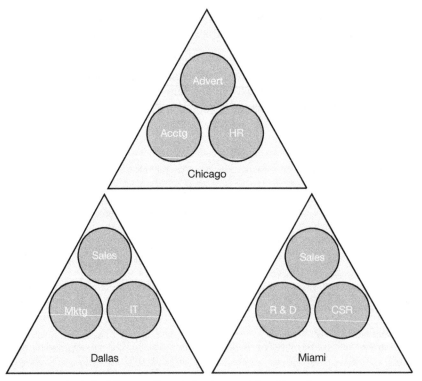

**FIGURE 3-26** An Active Directory Domain Services container hierarchy

Forests, trees, domains, and organizational units are all types of AD DS objects that contain other objects, such as users, groups, and computers, as shown in Figure 3-27. As with a file system, permissions flow downward through the hierarchy. Permissions granted to a container object are inherited by all the objects in that container and by all subordinate containers beneath it. Administrators can design the AD DS hierarchy however they wish.

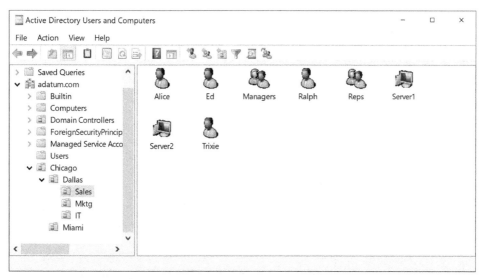

**FIGURE 3-27** AD DS objects in an organizational unit

In AD DS administration, there is a lot more work left to the network administrator than there is in Azure AD. In Azure AD, one can begin creating users and groups immediately after establishing a tenancy, with no need to install and maintain domain controllers or design an infrastructure. There are also no concerns about physical security with Azure AD, because Microsoft is responsible for its data centers and for maintaining the computers that provide the services. The initial cost outlay for an Azure AD directory is also minimal. AD DS requires the purchase of server computers and the Windows Server operating system, but there are no ongoing subscription fees.

Although AD DS uses an infrastructure that is substantially different from Azure AD, it performs the same basic services by authenticating users and authorizing their access to network resources. However, AD DS does not support many of the advanced security features found in Azure AD. For example, it has no internal support for multifactor authentication, although it is possible to use an external authentication service for some additional authentication factors. AD DS also does not include Azure AD Identity Protection, Conditional Access, and Azure Information Protection.

Because domain controllers are often connected to the same network as workstations and other less sensitive systems, they can be vulnerable to a lateral attack from an intruder who has gained access to another system on the network. As a result, even though the domain controllers themselves might be protected, any of the typical attack vectors to which on-premises computers are susceptible can pose a threat to the AD DS implementation. For example, any computer on the network that is not current in its operating system and application updates or that lacks virus or malware protection can be a target for attack and a launch point for a further invasion of the AD DS directory.

AD DS is also more vulnerable to credential theft than Azure AD because of unsafe use of privileged credentials. Administrators of an on-premises network can sometimes be careless about using their privileged identities to perform everyday tasks, such as browsing the Internet or signing on to computers that are not fully secured. In Azure Active Directory Premium P1, these are practices that can be addressed with the Privileged Identity Management feature, but Microsoft has not integrated the Azure AD security tools into AD DS.

**EXAM TIP**

For MS-900 examination candidates who are new to these technologies, it can be easy to confuse the capabilities of the cloud-based Azure Active Directory (Azure AD) and the on-premises Active Directory Domain Services (AD DS). It is important to know that AD DS is a hierarchical directory service, provided with the Windows Server operating system, that requires a fairly extensive design and implementation process. Azure AD, by contrast, is subscription-based, is not hierarchical, and requires virtually no setup. Candidates should also be conscious of which features are provided in the Azure Active Directory Premium P1 and Azure Active Directory Premium P2 plans, and with the different functionalities of the Azure Information Protection Premium P1 and Azure Information Protection Premium P2 plans.

## SCCM and Intune co-management

System Center Configuration Manager (SCCM) is Microsoft's Client Management Tool for on-premises networks. The product, first released in 1994 (under the name Systems Management Server), provides a comprehensive management solution for on-premises systems by providing the following features:

- **Operating system deployment**  Deploys operating system images to client workstations over the network using a variety of scenarios, both automated and interactive.
- **Software update management**  Deploys updates of operating systems, applications, device drivers, and system BIOS firmware to entire fleets of devices.
- **Hardware and software inventory**  Performs comprehensive inventories of the hardware in and the software installed on client computers.
- **Application deployment**  Provides user-based application deployment to multiple device types using various delivery mechanisms, including local installations, App-V, and RemoteApp.

- **Endpoint protection** For Windows 8.1 and earlier, provides a System Center Endpoint Protection antimalware client; for Windows 10, provides a management client for the built-in Windows Defender antimalware engine.

- **Client health monitoring** Provides centralized monitoring and reporting of client health and activities, with the ability to generate alerts and perform remediations.

- **Compliance management** Enables administrators to create a configuration state baseline for clients, evaluate them for compliance, and generate alerts or perform remediations.

SCCM is an excellent CMT solution for on-premises systems, but it doesn't support the management of cloud-based mobile devices by itself. Therefore, to achieve a true Unified Endpoint Management solution with Microsoft products, a combination of SCCM and Microsoft Intune is needed, in an arrangement called *co-management*.

An SCCM deployment consists of at least one server on the network, a Configuration Manager console, and the installation of a software agent on each client to be managed. The process of deploying SCCM on an on-premises network is not a simple one, requiring schema modifications to Active Directory Domain Services and a Microsoft SQL Server installation, as well as the installation of the SCCM server and the individual clients.

The typical scenario envisaged for co-management is an enterprise that has already made a significant investment in an SCCM infrastructure and is planning to add Microsoft 365. Microsoft Intune, the enterprise mobility management tool that is included in the Enterprise Mobility + Security component, provides advanced management capabilities that administrators often want to use for their on-premises systems, as well as their cloud-based mobile ones.

Co-management is an SCCM feature that links the on-premises systems to Microsoft Intune in the cloud and enables administrators to manage their on-premises computers with both the SCCM and Intune consoles. By adding co-management capabilities to their internal infrastructure, administrators can then take advantage of the following Microsoft 365 features:

- **Hybrid Azure AD** By creating hybrid identities for on-premises users, they can access both cloud-based and on-premises resources with a single sign-in, as well as use Microsoft 365 features such as Windows Hello for Business and Self-Service Password Reset. Administrators can take advantage of Intune's device-based conditional access and automatic device licensing.

- **Conditional access** The conditional access capability in Intune goes beyond the compliance management capabilities in SCCM by providing more comprehensive device evaluation, as well as detection and remediation of security threats.

- **Remote actions** Microsoft Intune enables administrators to manage devices connected to the network, wherever they are located, using cloud-based controls that can inventory, restart, or reset a device, delete company data, or take remote control.

- **Client health**  Client health monitoring in SCCM is limited to devices that are actively connected to the internal network. With Intune, client health is monitored whenever the device is accessible from the cloud. Intune provides timestamped records of each client's health and its readiness for application installations and updates.

- **Windows Autopilot**  Administrators can choose to deploy new devices using Windows Autopilot rather than the image deployment process that SCCM uses. This can eliminate the need for administrators to create and maintain boot and system images for various hardware combinations.

For Windows 10 devices to be co-managed, they must have the SCCM client agent software installed on them, and they must be enrolled in Microsoft Intune. For an existing SCCM installation, the process of implementing co-management with Intune consists of the following basic steps:

- Create hybrid identities for the SCCM client users by installing Azure AD Connect on the internal network and configuring it to replicate the AD DS users to the Azure AD tenant.

- Assign a Microsoft 365 license (or individual Intune and Azure AD Premium licenses) to the SCCM client users.

- In the Configuration Manager console in SCCM, enable the **Automatically Register New Windows 10 Domain Joined Devices With Azure Active Directory Client** setting.

- In the Azure portal, enable **MDM Automatic Enrollment** for some or all the Windows 10 devices on the network.

- In the Configuration Manager console, run the **Co-management Configuration Wizard** and enable the **Automatic Enrollment Into Intune** setting

> *NOTE*  **PILOT DEPLOYMENTS**
>
> As with all new technology implementations, Microsoft recommends a small pilot deployment for evaluation purposes before any product is rolled out to an entire enterprise.

The implementation of the co-management infrastructure is somewhat different for an enterprise seeking to co-manage new Windows 10 workstations deployed by an OEM or by using Windows Autopilot but does not provide users with hybrid AD DS/Azure AD identities. Administrators must deploy a cloud management gateway on the internal network and obtain a public SSL certificate for it, configure Intune to install the SCCM client agent on the new computers, and configure the clients to use the gateway.

Once the co-management setup is completed, SCCM and Microsoft Intune work together with AD DS and Azure AD, as shown in Figure 3-28.

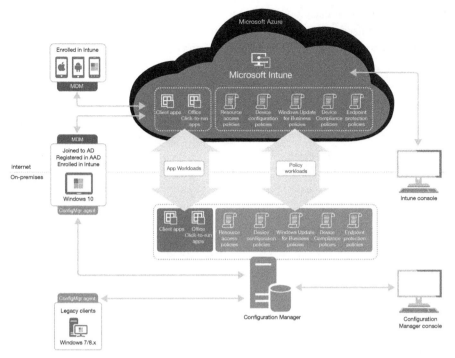

**FIGURE 3-28** System Center Configuration Manager and Microsoft Intune co-management

In the Co-management Configuration Wizard, it is also possible to select the workloads to be managed by Microsoft Intune, although administrators can also do this at any time after co-management is implemented. All the workloads remain managed by SCCM until they are explicitly shifted to Intune instead. The SCCM co-management feature supports the transfer of the following workloads to Intune:

- **Compliance policies** Specify the configuration settings and policies that the device must observe before it can be granted conditional access to network resources.

- **Windows Update policies** Enable administrators to define policies for Windows 10 feature and quality update deployments to devices using Windows Update for Business.

- **Resource access policies** Provide the management of devices' Wi-Fi, virtual private network (VPN), email, and certificate settings.

- **Endpoint Protection** Provide management over all the Windows Defender antimalware features on Windows 10 devices.

- **Device configuration** Provides management authority for device management settings, including those included in the Resource access policies and Endpoint protection workloads. Despite transferring this workload to Intune, it is still possible to configure device settings in Configuration Manager, such as settings in SCCM that have not yet been implemented in Intune.

- **Office click-to-run apps** Provide management authority for all the Office 365 applications.

- **Client apps** Provide application deployment capability. Transferring this workload to Intune enables devices to install applications from Intune, using the company portal, or from SCCM, using Software Center, as shown in Figure 3-29.

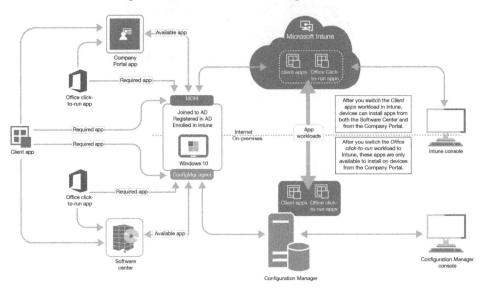

**FIGURE 3-29** The Client App workload in a co-managed environment

## Security usage scenarios

Management of the various types of endpoints presents administrators with a variety of issues that they must address, including the following:

- **User-owned devices** When workers use their own devices, administrators must define a policy specifying what degree of control the organization will have over the devices and what company resources the devices will be permitted to access. This can be a difficult task because, while the organization must protect its resources, users are often unwilling to turn over full control of their property to the company. Windows Intune provides administrators with both Mobile Device Management (MDM) and Mobile Administration Management (MAM) capabilities, which provide different levels of management control to suit the needs of the organization and the users.

- **Mobile device networking** Mobile users often connect to outside wireless networks, such as those in coffee shops and other businesses, which are unsecured by the enterprise. This leaves the devices open to the possibility of intrusion by outside persons, exposing them to potential threats that can jeopardize the device, the data stored on it, and the enterprise network. Administrators can use Microsoft Intune or other tools to create and enforce mobile device policies that require devices to have the malware prevention tools, software updates, and other forms of protection needed to repel the threats.

- **Device loss or theft** Any mobile device is liable to be lost or stolen, with the accompanying danger that any sensitive data stored on the device might be compromised.

There might also be users who leave the company under less-than-friendly circumstances, taking their personal devices with them. In some cases, the cost of replacing the device hardware can be less than that of identifying the data that has been lost and re-creating it. Administrators must prepare for these situations by devising a Microsoft Intune policy that can exercise remote protection of the organization's resources, even when the mobile device is in hostile hands.

- **Infected devices** Mobile devices that become infected with malware while connected to outside networks can bring that infection into the enterprise, damage documents, and pass the infection along to other systems. Administrators must classify all mobile devices connecting to the enterprise network as potential threats and protect them using tools such as Windows Defender and System Center Endpoint Protection.

- **Device data synchronization** While data stored in the Microsoft cloud is replicated to multiple data centers for protection, mobile devices working outside the company premises might not always be connected to the cloud. Therefore, when users work with company documents while offline, any revisions they make to the documents are not saved to the cloud or backed up until they next connect to a network. Therefore, this revised data can be lost if the device is damaged, lost, or stolen before it next connects to the cloud.

- **Password changes** One of the more common tasks for help desk personnel and administrators is the need to change users' passwords. This task is even more common when Azure AD Identity Protection is configured to require a password change when their authentication-based risk levels reach a certain value. Self Service Password Reset (SSPR) enables users who have been successfully authenticated to change their own passwords, rather than require the intervention of an administrator.

## Addressing common threats

Risk management is a highly specialized undertaking that is heavily dependent on the type and sensitivity of the information to be protected and the nature of the threats to which the network is most vulnerable. For example, an organization that consists mostly of IT professionals will not be overly susceptible to phishing attacks because they have more awareness of them and experience with them. On the other hand, an organization of users with little or no IT expertise will be far more vulnerable to this particular threat and will have to expend more effort in trying to prevent this type of attack.

Microsoft 365 includes a wide variety of security tools that make it possible to predict, prevent, and react to many different kinds of threats. Many of these tools are discussed individually, both in this chapter and elsewhere in this book. The nature of each tool's function is explained in relation to the types of threats it addresses. However, Microsoft recently announced an effort to organize Microsoft 365's security components under the single name *Microsoft Threat Protection*, which places the tools into the following five categories:

- **Identities** Tools that authenticate, authorize, and protect the accounts of standard users and privileged administrators, such as Windows Hello, Azure Active Directory Identity Protection, Privileged Identity Management, Azure Advanced Threat Protection, and Microsoft Cloud App Security

- **Endpoints**  Tools that protect user devices and sensors from the effects of loss, theft, and attack, such as Microsoft Intune, System Center Configuration Manager, Windows 10, Microsoft Advanced Threat Analytics, and Windows Defender Advanced Threat Protection

- **User data**  Tools that analyze documents and messages for sensitive or malicious content, such as Exchange Online Protection, Azure Information Protection, Data Loss Prevention, Windows Defender Advanced Threat Protection, Office 365 Advanced Threat Protection, Office 365 Threat Intelligence, and Microsoft Cloud App Security

- **Cloud apps**  Tools that protect Software as a Service (SaaS) applications like Office 365 and their data, such as Exchange Online Protection, Office 365 Advanced Threat Protection, and Microsoft Cloud App Security

- **Infrastructure**  Tools that provide protection to servers, both physical and virtual; databases; and network, such as Azure Security Center, Microsoft Advanced Threat Analytics, and SQL Server

However, Microsoft Threat Protection is meant to be more than just a list of individual tools. Microsoft 365 also gathers information from all these security components and accumulates them in a single Microsoft 365 security center, as shown in Figure 3-30.

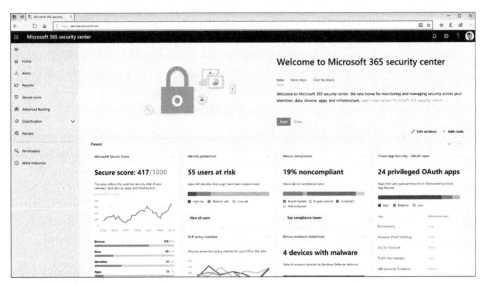

**FIGURE 3-30**  Microsoft 365 security center

The pages of the Microsoft 365 security center, accessible from the navigation pane on the left, provide the following:

- **Home**  Displays a dashboard with configurable tiles that contain status indicators for the security issues most important to a particular administrator or organization

- **Alerts**  Displays notifications generated by other Microsoft 365 security tools, including Microsoft Cloud App Security, Office 365 Advanced Threat Protection, Azure Active Directory, and Microsoft Defender Advanced Threat Protection

- **Reports**   Provides detailed information on the security status of the network's identities, devices, data, applications, and infrastructure

- **Secure score**   Provides a comprehensive assessment of the enterprise's current security status in a numerical score out of 1,000

- **Advanced Hunting**   Provides access to the analytical tools that can proactively identify potential threats to the network's identities, messages, data, and devices, such as the Advanced Threat Protection tools for Azure, Office 365, and Microsoft Defender

- **Classification**   Provides access to tools for creating classification labels for Microsoft 365's Information Protection tools

- **Policies**   Provides the ability to create policies for a variety of Microsoft 365 tools and purposes, including Advanced Threat Protection, Office 365 alerts, and Cloud App Security

Microsoft 365 also goes beyond the reactive approach to security and provides tools that can be proactive by detecting attacks and other security issues before they occur, or when they have barely begun. The Advanced Threat Protection tools for Azure, Office 365, and Microsoft Defender are all designed to monitor the behavior of users, devices, and other network resources and analyze the information they collect to detect and anticipate suspicious behavior. The intelligence the tools apply to the task is based on the Microsoft Intelligent Security Graph, a web of security relationships that spans the entire network. Microsoft's Cybersecurity Reference Architecture, shown in Figure 3-31, illustrates these relationships.

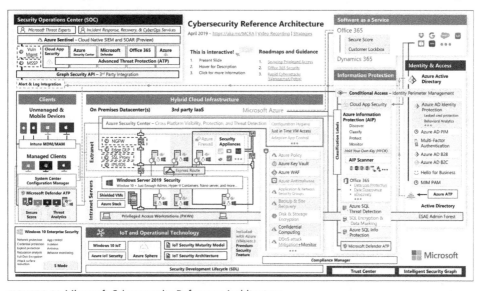

**FIGURE 3-31** Microsoft Cybersecurity Reference Architecture

---

**NEED MORE REVIEW?**   **MICROSOFT CYBERSECURITY REFERENCE ARCHITECTURE**

For an interactive PowerPoint version of the architecture shown in Figure 3-31, see *https://gallery.technet.microsoft.com/Cybersecurity-Reference-883fb54c*.

# Skill 3.4: Understand the Service Trust Portal and Compliance Manager

For many IT professionals, the prospect of implementing vital services and storing important company information in the cloud is met with a significant amount of trepidation. They might have an instinctive reluctance to trust an IT infrastructure that is not implemented on computers the company owns and housed in their own data centers. They might also hesitate to give up their personal control over those computers and their resources. Also, there might be statutes and standards to which the IT infrastructure must comply, whether because of contracted terms, company policies, or governmental requirements.

## Service Trust Portal

Microsoft is aware of these trust issues and has created a central storehouse for information about them, called the *Service Trust Portal (STP)*. STP is a website that is available to everyone at *http://aka.ms/stp*, although some parts of the site are restricted to registered users of Microsoft 365 and other products. Among the many resources on the site are links to documents in the following categories:

- **Audit Reports**   Provide independent audit and assessment reports of Microsoft's cloud services, evaluating their compliance with standards such as those published by International Organization for Standardization (ISO), Service Organization Controls (SOC), National Institute of Standards and Technology (NIST), Federal Risk and Authorization Management Program (FedRAMP), and General Data Protection Regulation (GDPR)

- **Documents & Resources**   Consist of a large library of documents, including white papers, FAQs, compliance guides, penetration test reports, Azure security and compliance blueprints, and other data protection resources
- **Compliance Manager**   Assesses and scores an organization's regulatory compliance, based on multiple published standards
- **Industries & Regions**   Provide documents containing compliance information for specific industries, such as education, financial services, government, health care, manufacturing, and retail; and specific countries, including Australia, Czech Republic, Germany, Poland, Romania, Spain, and United Kingdom
- **Trust Center**   Links to the Trust Center site, which provides documentation on the means by which Microsoft supports security, privacy, compliance, and transparency in its cloud services
- **Resources**   Provide information about Microsoft's global data centers, security and compliance information for Office 365, and a FAQ list for the Service Trust Portal
- **My Library**   Enables users to pin documents from the site onto a separate user page for quick reference later

## Compliance Manager

Compliance Manager is a risk assessment tool that enables an organization to track and record the activities they undertake to achieve compliance with specific certification standards. An assessment of an organization's compliance posture is based on the capabilities of the Microsoft 365 cloud services and the ways that the organization makes use of them, as compared to an existing standard, regulation, or law.

The home page for the Compliance Manager tool contains a dashboard that displays tiles representing the assessments of the Office 365 and Azure components against three different standards, as shown in Figure 3-32. Each tile specifies a cloud service and the standard to which it is being compared. The results of the comparison are stated as a numerical score.

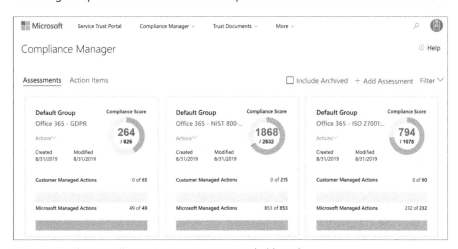

**FIGURE 3-32** The Compliance Manager assessments dashboard

Selecting a tile displays a detailed list of the controls tested for the assessment, along with the results for each individual control, as shown in Figure 3-33. The controls are broken down into those for which Microsoft is responsible and those for which the customer is responsible. Each control entry contains a reference to a section or article in the standard that corresponds to the control; information about who tested the control and when; and the results of the test, which is expressed as an individual Compliance Score value.

**FIGURE 3-33** A Microsoft Managed Control in Compliance Manager

In the default view of a Compliance Manager assessment, the Microsoft-managed controls are complete with results and compliance scores, but the customer-managed controls are not. It is up to the subscriber to complete these controls and use the guidance and recommendations in each one to finish the assessment and generate an overall score that reflects the compliance of both Microsoft and the organization to the selected standard.

## Cloud adoption showstoppers

For any organization contemplating or anticipating a movement to the cloud, there are issues that they must contemplate before making a final decision. It some instances, the company decision-makers might be unsure about whether cloud-based providers can deliver the services that the organization needs. In other cases, there might be no doubt that the cloud can provide the necessary services, but there is indecision about how to actually implement a transition from on-premises to cloud-based services.

Both types of issues can at times be "showstoppers" that prevent a cloud implementation from happening at all. Microsoft has considered many of these critical adoption issues, as shown earlier in the extensive documentation provided in the Service Trust Portal and Company Manager tools. However, sometimes the considerations involved in a cloud transition situation are unique to an industry or an individual company, or are more legal or financial than they are technical, and the solutions must be generated internally rather than provided by a product or service such as Microsoft 365.

The following sections address some of the most common cloud adoption showstoppers and provide approaches that companies can take to address them.

## Anticipating performance latency

Can cloud-based services provide the performance levels that the organization is accustomed to achieving with on-premises resources? IT professionals familiar with service issues to which Internet services providers and the Internet itself can be subject might question whether a consistently high level of performance is possible with cloud-based services. The comfortingly consistent performance of an internal cable plant, over which the company has complete control, is a difficult thing to lose. There might be concerns as to whether service outages or periods of increased latency might occur that can affect productivity and damage the company's reputation with its partners and clients.

When considering any cloud service provider, the potential subscriber should investigate the vendor's service performance record, both by examining any data they provide and by contacting their other clients. Most providers include a Service Level Agreement (SLA) in their contracts that account for service availability, but potential subscribers should inquire about the possibility of a performance level SLA as well.

An examination of the provider's hardware infrastructure is recommended as well, to determine where their data centers are located in proximity to the company's sites. Microsoft has addressed this issue by constructing a global network of data centers and by recommending that Microsoft 365 subscribers perform a detailed examination of their own network infrastructure. This is to ensure that each company location accesses the Microsoft cloud services through the Microsoft Global Network endpoint nearest to their physical location.

> **READERAID**   **NETWORKING INFRASTRUCTURE AND MICROSOFT 365**
>
> For more information on the network infrastructure examination recommended as part of the Microsoft 365 deployment, see the "Phase 1: Networking" section in Chapter 2, "Understand core Microsoft 365 services and concepts."

## Selecting service providers

The process of choosing service providers is, of course, critical to any cloud deployment. One of the first questions to consider is whether to use a single provider for all the services the organization requires or evaluate several providers for individual services. Choosing one provider for everything minimizes the chance of service gaps, but it also creates a single point of failure. The selected provider might also not provide the best price for each of the services needed.

For Microsoft 365 subscribers, of course, there is no choice of providers for the services included in the product, but this does not mean that an organization must use Microsoft for its entire cloud infrastructure. Using multiple providers for various services might enable the company to negotiate the best terms for each one, and it also allows the company to maintain relationships with more than one vendor, so that services can be moved to another provider if the circumstances call for it. However, dealing with multiple cloud service providers requires meticulous planning to ensure that the company receives all the services it needs.

The organization should have a complete network infrastructure design before engaging any providers, and a careful comparison of the contracts for the providers is necessary to make sure that all the services called for in the plan are available and accounted for. When adding a new service to an existing cloud-based infrastructure, administrators should compare the new contracts of prospective providers with all the existing contracts that are in force.

The worst-case scenario, in this instance, would be the late realization that a vital infrastructure component is not being supplied by any of the engaged service providers and that none of the providers can supply it. These service gaps can be both expensive and embarrassing to the people responsible.

## Avoiding vendor lock-in

Being locked into a single vendor is one of the concerns of many organizations considering a cloud-based infrastructure. Prices and other contract stipulations can change over time, and it might be necessary to switch providers when multiple vendors provide the same services in the future. To prepare for this eventuality, contracts with cloud service providers should always include an exit strategy and language regarding contract novation, whether early or not.

One particularly important concern should be the issue of data reclamation. A large cloud-based enterprise network can generate enormous amounts of data over the course of several years. In the event of a provider switch, the process of reclaiming that data from one provider's cloud service and moving it to that of another can be extremely lengthy. The organization's cloud infrastructure plan should account for this eventuality, as should the contracts with both the old and the new providers.

## Evaluating vendor robustness

At the time of this writing, the business of providing cloud networking services is dominated by three very large companies, none of which appears to be in danger of failing anytime soon. However, other smaller providers do exist and might offer tempting terms for their services. When considering smaller providers, prospective subscribers should investigate the state of their businesses thoroughly. Decision-makers should weigh the risk of contracting with a small provider—which might conceivably fail sometime in the future—with the business consequences of such a failure, such as possible network downtime and even data loss.

## Comparing cost models

Comparing the financial cost of a cloud-based infrastructure with an on-premises one is difficult because they use entirely different models. An on-premises network requires a large outlay for hardware and deployment expenses, but once that cost has been amortized, the network is the property of the company, and the ongoing expense is reduced substantially. A cloud-based infrastructure requires a much smaller initial outlay, but the subscriber fees can be substantial and persist as long as the company uses the service.

There are other cost factors to consider as well. In the on-premises model, the company must plan for future growth and adjust the entire deployment process to account for resources that might not be needed for years. With a cloud-based infrastructure, the subscriber can contract for what services they need right now and add more (or remove) functionality later, whenever it is necessary.

To anticipate the TCO (total cost of ownership) for a cloud-based versus an on-premises network infrastructure, one recommended practice would be to total all necessary expenditures for each model over a period of two to three years. However, the TCO does not necessarily provide the whole picture. The cloud solution can provide other benefits that are more difficult to quantify financially. For example, cloud-subscribed services can be scaled up or down with immediate effect. Typically, cloud providers can deploy new virtual servers, add resources to existing ones, or even supply entirely new services almost immediately. On an on-premises network, an expansion might require the purchase, installation, and deployment of new hardware, which can take weeks or months. Scalability can be an important factor for a company that experiences significant seasonal fluctuations in business.

## Securing company data

Arguably the greatest concern for many IT professionals considering a cloud-based network infrastructure is the risk of their data being lost or compromised. Microsoft—and presumably other reputable cloud service providers—note in their service descriptions the mechanisms they use to protect subscribers' data, such as replicated storage at multiple data centers. Contracts also routinely include an SLA that specifies a guaranteed uptime percentage (99.9 percent, in the case of Microsoft), which all but ensures the availability of the data. However, while the contract might impose a penalty on the provider if they do not meet the terms of the SLA, they will almost certainly not be financially responsible for any losses the subscriber incurs due to downtime.

There is no way around the fact that data stored in the public cloud does have a greater risk of being compromised than data stored on the subscriber's on-premises servers. To address this risk, Microsoft 365 includes security tools that, when used properly, can help to mitigate the risk of identities being penetrated and data being accessed by unauthorized individuals. However, the burden of applying this protection and of exposing sensitive data to the risk falls on the subscriber in the first place.

It is up to the network's administrators to assess the sensitivity of the company's data, classify the data using an agreed-upon taxonomy of sensitivity levels (as discussed in the "Protecting documents" section, earlier in this chapter), and decide what measures they should use to protect the data at each level. Therefore, sn organization that works with extremely sensitive data might choose to store it on-premises, rather than allow it in the cloud at all.

It should also be up to the subscriber to ensure that all data, whether stored in the cloud or on-premises, is backed up on a regular basis, whether the cloud provider includes this service or not. If backups are also to be stored in the cloud, then the best practice would be to use a different provider for the backups, so that the data is stored on a separate network of data centers.

## Locating company data

For organizations that are subject to data storage restrictions imposed by their clients or by government entities, the exact locations of a cloud service provider's data centers can be significant. The Microsoft Azure network is divided into 54 regions (shown in Figure 3-34) and 18 geographies that enable subscribers to maintain their data in places that can honor any specific residency, sovereignty, compliance, or resiliency requirements they might be compelled to observe. This is not necessarily true of all public cloud providers, however, and potential subscribers subject to such restrictions should require providers to include contract language specifying where their data is to be stored.

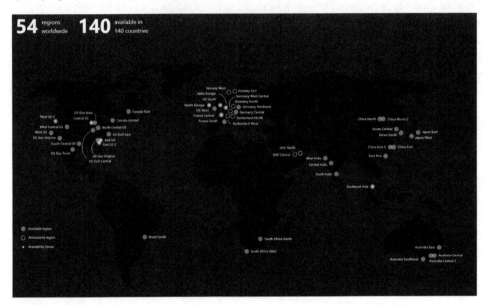

**FIGURE 3-34**  Map of Microsoft Azure regions

**NOTE**  **MICROSOFT AZURE GOVERNMENT**

Microsoft maintains a dedicated cloud for United States federal, state, and local government agencies and their partners, which is compliant with a large number of government standards, including FedRAMP, NIST 800.171 (DIB), ITAR, IRS 1075, DoD L4, and CJIS. The data centers for this government cloud are all located within the United States and are physically isolated, as are the networks inside them. In addition to the four dedicated U.S. government regions in Iowa, Texas, Arizona, and Virginia shown on the map, there are two other secret U. S. government regions at undisclosed locations.

## Obtaining skilled personnel

Because cloud-based services are a relatively new technology, there are not as many skilled administrators and support people for them as there are for traditional on-premises networking technologies. This can mean an enterprise that has an established on-premises network infrastructure but that is considering the addition of or migration to cloud services, the existing IT staff might lack the expertise needed to adequately support the cloud technologies.

One effective way of addressing this issue without replacing all or part of the IT staff is to train or recruit a core cloud network infrastructure design and planning team first. Then that team can function as mentors for the IT personnel that require a reorientation to cloud methodologies.

## Transitioning to the cloud

For traditional on-premises network administrators and support personnel, a transition to cloud-based services can be a major rethink in how they do almost everything, and many organizations are reticent to make the change for that reason. Cloud service providers have recognized this, however, and might provide help for subscribers moving into the cloud for the first time.

Microsoft's FastTrack program is designed for this exact purpose, providing organizations with a specified number of Microsoft 365 subscribers with a clearly defined path into the cloud and onboarding help, for no additional charge. Microsoft maintains its own FastTrack team, as well as a network of partners that can provide transition assistance by breaking the process down into the following three stages:

- **Envisioning**   Provides the subscriber with information about available resources and identifies business-specific scenarios to aid in the creation of an overall cloud deployment and migration plan catered to the organization's needs

- **Onboarding**   Realizes the plan created during the Envisioning phase by configuring the cloud services; migrating files, email stores, and web content; and creating users and groups, as shown in Figure 3-35

- **Driving value**   Helps the subscriber to develop efficient administration and maintenance practices and provides ongoing aid to the staff in working with Microsoft 365 technologies and adapting them to the organization's business model

Not all cloud service providers have a program like this, but some will provide assistance; also, there are third-party consultants who can help an organization deal with issues that arise during the transition to a cloud-based infrastructure. IT professionals who are hesitant to adopt cloud technologies, even after realizing the advantages they provide, have many resources available for assistance.

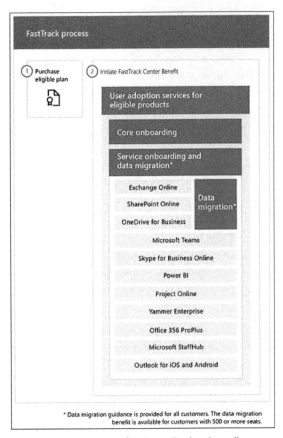

**FIGURE 3-35** The Microsoft 365 FastTrack onboarding process

## Summary

- The process of creating a security plan for an enterprise is known as *risk management*.
- Microsoft 365 includes security technologies that are divided into four areas: Security Management, Identity-based Protection, Information Protection, and Threat Protection
- A comprehensive security implementation must distribute protection among the four primary pillars supporting the enterprise infrastructure: Identity, Documents, Network, and Devices.
- An identity is a logical representation of a user in a network environment. To users, an identity is a name that they type to sign on to the network. To administrators, an identity is a collection of attributes associated with a particular individual.
- There are three basic means of authenticating an individual's identity. The individual must supply one or more of the following: something you know, something you are, or something you have.

- Unified endpoint management (UEM) is a management platform that can work with both on-premises and cloud-based devices, and be extendable to include new technologies as they develop, such as the Internet of Things (IoT).

- To achieve a true Unified Endpoint Management solution with Microsoft products, a combination of System Center Configuration Manager and Microsoft Intune is needed, in an arrangement called *co-management*.

- The Service Trust Portal (STP) is a central storehouse for information about cloud trust and standards compliance issues.

- Many company decision-makers are unsure about whether cloud-based providers can deliver the services that the organization needs or unclear about how to actually implement a migration to the cloud. These issues can at times be "showstoppers" that prevent a cloud implementation from happening at all unless solutions are carefully considered.

# Thought experiment

In this thought experiment, demonstrate your skills and knowledge of the topics covered in this chapter. You can find answer to this thought experiment in the next section.

Ralph is the Director of the Brooklyn data center at Contoso Corp. The company currently has three office buildings in in the New York area with a total of 600 users. There are data centers in all three buildings, all of which are based on Microsoft server products and managed using System Center Configuration Manager. The three data centers are all jammed with equipment and have no room for further expansion. Ralph is convinced that it would be better for the company to expand into the cloud and purchase Microsoft 365 subscriptions for the 600 users rather than purchase an additional property and build a fourth data center from scratch.

With the cost of real estate and construction in New York being what it is, the financial aspect of a cloud expansion is amenable to the company. However, there is still significant opposition to Ralph's proposal from the other two data center directors and from the chief technology officer:

1. None of the IT management staff—including Ralph—have much experience with cloud technologies.

2. There are fears that storing company data in the cloud will not be secure.

3. There are concerns that performance of the company's customer portal—a catalog database that took a great deal of effort to develop—will suffer because of cloud service downtime and Internet latency issues.

Ralph must prepare a presentation that promotes his cloud project and addresses these three concerns. Using what you have learned about cloud service trust and deployment issues, propose a solution for each of the three concerns that Ralph must address at his presentation.

# Thought experiment answer

Ralph can address the concerns of the other directors and the CTO in the following ways:

1. Microsoft's FastTrack program is designed to provide free support for new cloud subscribers during their infrastructure design and implementation processes, as well as ongoing support for the management staff.

2. Microsoft 365 includes tools such as Azure AD Identity Protection, Azure Information Protection, and Office 365 Advanced Threat Protection that enable administrators to protect user identities and elevate the security of the company data stored in the cloud based on its sensitivity.

3. Microsoft contracts include a service level agreement guaranteeing 99.9 percent uptime. The Microsoft 365 deployment process also includes a networking phase in which the company evaluates its Internet access infrastructure to ensure that all Microsoft 365 clients and administrators have sufficient Internet connectivity to access the cloud resources they require on a regular basis.

# CHAPTER 4

# Understand Microsoft 365 pricing and support

Microsoft 365 is designed to be a complete solution for organizations of various sizes that provides the operating system, productivity applications, and cloud-based services that most users need. For many businesses, Microsoft 365 can be a complete solution; other might have to install additional applications as well.

Candidates preparing for the MS-900 examination must understand the components included in the Microsoft 365 packages and the features and benefits they provide, as discussed in the preceding chapters. However, they must also be aware of the various licensing options available for Microsoft 365 subscribers, how they are priced, what support options are available, and what the expected lifecycle of the Microsoft 365 product is expected to be. This information is necessary for IT professionals to make an informed purchasing decision for their organizations.

### Skills in this chapter:

- Understand licensing options available in Microsoft 365
- Plan, predict, and compare pricing
- Describe support offerings for Microsoft 365 services
- Understand the service lifecycle in Microsoft 365

## Skill 4.1: Understand licensing options available in Microsoft 365

Microsoft 365 is not a "one-size-fits-all" product. It is intended to support a range of organization sizes and also organizations with different security and feature requirements. To do this, there are various editions of the product that have different feature sets and, of course, different prices. As with Office 365, Microsoft 365 is available only by subscription, but unlike Office 365, there is no need for subscribers to purchase an operating system.

All Microsoft 365 editions include the following three basic components:

- Windows 10 Enterprise
- Office 365 Pro Plus
- Enterprise Mobility + Security

However, all these components are available in their own plans, and the Microsoft 365 editions include them in various combinations.

# Microsoft 365 subscriptions

Most organizations interested in Microsoft 365 as an introduction to cloud-based networking, either as a new deployment or an addition to a traditional on-premises network, will opt for Microsoft 365 Business or one of the Microsoft 365 Enterprise subscription options described in the following sections. In addition, there are specialized versions of Microsoft 365 designed for educational and governmental environments.

## Microsoft 365 Business

Intended for small and medium-sized businesses with up to 300 users, the Microsoft 365 Business subscription includes Windows 10 Pro, Office 365 Pro Plus, and most (but not all) of the features included in Enterprise Mobility + Security E3. The intention behind the product is to create a comprehensive package for organizations that do not maintain a full-time IT staff, which is the case with many small businesses. The process of deploying Microsoft 365 workstations is largely automated, and the package includes the Microsoft 365 Admin Center, which provides a unified interface for the setup and management of identities and devices.

Microsoft 365 Business includes Windows Autopilot, which streamlines the process of deploying new Windows workstations or upgrading existing ones. For computers that already have Windows 7, Windows 8, or Windows 8.1 installed, Microsoft 365 provides an upgrade to Windows 10 Pro. In addition to Autopilot, Microsoft 365 includes device management settings in Azure Active Directory that can automatically apply policies to newly deployed workstations, including those for functions like the following:

- Activation of the Microsoft 365 subscription
- Windows 10 and Office 365 updates
- Automated installation of Office 365 applications on Windows 10
- Control of the device's screen when the system is idle
- Access control to Microsoft Store apps
- Access control to Cortana
- Access control to Windows tips and advertisements from Microsoft

Another priority of Microsoft 365 is to provide security in areas where small businesses often fall short, as shown in Figure 4-1. The suite of security functions and services included in the product provides protection for all the primary areas of a business network: identities, with multifactor authentication; devices, with management capabilities for on-premises and mobile devices; applications, with usage restrictions; email, with threat detection and data loss prevention; and documents, with classification, encryption, and access control.

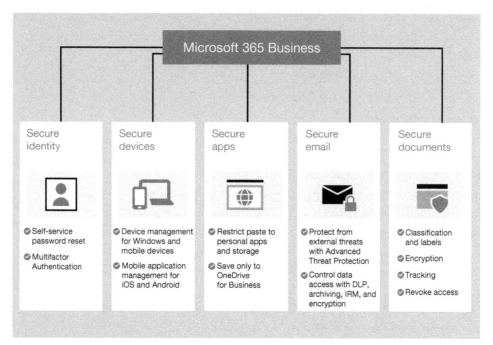

**FIGURE 4-1** Security functions in Microsoft 365 Business

Microsoft 365 Business allows up to 300 user subscriptions in one tenancy, but this does not mean than an organization's network is limited to 300 users. It is not required that every user on the network have a Microsoft 365 Business license, although only the license-holders can utilize the cloud services included with the product. It is also possible to combine license types in a single tenancy. This means that if an organization running Microsoft 365 Business expands to the point at which there are more than 300 users, it is possible to add more users with Microsoft 365 Enterprise licenses without having to upgrade the original 300 Business users.

## Microsoft 365 Enterprise

For organizations with more than 300 users, there are two subscription options, called Microsoft 365 Enterprise E3 and Microsoft 365 Enterprise E5. Both include Windows 10 Enterprise and Office 365 Pro Plus, as well as Enterprise Mobility + Security, and both support an unlimited number of users. The feature lists for the E3 and E5 subscriptions are largely identical, with Microsoft 365 Enterprise E5 including all the features of E3 plus more advanced security, threat protection, and analytics tools.

***EXAM TIP***

Candidates for the MS-900 exam should understand that while Microsoft 365 Enterprise is targeted at larger organizations, more than 300 users are not required. Small- or medium-sized businesses that require the additional security and analytical capabilities in the Enterprise E3 or E5 product can use it as well.

Several of the elements included in Microsoft 365 are also available as individual subscriptions and are available in two plans—referred to as Plan 1 (P1) and Plan 2 (P2)—and include the following:

- Azure Active Directory Premium
- Office 365 Advanced Threat Protection
- Azure Information Protection

In each case, Plan 2 includes all the features of Plan 1, plus some additional capabilities. Microsoft 365 Enterprise E5 includes Plan 2 for all three features, while Plan 1 is included in one or more of the other subscriptions, as shown later in Table 4-1.

For organizations subscribing to Microsoft 365 Enterprise E3, it is also possible to add certain advanced E5 features in two additional subscription packages, as follows:

- **Identity & Threat Protection** Includes Azure Advanced Threat Protection (ATP), Windows Defender Advanced Threat Protection, and Office 365 Advanced Threat Protection, as well as Microsoft Cloud App Security and Azure Active Directory Premium P2
- **Information Protection & Compliance** Includes Office 365 Advanced Compliance and Azure Information Protection P2

## Microsoft 365 F1

Microsoft envisions the Microsoft 365 product as a crucial step in an organization's transition from traditional on-premises computing to cloud-based services. For that transition to be complete, they consider it essential for workers at all levels of the business to participate. Microsoft 365 F1 is intended for *first-line workers*—that is, the segment of an organization's work force that provides that provides the first point of contact between the organization and the outside world. This refers specifically to workers in the field, in call centers, on shop floors, and in customer service roles.

The Microsoft 365 F1 subscription provides a streamlined version of the same basic functionality as the other Microsoft 365 subscriptions, including similar productivity, collaboration, and security tools but at a lower price and with limitations that are suitable to first-line workers' typical needs. The components in the Microsoft 365 F1 subscription are as follows:

- Windows 10 Enterprise
- Office 365 F1 (formally Office 365 Enterprise K1)
- Enterprise Mobility + Security

The primary difference in the F1 subscription, compared to the Enterprise and Business subscriptions, is that users receive access to the Office 365 productivity applications in their web and mobile versions only; the installable applications are not included. The product includes access to the Office 365 cloud-based services, including Exchange Online, SharePoint Online, OneDrive, Microsoft Teams, Microsoft Intune, Stream, Yammer, Sway, and Planner but with limitations that suit the tasks they typically perform and the devices that these workers employ, including the following:

- Exchange Online mailboxes are limited to 2 GB.
- SharePoint Online access is included, without personal sites, site mailboxes, or the ability to create forms.
- OneDrive is limited to 2 GB of cloud storage, without desktop synchronization.
- Microsoft Teams is limited to one-to-one calls only; users can join but not create meetings.
- Stream is limited to consumption only; users cannot create or upload video streams.
- Flow is limited to consumption only, with a limit of 750 flow runs per user per month.

Microsoft 365 F1 also includes many of the same threat protection and device management services as the Microsoft 365 Business and Enterprise E3 subscriptions. The end result is a package that enables first-line workers to fully participate in the culture and community of the organization, with access to the same productivity, collaboration, and security tools as users with Microsoft 365 Enterprise or Business subscriptions. At the same time, first-line workers can gain skills and experience with tools that can enable them to grow and develop within the work force.

## Microsoft 365 Business and Enterprise feature comparison

The components and features included in the main Microsoft 365 subscriptions are shown in Table 4-1.

**TABLE 4-1** Features and benefits in Microsoft 365 subscriptions

| FEATURES INCLUDED | MICROSOFT 365 BUSINESS | MICROSOFT 365 ENTERPRISE E3 | MICROSOFT 365 ENTERPRISE E5 | MICROSOFT 365 F1 |
|---|---|---|---|---|
| Windows 10 | Pro | Enterprise | Enterprise | Enterprise |
| Office 365 | Office 365 Pro Plus | Office 365 Pro Plus | Office 365 Pro Plus | Office 365 F1 (Office for Mobile apps and Office for the Web) |
| Exchange Online | Yes, with 50 GB mailbox | Yes, with 50 GB mailbox | Yes, with 50 GB mailbox | Yes, with 2 GB mailbox |
| SharePoint Online | Yes | Yes | Yes | Yes (without personal site, site mailbox, or form creation) |
| Microsoft Teams | Yes | Yes | Yes | Yes (one-to-one calls only, meetings join only) |
| OneDrive | 1 TB | 5 TB (five or more users) 1 TB (less than five users) | 5 TB (five or more users) 1 TB (less than five users) | 2 GB (without desktop synchronization) |
| OneDrive for Business | No | Unlimited | Unlimited | No |

| FEATURES INCLUDED | MICROSOFT 365 BUSINESS | MICROSOFT 365 ENTERPRISE E3 | MICROSOFT 365 ENTERPRISE E5 | MICROSOFT 365 F1 |
|---|---|---|---|---|
| Microsoft Stream | Yes | Yes | Yes | Yes (consume only) |
| Audio conferencing/ Phone System | No | No | Yes | No |
| Yammer | Yes | Yes | Yes | Yes |
| Planner | Yes | Yes | Yes | Yes |
| Flow | Yes | Yes | Yes | Yes (consume only, 750 runs per user per month) |
| Sway | Yes | Yes | Yes | Yes |
| Windows Hello | Yes | Yes | Yes | Yes |
| Azure Active Directory Premium | Plan 1 | Plan 1 | Plan 2 | Plan 1 |
| Azure Active Directory Privileged Identity Management | No | No | Yes | No |
| Microsoft 365 Admin Center | Yes | Yes | Yes | Yes |
| Microsoft Intune | Yes | Yes | Yes | Yes |
| System Center Configuration Manager | No | Yes | Yes | Yes |
| Windows Autopilot | Yes | Yes | Yes | Yes |
| Microsoft Advanced Threat Analytics | No | Yes | Yes | Yes |
| Microsoft Defender Advanced Threat Protection | No | No | Yes | No |
| Office 365 Advanced Threat Protection | Plan 1 | No | Plan 2 | No |
| Office 365 Threat Intelligence | No | No | Yes | No |
| Azure Advanced Threat Protection | No | No | Yes | No |
| Office 365 Data Loss Prevention | Yes | Yes | Yes | No |
| Azure Information Protection | Plan 1 | Plan 1 | Plan 2 | Plan 1 |
| Windows Information Protection | Yes | Yes | Yes | Yes |

| FEATURES INCLUDED | MICROSOFT 365 BUSINESS | MICROSOFT 365 ENTERPRISE E3 | MICROSOFT 365 ENTERPRISE E5 | MICROSOFT 365 F1 |
|---|---|---|---|---|
| Office 365 Privileged Access Management | No | No | Yes | No |
| MyAnalytics | No | Yes | Yes | Yes |
| Power BI Pro | No | No | Yes | No |
| Cloud App Security | No | No | Yes | No |
| Microsoft Security and Compliance Center | Yes | Yes | Yes | Yes |

> **NOTE   MICROSOFT 365 INTERNATIONAL USERS**
>
> The exact features included in the Microsoft 365 subscriptions, as well as their pricing and licensing requirements, can vary depending on the country or geographical region in which the subscription is purchased.

## Microsoft 365 Government

In addition to the core Microsoft 365 subscriptions mentioned earlier, Microsoft has also created specialized packages for governmental and educational organizations that are designed to suit their specific needs. The Microsoft 365 Government G3 and G5 subscriptions contain the same tools and services found in their Enterprise E3 and E5 equivalents, but the packages are designed to adhere to the additional compliance regulations and requirements to which United States government entities are often subject.

For all the Microsoft 365 Government products, data is stored under special conditions, including the following:

- All Microsoft 365 Government user content, including Exchange Online mailboxes, SharePoint Online site content, Skype for Business conversations, and Microsoft Teams chat transcripts, is stored in data centers located within the United States.

- The user content generated by Microsoft 365 Government subscribers is logically segregated from commercial Microsoft 365 user content within the Microsoft data centers.

- Access to Microsoft 365 Government user content within the Microsoft data centers is restricted to employees who have undergone additional security screening.

Access to the Microsoft 365 Government products is restricted to United States federal, state, local, tribal, or territorial government entities, as well as to other entities that are required to handle government data in compliance with the same regulations and requirements as a government entity. Eligibility to purchase these products is subject to verification by Microsoft using various government resources, including those of law enforcement agencies and the Department of State, as well as government standards, such as the International Traffic in Arms Regulations (ITAR) and the FBI's Criminal Justice Information Services (CJIS) Policy.

In addition to the Microsoft 365 Government G3 and G5 subscriptions, which define the products' feature sets, there are versions of Microsoft 365 Government that define various levels of security and compliance, including the following:

- **Microsoft 365 U.S. Government Community (GCC)** Intended for Federal Risk and Authorization Management Program (FedRAMP) moderate risk impact situations; also complies with the Internal Revenue Service Publication 1075 standard, the U.S. Criminal Justice Information Services (CJIS) Security Policy, and the U.S. Department of Defense (DoD) Defense Information Systems Agency (DISA) Level 2 requirement for noncontrolled unclassified information.

- **Microsoft 365 U.S. Government Community (GCC) High** Intended for FedRAMP high-impact situations; complies with the International Traffic in Arms Regulations (ITAR) and the Defense Federal Acquisition Regulation Supplement (DFARS).

- **Microsoft 365 DoD** Restricted to the exclusive use by U.S. Department of Defense agencies; complies with the U.S. DoD Defense Information Systems Agency (DISA) Level 5 requirement for controlled unclassified information and unclassified national security systems.

In addition to the Microsoft 365 Government subscriptions, Microsoft also maintains an alternative means of accessing Office 365 cloud services, called Azure Government ExpressRoute, which is a private, dedicated network connection to the Microsoft cloud services for eligible subscribers that have regulatory requirements that prevent them from using the public Internet.

## Microsoft 365 Education

Microsoft 365 Education is another specialized version of Microsoft 365 that includes additional tools and services that are specifically targeted at teachers and students. There are two subscription levels, called Microsoft 365 Education A3 and Microsoft Education A5, which correspond to the Enterprise E3 and E5 subscriptions in most of their features and services. The subscriptions include specialized versions of the three major components, as follows:

- Windows 10 Education
- Office 365 Education
- Management & Security

Some of the tools included in the Education subscriptions are specially modified for classroom use, and there are additional educational tools included as well.

> **NOTE  MICROSOFT 365 EDUCATION A1**
>
> In addition to Microsoft Education A3 and A5, there is also a Microsoft Education A1 product, which is a one-time, per-device license that includes the Office 365 for the web applications and cloud-based email, Teams, video conferencing, and compliance and information-protection tools; it does not include the installable Office 365 applications and also omits some of the educational, security, and analytics tools found in the A3 and A5 subscriptions.

The education-specific modifications in the Microsoft 365 Education A3 and A5 subscriptions include the following:

- **OneNote Class Notebook** A shared OneNote implementation that includes a collaboration space for class work, a content library for handout documents, and a personal notebook space for each student.

- **Yammer Academic** An implementation of the Yammer private social networking service that includes school branding capability, administration capabilities that provide content management and access control.

- **Minecraft Education Edition with Code Builder** An educational adaptation of the Minecraft game that enables students to learn how to code software by dragging and dropping visual code blocks.

- **Take a Test app** An application that enables teachers to deploy high-stakes or low-stakes tests to students in a distraction-free environment, as shown in Figure 4-2. Once students have begun taking a test, they are not able to browse the web, print or share the screen, open other applications, use the Windows clipboard, or change system settings.

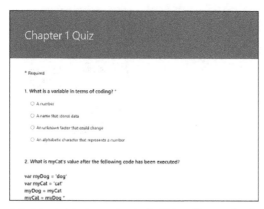

**FIGURE 4-2** A test question in the Take a Test application

- **Set Up School PCs app** An application that enables administrators or teachers to easily set up computers running Windows 10 by joining them to an Azure Active Directory tenant, installing approved applications (as shown in Figure 4-3), removing unapproved applications, configuring Windows Update to install updates outside of class time, and locking down the system to prevent its use for anything other than educational purposes.

- **School Data Sync (SDS)** A service that uses data synchronized from a school's Student Information System (SIS) to create Office 365 groups for Exchange Online and SharePoint Online, Microsoft Intune groups, class teams for Microsoft Teams, and class notebooks for OneNote, as shown in Figure 4-4. Also, SDS can populate many other third-party applications with student information.

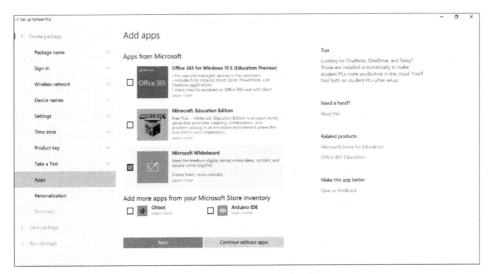

**FIGURE 4-3** Adding applications in the Set Up School PCs application

**FIGURE 4-4** School Information System data synchronization

- **Office Lens** A tool that uses the camera of a smartphone or tablet to take pictures of printed pages or whiteboards. This tool crops, straightens, and sharpens them, and it converts them to PDF, Word, or PowerPoint files and then saves them to a OneNote notebook, a OneDrive folder, or a local drive.

- **Intune for Education** A streamlined version of Microsoft Intune that provides device management and application-deployment services for teacher and student devices through a web-based portal, as shown in Figure 4-5.

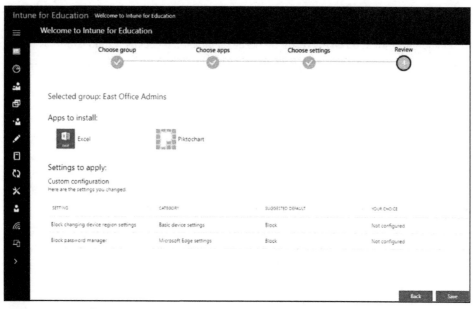

**FIGURE 4-5** Intune for Education application deployment

---

**Quick check**

- Which of the following is one of the features included in Microsoft 365 F1?
    - **a.** Install Office 365 on up to five devices
    - **b.** 50 GB Exchange Online mailboxes
    - **c.** 2 GB of OneDrive cloud storage
    - **d.** SharePoint Online personal sites

---

**Quick check answer**

- C. Microsoft 365 F1 does not include the installable versions of the Office 365 applications, includes only 2 GB Exchange Online mailboxes, and does not include SharePoint Online personal sites.

---

# Selling Microsoft 365

As noted elsewhere in this book, there are many IT professionals who are hesitant to buy into the idea of cloud-based services, and the cloud is the first and biggest buzzword for the Microsoft 365 product. As a result, Microsoft has devoted a great deal of time, effort, and expense to developing a product and a campaign that can convince people like these to adopt—or at least consider—Microsoft 365 as a viable route for the development of their enterprise infrastructures. The following sections discuss the key selling points for Microsoft 365 in four major areas.

## Productivity

Few IT professionals must be sold on the Microsoft Office productivity applications, such as Word, Excel, and PowerPoint; they are industry standards that are virtually without competition. However, there are those who do need to be sold on a cloud-based, subscription-based implementation such as Office 365 ProPlus, as opposed to on-premises versions like Office Professional Plus 2019. The selling points that make an effective case for Office 365 include the following:

- **Applications**   Some people might think that with Office 365, the productivity applications are accessible only from the cloud and that an Internet connection is required to run them. While the productivity applications are indeed accessible from the cloud with an Office 365 ProPlus subscription, such as that included in Microsoft 365, the product also includes fully installable versions of the productivity applications, just like those in Office 2019.

- **Devices**   An Office 2019 Professional Plus license enables a user to install the productivity applications on a single computer; however, with an Office 365 ProPlus subscription, a user can install the applications on up to five PC, Mac, or mobile devices and sign in to any or all them at the same time. This means that users can run the Office 365 applications on an office computer, a home computer, and a smartphone, plus two other devices, with a single license, while an Office 2019 user would need a separate license for each device.

- **Installation**   An Office 365 ProPlus license includes access to a cloud-based portal, with which users can install the productivity applications themselves on any computer. Office 2019 and other on-premises versions include no self-service portal access and require administrators to install the applications on each device.

- **Activation**   When users install the Office 365 productivity applications from the self-service portal, they are automatically activated. They remain activated as long as the computers connect to the Office Licensing Service in the cloud at least once every 30 days. If a device exceeds the 30-day requirement, Office 365 goes into reduced functionality mode, which limits the user to viewing and printing existing documents. Office 2019 and other on-premises versions in an enterprise environment require administrators to keep track of the product key for each individual license or utilize a network-based activation method, such as Key Management Service (KMS) or Multiple Activation Key (MAK). Once activated, Office 2019 installations do not require periodic reactivation.

- **Updates**   Office 365 installations are automatically updated either monthly or semi-annually with the latest security, quality, and feature updates. Office 2019 and other on-premises versions receive security updates but no feature updates. There is also no upgrade path to the next major on-premises version of Office. For example, Office 2016 users must pay full price for a new license to install Office 2019.

- **Support**  Office 2019 and other on-premises versions include free technical support for the installation process only. Office 365 subscriptions include free technical support for the life of the subscription.

- **Storage**  An Office 365 ProPlus subscription includes 1 TB of OneDrive cloud storage. Office 2019 and other on-premises versions do not include cloud storage.

- **Mobile apps**  Access to the Office mobile apps on devices with screens smaller than 10.1 inches with core editing functionality is free to everyone. Office 365 subscribers receive extra features on all the mobile apps. Users of Office 2019 or other on-premises versions do not receive the extra features.

## Collaboration

The nature of collaboration in the workplace has changed, so the tools that facilitate collaboration must change with it. One of the primary advantages of cloud-based computing is that it provides users with the ability to access enterprise resources from any location. Microsoft 365 takes advantage of that benefit by making it possible to access the cloud using nearly any device with an Internet connection. Azure Active Directory and Microsoft Intune are services, based in the cloud, which provide identity and device management functions that these user connections to the cloud secure. These components, along with the increased capabilities and emphasis on smartphones and other mobile devices in the business world, have made Microsoft 365 an unprecedented platform for collaboration.

With an infrastructure in place that can provide users with all but universal access to enterprise resources, the next step toward a collaboration platform is the applications and services that enable users to communicate and share data. Microsoft 365 includes four primary collaboration services—shown in Figure 4-6—that provide different types of communication for different situations. There are also additional services that provide more specific functions for the other services.

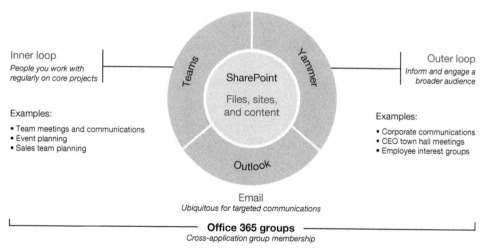

**FIGURE 4-6**  Microsoft 365 collaboration services

The services that contribute to the collaboration capabilities in Microsoft 365 are as follows:

- **SharePoint Online**  Provides content storage and publishing services for group and personal intranet websites and for all the other Microsoft 365 collaboration tools. A SharePoint site can be a collaboration platform of its own, or its elements can be embedded in other service publications.

- **Exchange Online/Outlook**  Provides standard email communication, as well as calendar and scheduling functions. Email is asynchronous communication that can be one-to-one, or with the aid of distribution lists, one-to-many. Scheduling functions can be embedded in other services.

- **Microsoft Teams**  Provides synchronous chat- and call-based communication among team members that must communicate quickly and frequently. By incorporating elements from other services, such as Exchange Online scheduling, SharePoint Online content, and Stream video, Teams can function as a comprehensive collaboration platform.

- **Yammer**  Provides a group-based or company-wide private social media service that is designed to accommodate larger groups than Teams or to foster a sense of community within the enterprise. Yammer also provides a platform for the functions provided by other services, such as content from SharePoint Online sites or scheduling with Exchange Online.

- **Stream**  Provides video storage and distribution services, both directly to users in web browsers or embedded in other Microsoft 365 collaboration services, including Exchange Online, SharePoint Online, Teams, and Yammer.

- **Planner**  Provides project management services that enable users to create schedules containing tasks, files, events, and other content from Microsoft 365 services.

- **OneDrive for Business**  Provides file storage for individual users that is private unless the user explicitly shares specific documents.

> **NEED MORE REVIEW?**  **MICROSOFT 365 COLLABORATION TOOLS**
>
> For more information about the collaboration capabilities of the Microsoft 365 services, see the "Understand collaboration and mobility with Microsoft 365" section in Chapter 2, "Understand core Microsoft 365 services and concepts."

Azure Active Directory and Office 365 Groups provide the identity-management infrastructure for all the Microsoft 365 collaborative services. This enables users and administrators to set up and use these services any way they want. However, the content from the various services is combined, there is only one set of user accounts and group memberships that applies to all of them. This turns the collection of Microsoft 365 collaboration services into a flexible and interoperable toolkit.

Microsoft has illustrated one possible scenario, shown in Figure 4-7, illustrating how workers and teams can use the Microsoft 365 collaboration services to work together by creating a digital daily plan containing specific tasks and the circumstances in which they might be performed.

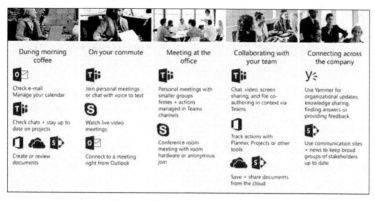

**FIGURE 4-7** A sample Microsoft 365 collaboration task schedule

## Security

For many IT professionals who are hesitant to move their operations to the cloud, security is the biggest issue that concerns them. The idea of storing sensitive company data on Internet servers, over which they have no direct control and of which they do not even know the exact location, can be frightening. However, Microsoft has invested an enormous amount of time, effort, and expense into securing its data centers, and Microsoft 365 includes an array of security tools that subscribers can utilize to provide defense in depth against outside intrusions.

Every security situation is a matter of judgment. Administrators must evaluate the organization's data and decide how much security it requires. In cases of highly sensitive data, the prospect of storing it in the cloud should rightly be frightening. In such cases, it might be necessary for an organization to maintain local storage and split the enterprise functionality between cloud-based and on-premises systems.

As noted elsewhere in this book, Microsoft maintains dozens of data centers around the world. The very fact that Microsoft's cloud services are storing data for thousands of organizations means that they have the incentive and the capital to build data centers with equipment and physical security that only the largest corporations could conceivably duplicate. For most prospective Microsoft 365 subscribers, the cloud will provide greater physical security, higher availability, and more fault tolerance than they could provide themselves.

Therefore, if the Microsoft data centers can be considered safe against physical theft and most natural disasters, the remaining security concerns are centered around the protection of identities, devices, and documents. These are concerns that are a threat to any enterprise network, whether on-premises or in the cloud. Unauthorized users can conceivably gain access to sensitive data wherever it is stored, and IT professionals might try to prevent that from happening.

Security is a continuously developing challenge, with threats growing as quickly as the means to protect against them. For administrators who want to use Microsoft products to keep up with the latest developing threats, there is no question that the latest and best security tools that Microsoft makes are to be found in cloud-based platforms, such as Microsoft 365.

On-premises products, such as Exchange Server and Office 2019, are being left behind in their security capabilities in favor of Software as a Service (SaaS) products like Office 365, Exchange Online, and SharePoint Online, all of which are part of the Microsoft 365 product.

The Microsoft 365 security components include the following:

- **Microsoft Intune**   Provides device and application management services that enable mobile devices to join the network if they comply with security policies that ensure they are appropriately equipped and configured

- **Azure Information Protection**   Enables users and administrators to apply classification labels to documents and implement various types of protection based on the labels, such as access restrictions and data encryption

- **Data Loss Prevention**   Enables the automated discovery of documents that contain common data patterns, such as those of credit cards and Social Security numbers, using preconfigured sensitive information types

- **Cloud App Security**   Analyzes traffic logs and proxy scripts to identify the apps that users are accessing and enables administrators to analyze app security and sanction or unsanction individual apps

- **Azure Active Directory Identity Protection**   Evaluates the sign-in activities of individual user accounts and assigns them risk levels that increment when multiple negative events occur

- **Azure Advanced Threat Protection**   Uses machine intelligence to prevent, detect, and remediate security threats unique to the Azure environment by analyzing user behavior and comparing it to known attack patterns

- **Microsoft Advanced Threat Analytics**   Captures network traffic and log information and analyzes it to identify suspicious behaviors related to known phases of typical attack processes

Another aspect of Microsoft 365 that might help to convince traditionalists that a cloud platform can be secure is its use of intelligent analysis to identify behavior indicative of an attack. Tools like Windows Defender Threat Protection gather information from Microsoft 365 devices, applications and services and use endpoint behavioral sensors, cloud security analytics, and threat intelligence to prevent, discover, investigate, and remediate potential and actual threats.

## Compliance

As the proliferation and value of data increases over time, businesses, agencies, and individuals are becoming increasingly concerned with the privacy and protection of their data. To quantify the nature of this data protection, there are hundreds of regulatory bodies—both private and governmental—that publish standards for data storage and handling.

Some of the most common data privacy standards in use today are as follows:

- **Federal Information Security Modernization Act (FISMA)**   Specifies how U.S. federal agencies must protect information

- **Health Insurance Portability and Accountability Act (HIPAA)**   Regulates the privacy of personal health information

- **Family Educational Rights and Privacy Act (FERPA)**   Regulates the disclosure of student education records

- **Personal Information Protection and Electronic Documents Act (PIPEDA)** Specifies how commercial business organizations can gather, retain, and share personal information

- **Gramm–Leach–Bliley Act (GLBA)**   Specifies how financial institutions must protect and share the personal information of their customers

- **General Data Protection Regulation (GDPR)**   Specifies data protection and privacy regulations for citizens of the European Union

These standards can define elements such as the following:

- The controls that organizations must exercise to protect the privacy of personal data

- The ways in which organizations can and cannot use personal data

- The rights of government and other official agencies to access personal data held by an organization

- The lengths of time an organization can and must retain individuals' personal data

- The rights of individuals to access their personal data held by organizations and correct it

Whether their adoption of certain standards is mandatory or voluntary, many organizations are concerned with whether the tools and procedures they use for storing and handling data are compliant with these standards.

Every organization must be responsible for assessing its own data resources and determining what standards should apply to them. The nature of the business in which the organization is engaged can often dictate compliance with particular standards. For example, companies in the health care industry or those with government contracts might be required by law to store, handle, and protect their data in specific ways. Indeed, there are regulatory standards to which the Microsoft 365 products on their own cannot possibly comply, such as those which require data to be stored on devices and in locations wholly owned and controlled by the organization, which preclude the use of cloud storage entirely.

However, many of the hundreds of privacy standards in use do allow the possibility of compliance when data is stored in the cloud, and Microsoft is well aware of the importance of adherence to these standards for many organizations considering a migration to the cloud. For IT professionals who are hesitant to become Microsoft 365 adopters because they fear that changing the location and the conditions of their data storage will negatively affect their compliance with standards like these, Microsoft has had their products' compliance with many different standards tested and has published documents certifying the results.

Microsoft divides the compliance effort into three phases, as shown in Figure 4-8. The phases are described as follows:

- **Assess**   The organization gathers the information needed to assess their current compliance status and produce a plan to achieve or maintain compliance with specific standards. Microsoft's Service Trust Portal website contains a vast library of documents specifying information about the testing processes and the third parties involved in compliance testing. In addition, the site provides access to Compliance Manager, a risk assessment tool that organizations can use to record the actions they take to achieve compliance with specific standards.

- **Protect**   The organization implements a protection plan for their data, based on its sensitivity, using the tools provided in the Microsoft 365 services, including access control permissions, file encryption, Information Protection, and Data Loss Prevention.

- **Respond**   The organization develops protocols for responding to regulatory requests using artificial intelligence tools such as Office 365 eDiscovery to perform complex searches of Exchange Online mailboxes, Office 365 Groups, SharePoint Online and OneDrive for Business sites, and Microsoft Teams conversations.

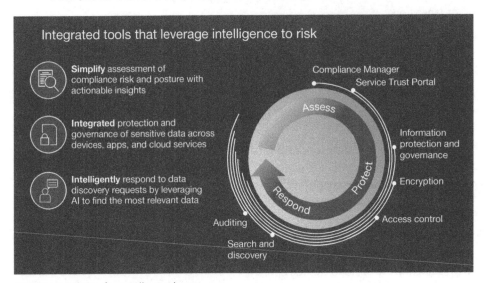

**FIGURE 4-8** Microsoft compliance phases

---

***NEED MORE REVIEW?***   **MICROSOFT 365 COMPLIANCE**

For additional information on Microsoft 365's compliance efforts, see the "Understand the Service Trust Portal and Compliance Manager" section in Chapter 3.

# Licensing Microsoft 365

To install and run the Microsoft 365 components and access the Microsoft 365 cloud services, each user in an organization must have a Microsoft 365 *user subscription license (USL)*. An administrator for an organization deploying Microsoft 365 typically creates a tenancy in Azure Active Directory, purchases a specific number of USLs and then assigns them to users in the Microsoft 365 Admin Center console by selecting Licenses in the **Billing** menu, as shown in Figure 4-9.

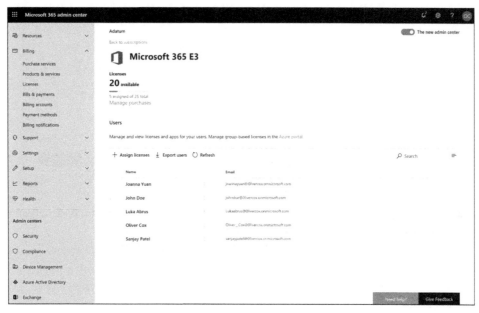

**FIGURE 4-9** The Licenses page in Microsoft 365 Admin Center

Global administrators or user management administrators can assign licenses to up to 20 users at once from this interface. It is also possible to assign licenses to hybrid user accounts created through Active Directory synchronization or federation, or while creating new user accounts in the Microsoft 365 Admin Center.

Assigning a Microsoft 365 license to a user causes the following events to occur:

- Exchange Online creates a mailbox for the user
- SharePoint Online grants the user edit permissions for the default team site
- Office 365 ProPlus enables the user to download and install the Office 365 productivity applications on up to five devices

From the **Purchase Services** page in the Admin Center, administrators can also purchase additional Microsoft 365 USLs or licenses for add-on products, as shown in Figure 4-10.

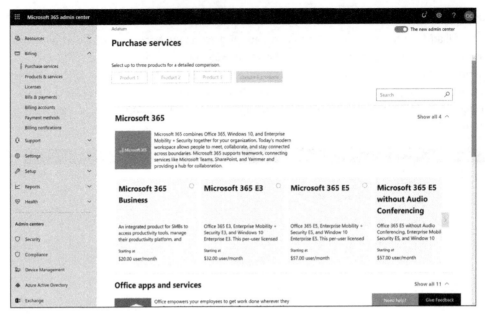

**FIGURE 4-10** The Purchase Services page in Microsoft 365 Admin Center

Microsoft offers four different USL types for each of the Microsoft 365 products, depending on the purchaser's existing relationship with the company, as follows:

- **Full USL**   A complete Microsoft 365 license for new purchasers that do not have existing Microsoft product licenses or for owners of on-premises Microsoft product licenses that do not include Software Assurance, Microsoft's software maintenance agreement.

- **Add-on USL**   A license for purchasers with existing on-premises Microsoft product licenses that include Software Assurance and who want to maintain their on-premises infrastructure while adding Microsoft 365 cloud services in a pilot or hybrid deployment.

- **From SA USL**   A license for purchasers with existing on-premises Microsoft product licenses that include Software Assurance and who want to transition to a cloud-based infrastructure with continued Software Assurance for the Microsoft 365 product. Qualifying purchasers can only obtain From SA USLs at their contract renewal time, and they must maintain their existing Software Assurance agreement. A Microsoft 365 Software Assurance agreement includes cloud-oriented benefits, such as Deployment Planning Services, Home Use Program, online user training courses, and additional support incidents.

- **Step-up USL**   A license for current Microsoft customers who want to upgrade their subscriptions during an existing enrollment or agreement period, such as from Office 365 to Microsoft 365 or from Microsoft 365 Business to Microsoft 365 Enterprise E3.

Because the Add-on USLs, From SA USLs, and Step-up USLs are intended for existing Microsoft customers, their prices reflect significant discounts from the Full USL price.

# Implementing best practices

As mentioned throughout this book, the Microsoft 365 product is a bundle consisting of Windows, Office 365, and Enterprise Mobility + Security, all of which continue to be available as separate subscriptions. In addition, there are subscriptions available for combinations of individual features within these products, such as the Identity & Threat Protection and Information Protection & Compliance packages.

Finally, to complicate the picture even further, it is possible to combine different licenses in a single Azure Active Directory tenancy. With all these options available, organizations that are contemplating a migration to a cloud-based infrastructure, or that are thinking of adding cloud services to an on-premises infrastructure, should undertake to design a licensing strategy that will fulfill all the following requirements:

- Provide the organization's users with the services they need
- Avoid providing users with unnecessary services that complicate the maintenance and support processes
- Minimize subscription costs

Generally speaking, a Microsoft 365 subscription will likely be significantly less expensive than purchasing subscriptions for each of its components separately. This might be true even if there are some users who do not need all the Microsoft 365 components.

Obviously, the simplest solution is to choose one Microsoft 365 product and purchase the same subscription for all the organization's users. This can easily fulfill the first of the requirements but might not be a solution for the other two.

Depending on the nature of the business the organization is engaged in, an Enterprise E5 subscription might be suitable for some users, but there might also be many workers who do not need all the applications and services included in Enterprise E5. Depending on the number of users in each group, the expense of purchasing E5 subscriptions for everyone could be extremely wasteful and require additional administrative effort to provide customized environments for the different user groups. This is one of the primary reasons why Microsoft offers the Microsoft 365 F1 subscription for first-line workers.

Therefore, the best practice is to compare the features included in each of the Microsoft 365 licenses with the requirements of the various types of users in the organization. In a large enterprise, this can be a complicated process, but in the case of a major migration like this, prior planning is crucial and can save a great deal of expense and effort.

# Skill 4.2: Plan, predict, and compare pricing

Cost is always a factor when considering the introduction of a new technology into a business network, and the question of whether Microsoft 365 is an economically sound choice when compared to a traditional on-premises network infrastructure is a complicated one. Every organization contemplating an entry into cloud-based computing must factor the results of a *cost-benefit analysis (CBA)* into its decision. However, in a comparison of Microsoft 365 to on-premises server products, it is not just a matter of how much the technologies cost but also when the costs are incurred.

## Cost-benefit analysis for cloud vs. on-premises networks

Evaluating the total cost of ownership (TCO) for a Microsoft 365 implementation is the relatively simple part of a cost-benefit analysis. There is a monthly or annual fee for each Microsoft 365 user subscription and those subscriber fees are predictable and ongoing. Contracts might be renewed with different prices at intervals, but those costs still remain predictable. It is possible that costs could rise precipitously in the future when the contracts are renewed, and the subscriber might feel locked in to one provider, but that is a risk with any software product.

Predicting the cost of an on-premises network is more difficult. It is common for businesses to categorize their expenses by distinguishing between two types of expenditures, as follows:

- Capital expenditures (CapEx) is money spent on fixed assets, such as buildings, servers and other hardware, deployment expenses, and purchased software.

- Operational expenditures (OpEx) is ongoing expenses, such as rent, utilities, staff, and maintenance.

The basic differences between CapEx and OpEx expenditures are shown in Table 4-2.

**TABLE 4-2** Capital expenditures versus operational expenditures

|  | CAPITAL EXPENDITURES (CAPEX) | OPERATIONAL EXPENDITURES (OPEX) |
|---|---|---|
| PURPOSE | Hardware and software assets with at least one year of usefulness | Ongoing business costs |
| PAYMENT | Initial lump sum | Recurring monthly or annual |
| ACCOUNTING | Three or more years of asset depreciation | Current month or year |
| DESCRIPTION | Property, equipment, software | Operating costs |
| TAXES | Multiple years of deduction based on depreciation | Current year deduction |

For a Microsoft 365 shop, nearly all the expenses are OpEx, including the subscription fees. There are virtually no CapEx expenses involved, except perhaps for things like initial cloud training for administrators. Businesses like working with OpEx expenses because they enable them to create accurate budgets and forecasts.

For an on-premises network, the CapEx outlay required to set up the infrastructure can be enormous, including the cost of building and equipping data centers and purchasing server software products. Depending on the nature of the business and the sensitivity of the data involved, these expenses can by multiplied by the need for redundant data centers and equipment. These are big expenses that must be paid before the network can even go live. These CapEx costs can be amortized or depreciated in the company's accounts over a period of years, but the initial investment is substantial compared to that of a cloud-based network, which requires almost none.

An on-premises network has OpEx expenses as well, including rent, power and other utilities data centers require, and the salaries of the staff needed to operate and maintain the data center equipment. There are also expensive software upgrades to consider every two to three years. The main cost benefit of an on-premises network is that hardware and software are purchased outright and do not require monthly subscription fees.

There are other factors to consider as well. When designing an on-premises network, the organization must consider the possibility of future growth, as well as seasonal business fluctuations. Therefore, the already substantial CapEx outlay can be increased by the cost of the additional data center space and equipment needed to support the busiest times of the year, as well as several years of predicted growth.

A cloud-based infrastructure like that of Microsoft 365 uses a pay-as-you-go model, which can accommodate virtually unlimited growth and occasional business fluctuations with no extra expenses other than the increased subscription fees for the extra services. The organization is never paying for hardware and software that isn't being used. In addition, the growth and fluctuations can be accommodated almost immediately and downsized when necessary, while on-premises resources can require months to approve, obtain, and install.

The entire cost-benefit analysis can be complicated further if the organization has already made a substantial investment in on-premises infrastructure. For example, if the company that is expanding already has sufficient space in its data centers and sufficient IT staff, the CapEx needed for a network expansion can be much less than it would be for an entirely new network installation. The question then becomes whether it is more economical to add to the existing on-premises infrastructure or expand into the cloud, creating a hybrid network that might require additional planning and training to bring personnel up to speed in cloud technologies.

Therefore, the end result can only be that every organization must consider its own economic, personnel, and business situations and calculate the TCO of its network options for itself. In a new deployment, a subscription-based, cloud-based option, such as Microsoft 365, can be faster and less expensive to implement, but there are many situations in which organizations might be compelled to consider an on-premises network instead.

***EXAM TIP***

Candidates for the MS-900 exam seeking greater familiarity with the characteristics of cloud-based services versus on-premises services should also consult the "Compare core services in Microsoft 365 with corresponding on-premises services" section in Chapter 2.

## Volume licensing

It is possible for organizations to purchase Microsoft 365 subscriptions directly from Microsoft individually or by using a variety of volume licensing agreements, including the following:

- **Enterprise Agreement (EA)**  A volume licensing agreement for organizations with at least 500 users or devices seeking to license software for a period of at least three years, which provides discounts of 15 to 45 percent based on the number of users. Available with up-front or subscription payment terms, the agreement includes Software Assurance and the ability to add users and services during the life of the agreement.

- **Microsoft Products and Services Agreement (MPSA)**  An ongoing, partner-based, transactional license agreement for organizations with 250 to 499 users or devices that optionally includes Software Assurance and requires no organization-wide commitment.

- **Cloud Solution Provider (CSP)**  A partner-based licensing channel that enables organizations of all sizes to obtain Microsoft 365 products through an ongoing relationship with a selected partner.

### Software assurance

For Enterprise Agreement and, optionally, for Microsoft Products and Services Agreement customers, Software Assurance provides a variety of additional services, including the following, which can benefit Microsoft 365 licensees:

- **Planning Services**  Provides a number of partner service days, based on the number of users/devices licensed, for the purpose of deploying Microsoft operating systems, applications, and services.

- **Microsoft Desktop Optimization Pack (MDOP)**   Provides a suite of virtualization, management, and restoration utilities, including Microsoft Application Virtualization (App-V), Microsoft User Experience Virtualization (UE-V), Microsoft BitLocker Administration and Monitoring (MBAM), and Microsoft Diagnostics and Recovery Toolset (DaRT).

- **Windows Virtual Desktop Access Rights (VDA)**   Provides users with the rights needed to access virtualized Windows instances.

- **Windows to Go Use Rights**   Enables administrators to create and furnish users with USB storage devices containing bootable Windows images that include line-of-business applications and corporate data.

- **Windows Thin PC**   Enables administrators to repurpose older computers as Windows Virtual Desktop Interface (VDI) terminals.

- **Enterprise Source Licensing Program**   Provides organizations with at least 10,000 users or devices with access to the Windows source code for their own software development projects.

- **Training Vouchers**   Provides a number of training days based on the number of users/devices licensed for the technical training of IT professionals and software developers.

- **24x7 Problem Resolution Support**   Provides 24x7 telephone support for business-critical issues and business hours or email support for noncritical issues. The number of incidents allowed is based on the type of volume licensing agreement and the products licensed.

- **Step-up License Availability**   Provides licensees with the ability to migrate their licensed software products to a high-level edition.

- **Spread Payments**   Enables organizations to pay for three-year license agreements in three equal, annual payments.

> **NOTE   ADDITIONAL SOFTWARE ASSURANCE BENEFITS**
>
> There are additional Software Assurance benefits included that are intended for on-premises server software licensees, such as New Version Rights, which provides the latest versions of the licensed software released during the term of the agreement, and Server Disaster Recovery Rights and Fail-Over Rights, which provide licensees the right to maintain passive redundant servers for fault-tolerance purposes.

## Cloud solution providers

The *Cloud Solution Provider (CSP)* program enables partners to establish ongoing relationships with end-user organizations of all sizes and provide them with sales and support for Windows 10 and all the Microsoft 365 Enterprise, Business, and Education products. Members of the Microsoft Partner Network can become CSPs and play a more prominent part of their customers cloud solutions.

Rather than simply reselling products, such as Windows 10 and Microsoft 365, a CSP can be a customer's single contact for everything from providing solutions, to billing, to providing technical support. CSP partners can enhance their relationships with their customers by adding value to the Microsoft products, such as by bundling industry-specific software products with Microsoft 365 or by offering managed services, such as data migrations and internal help desk support. CSP partners can also offer Microsoft products that were previously unavailable to smaller companies. For example, at one time, Windows 10 Enterprise was available only to customers with a Microsoft Volume Licensing Agreement; CSP partners can now offer the Enterprise edition of the operating system to small- and medium-sized companies.

Depending on the capabilities of the Microsoft partner, the CSP program operates in two ways—direct (Tier 1) and indirect (Tier 2)—as shown in Figure 4-11.

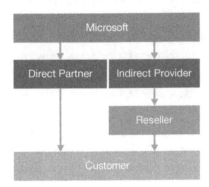

**FIGURE 4-11** The Microsoft Cloud Solution Provider partner options

The CSP direct model enables the partners to work directly with Microsoft and function as their customers' sole point of contact. The CSP direct partner is the only conduit between Microsoft's products and services and the customer. For a partner to participate in the CSP direct model, the partner's company must have existing billing and technical support infra-structures. The customer's entire relationship is with the partner; they have no direct contact with Microsoft at all. The CSP partner's relationship with Microsoft and with their customers proceeds as follows:

1. The CSP partner cultivates customers, sells them on Microsoft 365 and/or other Microsoft cloud-based subscription products, and sets them a price based on both the cost of the subscriptions and the added value the CSP partner provides.

2. The CSP partner sets up the customer's tenancy in Azure Active Directory and provides them with the necessary software, such as Windows 10 and any other products they might include in the customer's negotiated package.

3. The customer uses the supplied Microsoft products and contacts the CSP partner for any support issues they might have.

4. Each month, Microsoft uses the Partner Center portal to bill the CSP partner for all the user subscriptions they have sold to their customers.

5. The CSP partner bills the customers at their negotiated rate for the Microsoft subscriptions, technical support, and other services.

The upside of this model is that the relationship with the customers is wholly in the hands of the CSP partners. They are responsible for building and maintaining relationships with their customers, and they can establish whatever prices they feel are appropriate for their services. However, this responsibility also means that a CSP partner must have a company infrastructure that can fulfill all the customers' needs without any help from Microsoft.

For partners that do not have the infrastructure to handle all the billing and support issues that their customers might require, there is the CSP indirect model, which defines two levels of partners, as follows:

- **Indirect provider**   Typically, this is a larger company engaged by indirect resellers to take on the responsibility for supplying products, customer service, billing, and technical support services to customers. Some indirect providers are also willing to provide indirect resellers with other types of assistance, such as technical training and marketing; some also provide financing and credit terms.

- **Indirect reseller**   Typically, these are smaller companies or individuals who concentrate on locating, cultivating, and signing customers for Windows 10, Microsoft 365, and other cloud-based products and services. To become an indirect reseller, an individual or firm must do the following:

  - Join the Microsoft Partner Network (MPN) and obtain an ID

  - Enroll in the CSP program as an indirect reseller by supplying an MPN ID, business address, banking information, and a contact email address

  - Establish a relationship with an indirect provider, to obtain product, billing, and support services

The CSP indirect partner model enables individual consultants or small consulting companies to sign up as indirect resellers and concentrate on locating customers and developing relationships with them, rather than concentrating on back-end services, such as billing and support.

### Quick check

- What is the difference between a Cloud Solution Provider that is an indirect reseller and one that is an indirect provider?

### Quick check answer

- Typically, an indirect reseller is a smaller company that concentrates on locating, cultivating, and signing customers for Microsoft cloud-based products and services. An indirect provider is a larger company engaged by indirect resellers to take on the responsibility for supplying products, customer service, billing, and technical support services to customers.

# Billing and bill management

Subscription-based products like Microsoft 365 require regular attention to billing to keep them current. If subscriptions are allowed to lapse, they become unusable. For example, if an Office 365 subscription is allowed to lapse, or if the computer does not connect to the cloud at least every 30 days, it deactivates and goes into reduced functionality mode. In this mode, users can view or print their existing documents, but they cannot create or edit new ones.

The **Billing** menu in the Microsoft 365 Admin Center is where administrators can manage all aspects of the billing process. The menu contains the following items:

- **Purchase Services**  Contains tiles with cloud-based subscription products that administrators can add to their tenancies

- **Products & Services**  Lists the subscriptions that are currently active and specifies how many licenses have been assigned and any balance that is due, as shown in Figure 4-12

**FIGURE 4-12** The Products & services page in the Microsoft 365 Admin Center

- **Licenses**  Contains a list of the subscriptions the tenancy currently possesses and specifies how many licenses are assigned. Selecting a subscription displays a list of the users to which licenses have been assigned and enables administrators to create new assignments.

- **Bills & Payments**  Displays a history of the invoices for the current subscriptions, the payment methods configured by the administrator, and the payment frequency (monthly or annual).

- **Billing Accounts**  Displays the account profile of the legal entity in the subscriber's organization responsible for signing software agreements and making purchases, as well as a list of the subscriber's partnerships.

- **Payment Methods**  Displays a list of the subscriber's current payment methods and enables the addition of new ones.

- **Billing Notifications**  Displays a list of the users who will receive billing notifications and renewal reminders from Microsoft, as shown in Figure 4-13.

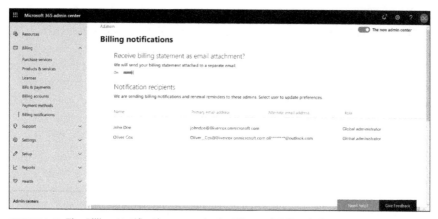

**FIGURE 4-13** The Billing Notifications page in the Microsoft 365 Admin Center

For Microsoft partners, there is a **Billing** menu in the **Partner Center** console that displays the invoices from Microsoft for the products that the partners have resold to customers. Microsoft bills partners for the license and usage fees of their customers 60 days in arrears, so that the partners have time to collect. This **Billing** menu only handles the charges that partners remit to Microsoft. There are no conditions or requirements in the partnership agreement about how or when the partners invoice their customers and collect their payments.

# Skill 4.3: Describe support offerings for Microsoft 365 services

For many IT professionals, there are important concerns about what happens after their organization commits itself to the use of cloud-based applications and services. These issues include concerns about downtime, monitoring the continuity of the Microsoft services, and the product support provided by Microsoft and its partners.

## Service level agreements

When an enterprise uses on-premises servers, they know issues they experience that prevent the servers from functioning are their problem, and they must have the resources to resolve them. This is why organizations often use redundant components, servers, or even data centers to keep business-critical services available. Many IT professionals prefer this self-reliance; by planning and implementing their services correctly, they can be confident of their continued functionality. An enterprise that uses cloud-based services, however, must rely on others to keep its services running.

For IT professionals, service outages are one of the potential showstopper issues for the adoption of Microsoft 365 and other cloud-based services. If the services suffer downtime, business stops. While it might not be the IT professionals' fault, it is their responsibility. What is worse, there is nothing they can do about it except call the provider and shout at them. Depending on the nature of the organization's business, service downtime can result in lost productivity, lost income, and in extreme cases, even lost lives.

To address this issue, contracts with cloud service providers typically include a *service level agreement (SLA)*. The SLA guarantees a certain percentage of uptime for the services and specifies the consequences if that guarantee is not met. It is important to remember that an organization usually has more than one service provider that is needed to access the cloud. For example, an organization can contract with Microsoft for a certain number of Microsoft 365 subscriptions, but the reliability specified in Microsoft's SLA means nothing if the organization's Internet service provider (ISP) fails to provide them with access to the cloud. Therefore, an organization should have a contract with every cloud service provider they use that includes SLA terminology.

When negotiating an SLA with any cloud service provider or Internet service provider, there should be language included to address questions like the following:

- What formula is used to calculate the service levels that are actually achieved?
- Who is responsible for maintaining records of service levels?
- How and when is the subscriber provided with written reports of the service levels achieved?
- Are the exceptional circumstances specified in the SLA under which service outages are not classified as downtime?
- How much downtime is expected or allowable for the provider's maintenance, both scheduled and emergency?
- What are the terms of the agreement regarding service interruptions that are the result of acts of war, extreme weather, or natural disasters?
- What are the terms of the agreement regarding service interruptions that are caused by third-party services, such as power outages?
- What are the terms of the agreement regarding service interruptions that are the result of malicious cyberattacks against the provider?
- What are the terms of the agreement regarding service interruptions that are the result of malicious cyberattacks against the subscriber?
- What remedy or penalty does the provider supply when they fail to meet the agreed upon service levels?
- What is the liability to which the provider is subject when service interruptions cause a loss of business or productivity?

These questions are designed to quantify the nature of the SLA and how it can legally affect the relationship between the provider and the subscriber. For example, a provider can guarantee a 99 percent uptime rate. However, without specific language addressing the point, there is no way to determine exactly what constitutes uptime or downtime. What if a service is only partially operational, with some tasks functional and others not? Does that constitute downtime? There is also the question of what happens when downtime in excess of the guaranteed amount does occur. Is it the responsibility of the subscriber to make a claim? If excessive downtime does occur, is the provider responsible for the subscriber's lost business during that downtime or just for a prorated amount of the subscription fee? If issues like these are not discussed with specific language in the SLA, then they are potential arguments that the provider can use to avoid supporting their uptime guarantee.

## SLA Limitations

As an example of the terms that might appear in an SLA to limit the responsibility of the cloud service provider, consider the following excerpt from Microsoft's SLA for Azure Active Directory:

This SLA and any applicable Service Levels do not apply to any performance or availability issues:

1. *Due to factors outside our reasonable control (for example, natural disaster, war, acts of terrorism, riots, government action, or a network or device failure external to our data centers, including at your site or between your site and our data center);*

2. *That result from the use of services, hardware, or software not provided by us, including, but not limited to, issues resulting from inadequate bandwidth or related to third-party software or services;*

3. *That results from failures in a single Microsoft Datacenter location, when your network connectivity is explicitly dependent on that location in a non-geo-resilient manner;*

4. *Caused by your use of a Service after we advised you to modify your use of the Service, if you did not modify your use as advised;*

5. *During or with respect to preview, pre-release, beta or trial versions of a Service, feature or software (as determined by us) or to purchases made using Microsoft subscription credits;*

6. *That result from your unauthorized action or lack of action when required, or from your employees, agents, contractors, or vendors, or anyone gaining access to our network by means of your passwords or equipment, or otherwise resulting from your failure to follow appropriate security practices;*

7. *That result from your failure to adhere to any required configurations, use supported platforms, follow any policies for acceptable use, or your use of the Service in a manner inconsistent with the features and functionality of the Service (for example, attempts to perform operations that are not supported) or inconsistent with our published guidance;*

8. *That result from faulty input, instructions, or arguments (for example, requests to access files that do not exist);*

9. *That result from your attempts to perform operations that exceed prescribed quotas or that resulted from our throttling of suspected abusive behavior;*

10. *Due to your use of Service features that are outside of associated Support Windows; or*

11. *For licenses reserved, but not paid for, at the time of the Incident.*

These limitations are not standard for all SLAs, but they are typical.

As with any contract, an SLA is a contract, and the language should be negotiable; both parties must agree to all the final terms. If a provider refuses to negotiate the terms of the SLA or modify any of its language, this should set off alarms for the potential subscriber. The alternatives in this instance are to either find a different service provider or purchase insurance to cover the organization for any losses they might incur as a result of service interruptions that are not covered by the SLA.

In the *Microsoft Volume Licensing Service Level Agreement for Microsoft Online Services* document, dated August 1, 2019, the terms for each of the individual cloud services are listed with the following information:

- **Downtime**   Specifies exactly what type or types of service interruption legally constitute downtime in the terms of the agreement. Some of the definitions of downtime for cloud services included in Microsoft 365 are shown in Table 4-3.

- **Monthly Uptime Percentage**   Specifies the formula by which the percentage of uptime is calculated for each month, taking into account the number of minutes the service was considered to be down, and the number of user licenses affected by the outage. For example, the following formula subtracts the total number of downtime minutes for all the users from the total user minutes and calculates a percentage from that:

$$\frac{User\,Minutes - Downtime\,Minutes}{User\,Minutes} \times 100$$

- **Service Credit**   Specifies the percentage of the monthly subscription fee that will be credited to the subscriber's account, based on the calculated monthly uptime percentage. Microsoft's SLA guarantees 99.9 percent uptime, so the service credit for months that do not meet that percentage are calculated as shown in Table 4-4.

- **Additional Terms**   Identifies other parts of the document that might define other conditions constituting a refundable service outage. For example, a failure of Exchange Online to detect viruses or filter spam as agreed in the SLA can qualify for a service credit, even if no downtime occurs.

**TABLE 4-3** Definitions of downtime in the Microsoft Volume Licensing Service Level Agreement for Microsoft Online Services

| CLOUD SERVICE | DEFINITION OF DOWNTIME |
| --- | --- |
| Azure Active Directory Premium | Any period of time when users are not able to log in to the service, log in to the Access Panel, access applications on the Access Panel and reset passwords or any period of time IT administrators are not able to create, read, write and delete entries in the directory and/or provision/deprovision users to applications in the directory. |
| Exchange Online | Any period of time when users are unable to send or receive email with Outlook Web Access. |
| Microsoft Teams | Any period of time when users are unable to see presence status, conduct instant messaging conversations, or initiate online meetings. |
| Office 365 ProPlus | Any period of time when Office applications are put into reduced functionality mode due to an issue with Office 365 activation. |

| CLOUD SERVICE | DEFINITION OF DOWNTIME |
| --- | --- |
| Office Online | Any period of time when users are unable to use the web applications to view and edit any Office document stored on a SharePoint Online site for which they have appropriate permissions. |
| OneDrive for Business | Any period of time when users are unable to view or edit files stored on their personal OneDrive for Business storage. |
| SharePoint Online | Any period of time when users are unable to read or write any portion of a SharePoint Online site collection for which they have appropriate permissions. |
| Yammer Enterprise | Any period of time greater than 10 minutes when more than 5 percent of users are unable to post or read messages on any portion of the Yammer network for which they have appropriate permissions. |
| Microsoft Intune | Any period of time when the customer's IT administrator or users authorized by customer are unable to log in with proper credentials. Scheduled downtime will not exceed 10 hours per calendar year. |
| Microsoft Defender Advanced Threat Protection | The total accumulated minutes that are part of the maximum available minutes in which the customer is unable to access any portion of a Microsoft Defender Advanced Threat Protection portal site collections for which they have appropriate permissions and customer has a valid, active license. |

**TABLE 4-4** Service credit for monthly uptime percentages in the Microsoft Volume Licensing Service Level Agreement for Microsoft Online Services

| MONTHLY UPTIME PERCENTAGE | SERVICE CREDIT |
| --- | --- |
| Greater than or equal to 99.9 percent | 0 percent |
| Less than 99.9 percent | 25 percent |
| Less than 99 percent | 50 percent |
| Less than 95 percent | 100 percent |

Microsoft requires subscribers to file a claim for service credits, containing evidence of the outages, as described in the following SLA excerpt:

*In order for Microsoft to consider a claim, you must submit the claim to customer support at Microsoft Corporation including all information necessary for Microsoft to validate the claim, including but not limited to: (i) a detailed description of the Incident; (ii) information regarding the time and duration of the Downtime; (iii) the number and location(s) of affected users (if applicable); and (iv) descriptions of your attempts to resolve the Incident at the time of occurrence.*

Generally speaking, it appears as though the SLA for Microsoft's online services is rarely even needed. Table 4-5 lists the worldwide quarterly uptime percentages for the Office 365 cloud services since 2017, and none of the figures even comes close to dropping below the guaranteed 99.9 percent. This is not to say that there weren't a few isolated outages resulting in service credits, but the overall record for the Office 365 products is an impressive one.

**TABLE 4-5** Quarterly Uptime Percentages for Office 365, 2017 to 2019

| YEAR | QUARTER 1 | QUARTER 2 | QUARTER 3 | QUARTER 4 |
|------|-----------|-----------|-----------|-----------|
| **2017** | 99.99 percent | 99.97 percent | 99.98 percent | 99.99 percent |
| **2018** | 99.99 percent | 99.98 percent | 99.97 percent | 99.98 percent |
| **2019** | 99.97 percent | 99.97 percent | | |

## Creating support requests

The support that subscribers receive for Microsoft 365 depends on their subscription level and how they obtained it. Nearly every page in the Microsoft 365 Admin Center console has a **Need help?** button in the bottom-right corner, and there is a **Support** menu that enables administrators to search for help with specific problems and create a support request when a solution is not available in the existing help information. Telephone and email support are also available.

To prevent excessive use and abuse of its support services, Microsoft carefully defines the division of responsibilities between the Microsoft support team and the administrators at Microsoft 365 subscription sites. Table 4-6 lists some of the responsibilities for each of these entities.

**TABLE 4-6** Responsibilities of Microsoft 365 administrators and Microsoft Support

| MICROSOFT 365 ADMINISTRATOR RESPONSIBILITIES | MICROSOFT SUPPORT RESPONSIBILITIES |
|---|---|
| Service setup, configuration, and maintenance | Respond to support issues submitted by subscribers |
| User account creation, configuration, and maintenance | Gather information about technical support issues from subscribers |
| Primary support contact for enterprise users | Provide subscribers with technical guidance for submitted issues |
| Gather information from users about technical support issues | Troubleshoot subscriber issues and relay pertinent solution information |
| Address user software installation and configuration issues | Maintain communication with subscribers regarding ongoing service issues |
| Troubleshoot service availability issues within the bounds of the organization | Provide guidance for presales and trial-edition evaluators |
| Utilize Microsoft online resources to resolve support issues | Provide licensing, subscription, and billing support |
| Authorization and submission of support issues to Microsoft | Gather customer feedback for service improvement purposes |

Microsoft 365 administrators are expected to do what they can to address a support issue before submitting a support request to Microsoft. There are considerable Microsoft online support, training, blog, and forum resources available for this purpose, including the following:

- Microsoft Support (*support.microsoft.com*)
- Office Help & Training (*support.office.com*)
- Microsoft Community (*answers.microsoft.com*)
- Microsoft 365 Tech Community (*techcommunity.microsoft.com/t5/Microsoft-365/ct-p/ microsoft365*)

When an administrator clicks the **Need Help?** button in the Microsoft 365 Admin Center console or opens the **Support** menu and selects **New Service Request**, a **Need Help?** pane appears, prompting you for a description of the issue. Based on the furnished description, relevant material appears, such as step-by-step procedures and links to product documentation that might be helpful, as shown in Figure 4-14.

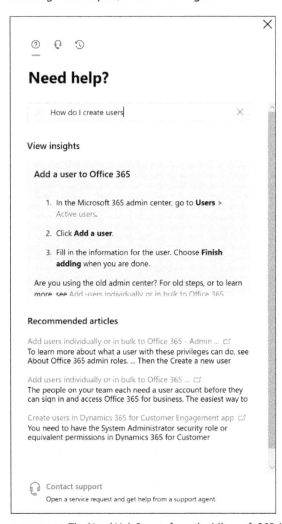

**FIGURE 4-14** The Need Help? pane from the Microsoft 365 Admin Center

At the bottom of the **Need Help?** pane is a **Contact Support** link that opens the pane shown in Figure 4-15. In this pane, the administrator can provide a more detailed description of the issue, add contact information, specify time zone and language references, and attach documents pertinent to the issue.

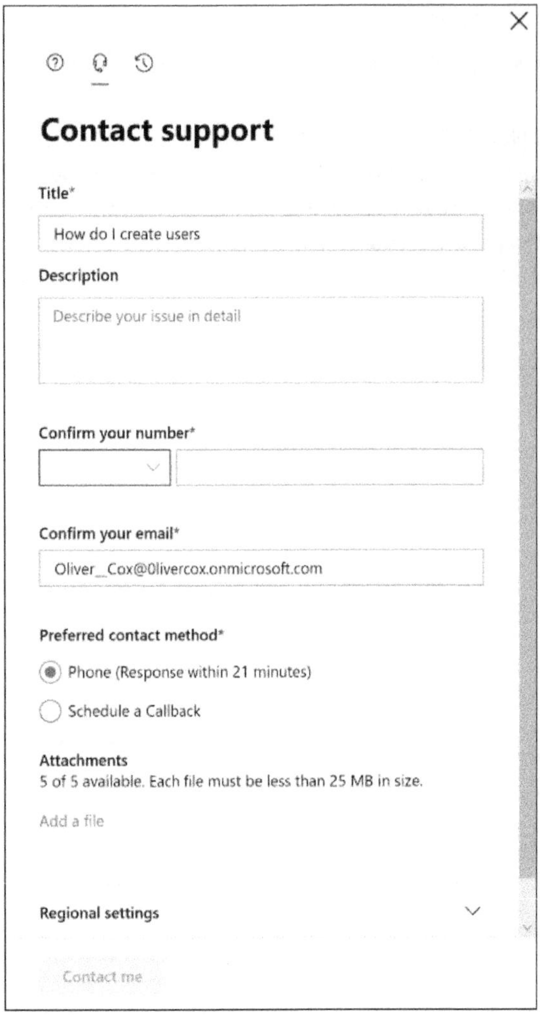

**FIGURE 4-15** The Contact support pane from the Microsoft 365 Admin Center

The support that Microsoft provides with the Microsoft 365 product is intended primarily to provide help with service installation and configuration issues, such as the following:

- **Azure Active Directory**   Domain setup, synchronization with on-premises Active Directory Domain Services, and single sign-on configuration
- **Microsoft 365**   Service configuration issues
- **Exchange Online**   Mailbox migration and configuration, autodiscover configuration, setting mailbox permissions, sharing mailboxes, and creating mail forwarding rules

- **SharePoint Online**   Creation of user groups, assigning site permissions, and external user configuration
- **Office 365 ProPlus**   Office application installation on various device platforms
- **Microsoft Teams**   Setup of a Teams environment and creating contacts
- **Microsoft Intune**   Mobile device and application management setup

When subscribers submit support requests to Microsoft, they go through a triage process and are assigned a severity level, using the values shown in Table 4-7.

**TABLE 4-7** Microsoft Support severity levels

| SEVERITY LEVEL | DESCRIPTION | EXAMPLES |
| --- | --- | --- |
| Critical (Sev A) | <ul><li>One or more services is inaccessible or nonfunctional.</li><li>Productivity or profit is impacted.</li><li>Multiple users are affected.</li><li>Immediate attention is required.</li></ul> | <ul><li>Problems sending or receiving email with Outlook/Exchange Online.</li><li>SharePoint Online or OneDrive for Business sites inaccessible.</li><li>Inability to send or receive messages or calls in Microsoft Teams.</li></ul> |
| High (Sev B) | <ul><li>One or more services is impaired, but still usable.</li><li>A single user or customer is affected.</li><li>Attention can wait until business hours.</li></ul> | <ul><li>Critical service functionality is delayed or partially impaired, but operational.</li><li>Noncritical functions of a critical service are impaired.</li><li>A function is unusable in a graphical interface but accessible using PowerShell.</li></ul> |
| Non-critical (Sev C) | <ul><li>One or more functions with minimal productivity or profit impact are impaired.</li><li>One or more users are affected, but a workaround allows continued functionality.</li></ul> | <ul><li>Problems configuring password expiration options.</li><li>Problems archiving messages in Outlook/Exchange Online.</li><li>Problems editing SharePoint/Online sites.</li></ul> |

After submitting support requests, administrators can monitor their progress in the Microsoft 365 Admin Center by selecting **View Service Requests** from the **Support** menu to display a list of all the support tickets associated with the account.

All Microsoft 365 subscriptions include access to basic support services, but for some types of subscribers or subscribers with special needs, there are alternative methods for obtaining support, such as the following:

- **FastTrack**   Microsoft's FastTrack program uses a specialized team of engineers and selected partners to provide subscribers transitioning to the cloud with assistance in the envisioning, onboarding, and ongoing administration processes. Subscribers participating in this program are provided with a contact to which they can turn for support issues during the FastTrack transition.

- **Volume Licensing**   Subscribers with an Enterprise Agreement or a Microsoft Products and Services Agreement that includes Software Assurance receive a specified number of support incidents as part of their agreement. The Software Assurance program includes 24x7 telephone support for business-critical issues and business hours or email support for noncritical issues.

- **Cloud Solution Providers**   For subscribers that obtain Microsoft 365 through a Cloud Solution Provider (CSP), the CSP should be their first point of contact for all service and support issues during the life of the subscription. The reseller agreement between CSPs and Microsoft calls for the CSP to take on full responsibility for supporting their customers, although the CSP can still escalate issues to Microsoft when they cannot resolve them on their own.

- **Microsoft Professional Support**   Subscribers with support issues that go beyond the standard service provided with Microsoft 365 can use Microsoft Professional Support to open support requests on a pay-per-incident basis, as shown in Figure 4-16. Individual incidents are available, as are five-packs of incidents.

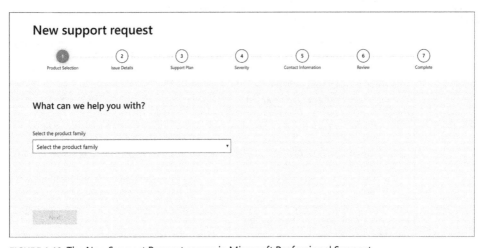

**FIGURE 4-16**   The New Support Request screen in Microsoft Professional Support

- **Microsoft Unified Support**   Subscribers can purchase a Microsoft Unified Support plan in addition to their Microsoft 365 subscriptions. Microsoft Unified Support is available at three levels: Core Support, Advanced Support, and Performance Support; each level provides increasing levels of included support hours, incident response times, and access to a technical account manager (TAM), along with increasing prices. Customers also receive access to the Microsoft Services Hub, a support portal that provides forms for submitting support requests (as shown in Figure 4-17), access to ongoing Microsoft support incidents, tools for assessing enterprise workloads, and on-demand education and training materials.

## Determining service health

Monitoring the continuous operation of the Microsoft 365 services is a critical part of the administration process, and the Microsoft 365 Admin Center includes a **Health** menu that provides a real-time display of the status of the individual services when administrators select the **Service Health** option, as shown in Figure 4-18.

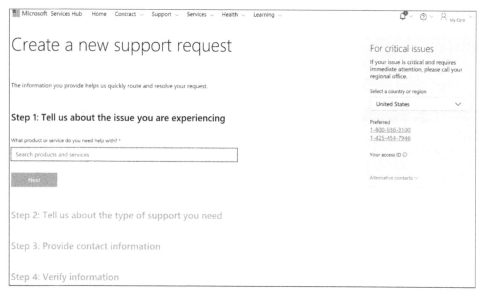

**FIGURE 4-17** The Create A New Support request screen from the Microsoft Services Hub

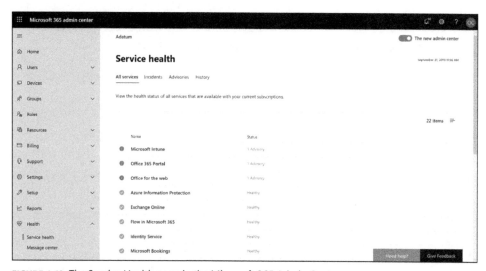

**FIGURE 4-18** The Service Health page in the Microsoft 365 Admin Center

In addition to displaying the services that are healthy, the **Service Health** screen also lists other service status conditions, as follows:

- **Advisories**    Indicates that the service is still available but that there is a known condition inhibiting its performance. The condition might cause intermittent interruptions, affect only some users, or be limited in scope. In some cases, a workaround might be available.

- **Incidents**    Indicates that a critical issue has been discovered that is rendering all or a significant part of the service unavailable or unusable. Typically, incidents are updated on their detail pages with information about the investigation, mitigation, and resolution of the issue.

Selecting the **Advisories** tab on the **Service Health** page displays details about the current advisories, as shown in Figure 4-19, including the service affected, its current status, and the time the advisory was posted. The **Incidents** page displays the same information about more serious occurrences. The **History** page lists all the incidents and advisories that have occurred during the last 7 or 30 days.

**FIGURE 4-19** The Advisories tab of the Service Health page in the Microsoft 365 Admin Center

The **Status** indicators on the **Service Health** pages can have values such as the following:

- **Investigating**   Indicates that Microsoft is aware of the issue and is currently gathering information prior to taking action
- **Service Degradation**   Indicates that the service is experiencing intermittent interruptions, performance slowdowns, or failure of specific features
- **Service Interruption**   Indicates that a significant, repeatable issue is occurring, which is preventing users from accessing the service
- **Restoring Service**   Indicates that the cause of the issue has been determined and remediation is underway, which will result in service restoration
- **Extended Recovery**   Indicates that remediation of the issue is in progress, but restoring service for all users may take some time or that an interim fix is in place that restores service until a permanent solution is applied
- **Investigation Suspended**   Indicates that Microsoft is awaiting information from subscribers or other parties before the issue can be diagnosed or further action can be taken
- **Service Restored**   Indicates that Microsoft has taken corrective action to address the issue and has successfully brought the service back to a healthy state
- **Post-Incident Report Published**   Indicates that documentation on the issue has been published containing an explanation of the root cause and steps to prevent a reoccurrence

Each advisory or incident includes a detail page containing more information, as shown in Figure 4-20. This information may include a greater elaboration on the user impact of the advisory or incident and a log of its status as it proceeds through the process of being addressed, documented, and resolved.

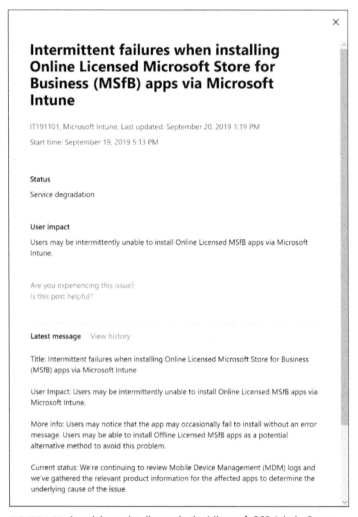

**FIGURE 4-20** An advisory detail page in the Microsoft 365 Admin Center

When an incident that prevents administrators from signing in to the Microsoft 365 Admin Center console, there is a separate Microsoft 365 Service Health Status page available at *status.office365.com* that indicates the health of the Microsoft 365 service itself, as shown in Figure 4-21.

The **Service Health** pages in the Microsoft 365 Admin Center do not contain planned maintenance events that might cause interruptions in service. For information about these interruptions, see the **Message Center** page, accessible from the **Health** menu, as shown in Figure 4-22.

**FIGURE 4-21** The Microsoft 365 Service Health Status page

**FIGURE 4-22** The Message Center page in the Microsoft 365 Admin Center

# Skill 4.4: Understand the service lifecycle in Microsoft 365

With the introduction of their subscription-based software products, such as Microsoft 365, Microsoft has had to redefine its service lifecycle policies. The service lifecycle defines how long a particular product continues to be supported by Microsoft through the release of software updates, the acceptance of feature design requests, and the availability of product support. Microsoft now has two lifecycle policies, as follows:

- **Fixed Lifecycle Policy** Applies to permanently licensed products available through retail purchase or volume licensing channels and defines a 10-year period of support; the license remains valid after this time, but support is discontinued.
- **Modern Lifecycle Policy** Applies to subscription-based products and services that are licensed continuously and for which the support is ongoing, as long as the customer stays current by applying all servicing updates within a specified time period.

In the Fixed Lifecycle policy, the 10-year support period is split into two phases: Mainstream Support and Extended Support.

- **Mainstream Support** During the five-year Mainstream Support phase, the product receives both security and feature updates, incident support is available, and feature enhancement requests are accepted.
- **Extended Support** After the Mainstream Support period expires, the product enters a five-year Extended Support phase in which only security updates are released, and support is only available on a paid basis. At the end of the Extended Support phase, the product enters the Beyond End of Support phase, in which no updates are released, and only paid support is available.

The Modern Lifecycle Policy is intended for products for which development and support is ongoing, such as Microsoft 365. There is no set end to the lifecycle, so subscribers continue to receive both security and nonsecurity updates, feature updates, and new product builds. Telephone and online support is ongoing. When Microsoft decides to end support for a product governed by the Modern Lifecycle Policy without providing a replacement or successor product, they provide a minimum of 12 months' notice of the end of the lifecycle.

The only customer requirements for a modern lifecycle product are as follows:

- The customer must maintain a license for the product by paying the required subscription fees.
- The customer must stay current by accepting all service updates for the product before a specified time frame has expired.

Because subscription-based modern lifecycle products like Microsoft 365 do not have major version upgrades, new and enhanced features are released as they become available. Because Microsoft 365 is a bundled product consisting of many applications and services, new features for individual components are developed and released separately.

In some cases, features and feature updates undergo a preview release cycle, so that customers can evaluate the technology and provide feedback to the developers at Microsoft. Depending on the product and the feature, the release cycle might include the following phases:

- **Private preview** An invitation-only preview distributed to a small number of selected customers for evaluation purposes by the product or feature's development team.
- **Public preview** A prerelease version of a product or feature released to all users by the development team that the customer can activate or deactivate as needed. For example, the Microsoft 365 Admin Center includes a **Try The New Admin Center** switch in the upper-right corner of most of its screens enabling administrators to switch between the original and the new Admin Center interface, as shown in Figure 4-23.

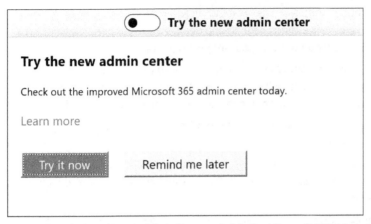

**FIGURE 4-23** The Try The New Admin Center switch in the Microsoft 365 Admin Center

- **General Availability (GA)**   Based on testing and customer feedback, preview releases might be withdrawn and returned for further development and additional previews. However, when the preview phases are completed successfully, the product or feature might be released to General Availability, meaning that it is provided to all customers as an official component of the product.

The terms and conditions of preview releases are specific to the product being tested. In nearly all cases, they are free, and they might or might not be covered by the customer support terms specified in the product license. However, in most cases, there is a mechanism to provide feedback to the developers regarding the performance or usability of the preview release.

To provide information to customers about the status of the update releases for specific products, Microsoft maintains roadmap sites that lists the updates in various phases of completion. The updates are listed as being in one of the following categories:

- **In Development**   Updates that have not yet been released because they are currently in the process of being developed or tested

- **Rolling Out**   Updates that have entered the release process, but which might not yet be available to all customers

- **Launched**   Updates that have completed the development and any preview phases and have now entered the General Availability phase, which makes them available to all customers

The Microsoft 365 Roadmap site, shown in Figure 4-24, contains a total of 644 updates at the time of this writing. The **Filters** on the left side of the screen enable the user to narrow down the list of updates displayed, based on products, platforms, cloud instances, and feature date.

Each update in the list contains a description, a status indicator, tags or keywords that pertain to the release, and an anticipated release date. When a user selects one of the updates, it expands to display additional information about its function and pertinent dates, as shown in Figure 4-25. In some cases, the expanded description includes a **More Info** link to additional Microsoft documentation of the feature and a **Mail** to link to forward the information to another user.

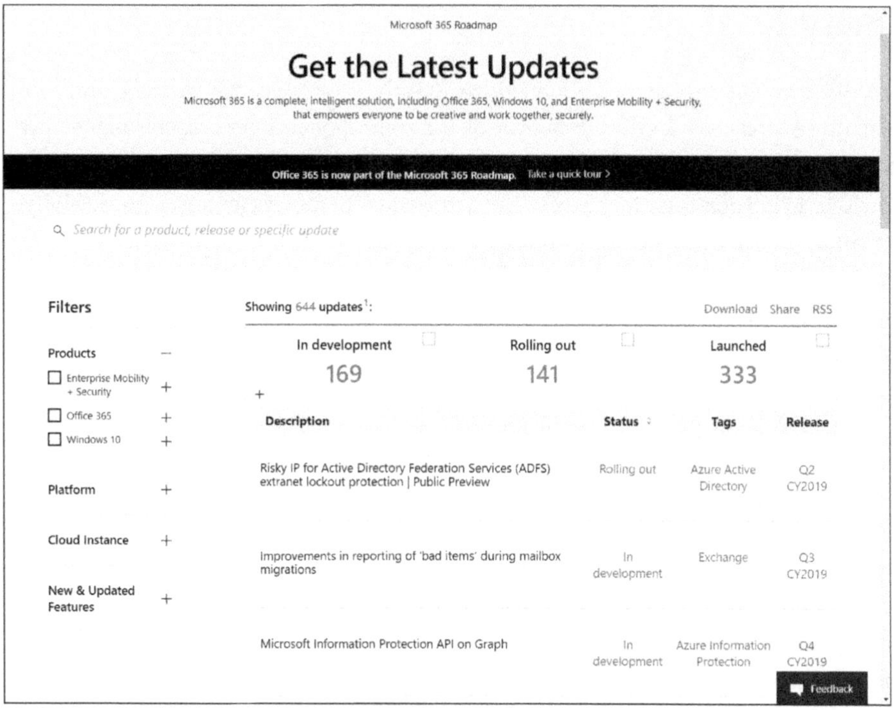

**FIGURE 4-24** The Microsoft 365 Roadmap site

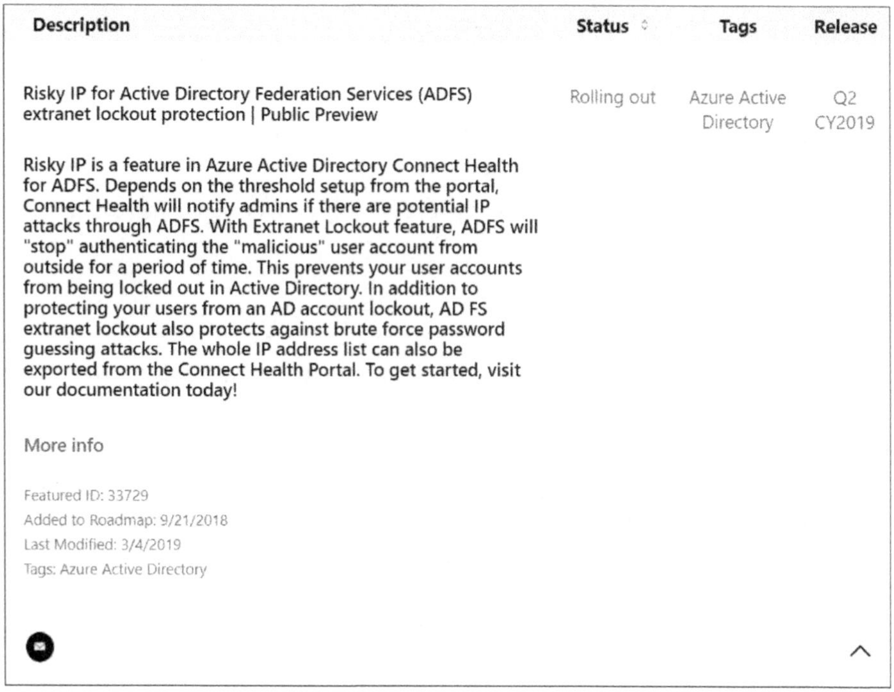

**FIGURE 4-25** Update detail from the Microsoft 365 Roadmap site

# Summary

- All Microsoft 365 editions include Windows 10 Enterprise, Office 365 Pro Plus, and Enterprise Mobility + Security. However, all these components are available in their own plans, and the Microsoft 365 editions include them in various combinations.

- The key selling points for Microsoft 365 are divided into four major areas: productivity, collaboration security, and compliance.

- To install and run the Microsoft 365 components and access the Microsoft 365 cloud services, each user in an organization must have a Microsoft 365 *user subscription license (USL)*.

- Evaluating the total cost of ownership (TCO) for a Microsoft 365 implementation is relatively simple; there is a monthly or annual fee for each Microsoft 365 user subscription and those subscriber fees are predictable and ongoing. Predicting the cost of an on-premises network requires businesses to categorize their expenses by distinguishing between capital expenditures (CapEx) and operational expenditures (OpEx).

- Organizations can purchase Microsoft 365 subscriptions directly from Microsoft individually or by using a variety of volume licensing agreements, including Enterprise Agreements (EA), Microsoft Products and Services Agreements (MPSA), or arrangements with Cloud Solution Providers (CSP).

- Typically, contracts with cloud service providers include a *service level agreement (SLA)*, which guarantees a certain percentage of uptime for the services and specifies the consequences if that guarantee is not met.

- Microsoft carefully defines the division of responsibilities between the Microsoft support team and the administrators at Microsoft 365 subscription sites.

- The Service health page in the Microsoft 365 Admin Center, displaying a list of the Microsoft 365 services with a status indicator for each one.

- Microsoft has two lifecycle policies: Fixed Lifecycle Policy and Modern Lifecycle Policy.

# Thought experiment

In this thought experiment, demonstrate your skills and knowledge of the topics covered in this chapter. You can find the answer to this thought experiment in the next section.

Ralph is responsible for planning the IT deployment for his company's new branch office, which will have 50 users. He is currently trying to determine which is the more economically viable choice: a cloud-based solution or on-premises servers. For the cloud-based solution, Ralph is considering Microsoft 365 Business, which has a price of $20.00 per user, per month. For an on-premises alternative providing the services his users need most, Ralph has searched through several online sources and found the software licensing prices shown in Table 4-8.

**TABLE 4-8** Sample software licensing prices

| QUANTITY NEEDED | PRODUCT | PRICE EACH |
|---|---|---|
| 2 | Microsoft Windows Server 2019 Standard (16 core) | $976.00 |
| 1 | Microsoft Windows Server 2019 Client Access Licenses (Pack of 50) | $1,869.99 |
| 50 | Microsoft Office Home & Business 2019 | $249.99 |
| 1 | Microsoft Exchange Server 2019 Standard | $726.99 |
| 50 | Microsoft Exchange Server 2019 Standard CAL | $75.99 |
| 1 | Microsoft SharePoint Server | $5,523.99 |
| 50 | Microsoft SharePoint Client Access License | $55.99 |

It is obvious to Ralph that the on-premises solution will require a much larger capital expenditure, but he is wondering whether it might be the more economical solution in the long term. Based on these prices and disregarding all other expenses (including hardware, facilities, and personnel) how long would it be before the ongoing Microsoft 365 Business subscription fees for 50 users become more expensive than the on-premises software licensing costs?

# Thought experiment answer

Ralph has calculated the total software licensing costs for his proposed on-premises solution and has arrived at a total expenditure of $29,171.47, as shown in Table 4-9.

**TABLE 4-9** Sample software licensing prices (with totals)

| QUANTITY NEEDED | PRODUCT | PRICE EACH | TOTAL |
|---|---|---|---|
| 2 | Microsoft Windows Server 2019 Standard (16 core) | $976.00 | $1,952.00 |
| 1 | Microsoft Windows Server 2019 Client Access Licenses (Pack of 50) | $1,869.99 | $1,869.99 |
| 50 | Microsoft Office Home & Business 2019 | $249.99 | $12,499.50 |
| 1 | Microsoft Exchange Server 2019 Standard | $726.99 | $726.99 |
| 50 | Microsoft Exchange Server 2019 Standard CAL | $75.99 | $3,799.50 |
| 1 | Microsoft SharePoint Server | $5,523.99 | $5,523.99 |
| 50 | Microsoft SharePoint Client Access License | $55.99 | $2,799.50 |
| | **Grand Total** | | **$29,171.47** |

The Microsoft 365 Business subscription fees for 50 users amount to $1,000.00 per month. Therefore, Ralph has concluded that after 30 months, the ongoing cost for the subscriptions will exceed the one-time cost for the on-premises server licensing fees.

# Index

## A

A1/A3/A5 subscriptions. *See* Microsoft 365 Education
Abnormal Behavior Machine Learning, 89
access control lists (ACLs), 116–117
Access from anywhere chart (Usage Analytics), 94
ACLs (access control lists), 116–117
activating applications, 178
Active Directory. *See* AD DS (Active Directory Domain Services);
AD FS (Active Directory Federation Services); Azure AD (Active
Directory)
AD DS (Active Directory Domain Services)
    Active Directory Users and Computers, 125
    compared to on-premises services, 40–41
    features and capabilities of, 114–116, 146–148
    password policies, 133–134
    on-premises identities, 124–125
    structure and hierarchy of, 146–148
    user accounts, creating, 114–116
AD FS (Active Directory Federation Services), 52, 131
Add-on USL (user subscription license), 186
Admin Center
    Billing menu, 185, 194–195
    Exchange Online settings, 26–27
    features and capabilities of, 46–47
    Health menu, 204–208
    Licenses page, 185
    New Group interface, 71
    Purchase Services page, 185–186
    Service Health page, 204–208
    Support menu, 200–205
    Try The New Admin Center option, 209
Admin Centers menu (Admin Center), 47
administration, 36
Adoption chart (Usage Analytics), 94
Advanced Threat Analytics (ATA), 33–34, 85, 88–91, 143
Advanced Threat Protection (ATP), 22, 35, 143, 182
advisories, 205
AIP (Azure Information Protection), 33, 85, 105–106, 117–118,
139–143, 182
alerts, 154
analytics
    Microsoft 365 Usage Analytics, 92–94
    Microsoft ATA (Advanced Threat Analytics), 33–34, 85,
    88–91, 143
    MyAnalytics, 94–96
    Workplace Analytics, 96–99
anomalous logins, 89
anticipation of threats, 111

Application Proxy, 129
Application Proxy Connector, 129
application scans, 112
Application Virtualization (App-V), 24, 64
applications, defined, 13. *See also individual applications
and services*
App-V (Application Virtualization), 24, 64
architecture, cloud, 8
    architecture, cloud services, 9–11
    hybrid cloud, 12–13
    private cloud, 11–12
Assess phase (compliance), 184
asset inventory, 104–106
ATA (Advanced Threat Analytics), 33–34, 85, 88–91, 143
ATP (Advanced Threat Protection), 22, 35, 143, 182
audit reports, 156
authentication
    with Azure AD (Active Directory), 130–132
        federated authentication, 131
        pass-through authentication, 130
        password authentication, 128
    definition of, 113–114
    multifactor
        biometric scans, 134
        cell phone-based, 134
        definition of, 134
    overview of, 132
    password
        Azure AD (Active Directory), 128
        password changes, 153
        password hash synchronization, 129
        password policies, 133–134
        SSPR (Self Service Password Reset), 52–53, 153
authorization, 113–114
automatic feature updates, 61
Automatically Register New Windows 10 Domain Joined Devices
With Azure Active Directory Client setting, 150
Autopilot, 24
availability
    definition of, 105
    high, 108
Azure. *See also* Azure AD (Active Directory); cloud services
    AIP (Azure Information Protection), 33, 85, 105–106, 117–118,
    139–143, 182
    ATP (Advanced Threat Protection), 22, 35, 143, 182
    management interface, 6
    regions, 162

# D

# G

GA (General Availability) releases, 210
Gateway (ATA), 90
GDPR (General Data Protection Regulation), 156, 183
Geography button (Microsoft Graph), 81
Golden Ticket attacks, 88
government subscriptions. *See* Microsoft 365 Government
Gramm-Leach-Bliley Act (GLBA), 183
Graph (Microsoft), 81–82
groups
    Group Policy, 133–134
    group-by-group transition, 43
    Group-to-group queries (Workplace Analytics), 98
    modification of, 89
    Office 365, 69–73
Groups menu (Admin Center), 46

# H

hardware inventory, 106–108
hardware requirements, 3
hashes, 128–129
Health Insurance Portability and Accountability Act (HIPAA), 11–12, 183
Health menu (Admin Center), 47, 204–208
High (Sev B) severity level, 203
high availability, 108
HIPAA (Health Insurance Portability and Accountability Act), 11–12, 183
horizontal scaling, 5
host scans, 112
Hunting tools, 155
Hybrid Azure AD, 149
hybrid cloud, 12–13
hybrid identities, 127–132
    in Azure AD (Active Directory)
        Application Proxy, 129
        authentication, 130–132
        passwords, 128
        SSO (single sign-on), 129
    definition of, 127
    first synchronization, 128–129
hybrid service deployments, 40
hypervisors, 14

# I

IaaS (Infrastructure as a Service), 14–16
Identity phase (deployment), 51–53
identity protection
    in AD DS (Active Directory Domain Services)
        hybrid identities, 127–132
        on-premises identities, 124–125
        user accounts, creating, 114–116

authentication
    definition of, 113–114
    multifactor, 134–136
    overview of, 132
    password, 128–129, 133–134
authorization, 113–114
in Azure AD (Active Directory), 13, 114–116
    Application Proxy, 129
    authentication, 130–132
    cloud identities, 126–127
    hybrid identities, 127–132
    Identity Protection, 136–139, 182
    passwords, 128
    SSO (single sign-on), 129
    user accounts, creating, 114–116
cloud identities, 126–127
hybrid identities, 127–132
modern management processes, 43
overview of, 113–116, 123, 170
password authentication
    in Azure AD (Active Directory), 128
    password changes, 153
    password hash synchronization, 129
    password policies, 133–134
    SSPR (Self Service Password Reset), 52–53, 153
on-premise identities, 124–125
risk levels, 136–139
Windows Hello for Business, 116
In Development release status, 210
incidents, 205
indirect providers, 193
indirect resellers, 193
Individual service usage chart (Usage Analytics), 94
Industries & Regions (Service Trust Portal), 157
infected devices, 153
information protection, 58–59, 170
infrastructure, cloud services, 7–8
Infrastructure as a Service (IaaS), 14–16
Insert Data button (Microsoft Graph), 82
Insert From File pane (Microsoft Graph), 81
installation. *See* deployment
integrity, data, 105
Internal networks metrics (Workplace Analytics), 97
International Organization for Standardization (ISO), 156
International Traffic in Arms Regulations (ITAR), 173–174
international users, 173
Internet of Things (IoT), 141–142
Intune. *See* Microsoft Intune
inventory
    assets, 104–106
    hardware, 106–108
Investigating indicator (Service Health), 206
Investigation Suspended indicator (Service Health), 206
IoT (Internet of Things), 141–142
ISO (International Organization for Standardization), 156
ITAR (International Traffic in Arms Regulations), 173–174

# Q-R

# S